BEYOND MAXIMUS

BEYOND MAXIMUS

*The Construction of Public Voice
in Black Mountain Poetry*

Anne Day Dewey

STANFORD UNIVERSITY PRESS

STANFORD, CALIFORNIA

2007

Stanford University Press
Stanford, California

Printed in the United States of America
on acid-free, archival-quality paper

Library of Congress Cataloging-in-Publication Data

Dewey, Anne Day.
    Beyond Maximus: the construction of public voice in Black Mountain poetry /
Anne Day Dewey.
        p. cm.
    Includes bibliographical references and index.
    ISBN 978-0-8047-5647-1 (cloth : acid-free paper)
    1. American poetry—North Carolina—Black Mountain—History and criti-
cism.   2. American poetry—20th century—History and criticism.   3. Black
Mountain school (Group of poets)   4. Poets, American—20th century—Political
and social views.   5. Politics and literature—United States—History—20th
century.   6. Black Mountain (N.C.)—Intellectual life.   I. Title.
PS266.N8D48 2007
811'.54099756—dc22   2006100990

Typeset by Westchester Book Group in 11/13.5 Garamond

For my mother and in memory of my father

Contents

Acknowledgements

Many people have helped to make this book possible. I wish first to thank the teachers who supported this project in its early stages and have continued to provide me with thoughtful advice, encouragement, and models of scholarship: Albert Gelpi, Marjorie Perloff, and George Dekker. I am extremely grateful for their wisdom, guidance, and teaching. Sincere thanks as well to Helen Brooks, Sabine MacCormack, and Donna Hollenberg for their inspiration and kindness and to other teachers who taught me to read poetry: Wade Evey, Harold Bloom, and Brigitte Peucker. I am deeply indebted to Burton Hatlen for his careful, generous reading of my work and his dedication and labor in helping to create the body of scholarship and the community of scholars that make this book possible.

I am tremendously thankful for the friends and colleagues whose valuable conversation and careful reading have given me spiritual and physical homes in which to work and contributed helpful advice: Joan Pong Linton and Ranen Omer-Sherman for their extraordinary patience and encouragement, Randall Costa and Lisa Ihde Costa for deep friendship, Jo Ellen Green, Antonia Holdegel Fore, Michele Pridmore-Brown, Michael Saler, Julie Inness, Rob Michalski, Derede Arthur, Mary Barker, and Paul Vita. Special thanks also to Rick Chaney for his deanly support of family and research.

I am grateful for the expertise and hard work of the staffs of several libraries and archives, many of whom provided valuable material crucial to the development of this project. I would like especially to thank Margaret Kimball and William McPheron of Stanford University's Special Collections and Robert Bertholf and Michael Basinski of The Poetry Collection of the State University of New York at Buffalo. Their knowledge has enriched this work and at times saved me from grave error. I wish also to thank the staffs of the Lilly Library at the University of Indiana, the Poetry Collection of the State University of New York at Buffalo, the Thomas J. Dodd Research Center at the University of Connecticut at Storrs, the Special Collections of the Stanford University and Washington University Libraries, and Jennifer Buch and Mary Shelly of Franklin and Marshall College Library. Thanks also to Susan Kenney for her help in preparing the final manuscript.

My family has shared this book with me for a long time. I am indebted to their patience and sacrifices. Words are not enough to express my gratitude to my parents, to whom this book is dedicated, for their lifelong contributions to my education; to my sister Jane for her clear wisdom and compassion; to José Luis, Mario, and Gracian for their vital, constant presence and for their patience and impatience; and to Fermina Aparicio Salvador and Santos Pérez Requejo for their support and understanding. The editorial staff at Stanford University Press has worked hard to improve and produce this book. I very much appreciate their helpful suggestions for revision and careful editing.

Parts of the following chapters were first published in different form: Chapter 1 as "History as Force Field in Pound, Zukofsky, and Olson," *Sagetrieb* 13.3 (Winter 1994): 83–116; part of Chapter 4 as "Poetic Authority and the Public Sphere of Politics in the Activist 1960s: The Duncan-Levertov Debate," in *Robert Duncan and Denise Levertov: The Poetry of Politics, the Politics of Poetry*, ed. Albert Gelpi and Robert Bertholf (Stanford: Stanford University Press, 2006); and parts of Chapter 5 as " 'The Art of the Octopus': The Maturation of Denise Levertov's Political Vision," *Renascence: Essays on Values in Literature* 50.1 and 2 (Fall 1997/ Winter 1998): 65–81 and "Public Idiom and Private Voice in John Ashbery's *Three Poems* and Ed Dorn's *Gunslinger*," *Sagetrieb* 11.1 and 2 (Spring/Fall, 1992): 47–66. This book began as a dissertation, "The Transformation of the Field in Black Mountain Poetry: Poetic Agency and Public Authority in a Culture of Mass Communication" (1994) at Stanford University.

I gratefully acknowledge permission to reprint the following published and unpublished material:

For published work by Robert Creeley: "A Method," "Still Life Or," "The Awakening," "The Bed," "The Chance," "The Place," "They,"

"Waiting," and other excerpts from *The Collected Poems of Robert Creeley, 1945–1975*, by Robert Creeley, copyright © 1982, The Regents of the University of California. Published by the University of California Press. Reproduced with permission. All rights reserved.

For unpublished work by Robert Creeley: Permission to quote the following unpublished material by Robert Creeley has been granted by Penelope Creeley and by the archives at which the material is held:

Archives and Special Collections at the Thomas J. Dodd Research Center, University of Connecticut Libraries: Draft response by Robert Creeley to Olson's letter of May 7, 1952, Charles Olson Research Collection. Letter from Robert Creeley to Jacob Leed, [194?], Folder 23, Robert Creeley Papers. Letter from Robert Creeley to Jacob Leed from Hotel Brunswick, [194?], Folder 23, Robert Creeley Papers. Original typed mss. in letter from Robert Creeley to Charles Olson, February 12, 1965, Charles Olson Research Collection. "The Painters," Robert Creeley Papers.

Lilly Library, Indiana University, Bloomington: Robert Creeley, "Alfred North Whitehead," Robert Creeley Papers. Letter from Robert Creeley to Cid Corman, March 9, 1951, Cid Corman Manuscripts.

The Poetry Collection of the University Libraries, State University of New York at Buffalo: Letter from Robert Creeley to Robert Duncan, October 6, 1955, Robert Duncan Papers. Letter from Robert Creeley to Robert Duncan, August 20, 1959, Robert Duncan Papers. Letter from Robert Creeley to Robert Duncan, February 24, 1964, Robert Duncan Papers. Letter from Robert Creeley to Robert Duncan, December 6, 1978, Robert Duncan Papers.

Department of Special Collections, University Libraries, Stanford University: Robert Creeley, "ROBERT DUNCAN: talking late July, 74 – S.F.," Robert Creeley Papers.

For published work by Edward Dorn: The following material is reprinted with permission of Jennifer Dunbar Dorn: excerpt from "On the Debt My Mother Owed to Sears Roebuck," by Edward Dorn, *The Collected Poems, 1956–1974*, expanded edition, copyright ©1964 by Edward Dorn. "Something we can all agree on," by Edward Dorn, from *Abhorrences*, copyright ©1990, by Edward Dorn.

Excerpts from *Gunslinger* by Edward Dorn, copyright ©1968, 1969, 1971, 1972, 1975, and 1989 by Edward Dorn are reprinted by permission of Duke University Press.

For unpublished work by Edward Dorn: Letter from Edward Dorn to Denise Levertov, November 24, 1958, Denise Levertov Papers. Reprinted by permission of Jennifer Dunbar Dorn and used with permission of Department of Special Collections, University Libraries, Stanford University.

For published work by Robert Duncan: The following material by Robert Duncan is reprinted by permission of New Directions Publishing Corp.: "For A Muse Meant," by Robert Duncan, from *Selected Poems*, copyright © 1950 by Robert Duncan. Excerpts by Robert Duncan, from *The Opening of the Field*, copyright ©1960 by Robert Duncan. Excerpts by Robert Duncan, from *Roots and Branches*, copyright ©1964 by Robert Duncan. Excerpts by Robert Duncan, from *Bending the Bow*, copyright ©1968 by Robert Duncan. Excerpt from "The Homosexual in Society," by Robert Duncan, from *A Selected Prose*, copyright ©1968 by Robert Duncan. Excerpts by Robert Duncan, from *Ground Work: Before the War*, copyright ©1984 by Robert Duncan. Excerpts by Robert Duncan, from *Ground Work: In the Dark*, copyright ©1987 by Robert Duncan.

Excerpts from *The Years As Catches: First poems (1939–1946)* by Robert Duncan (Berkeley: Oyez Press, 1966), copyright © 1966 by Robert Duncan is reprinted by permission of the Literary Estate of Robert Duncan and the Jess Collins Trust.

For unpublished material by Robert Duncan: Permission to quote unpublished material by Robert Duncan is granted by the Literary Estate of Robert Duncan and the Jess Collins Trust, copyright © the Literary Estate of Robert Duncan, and by permission of the archives at which it is held:

Archives and Special Collections at the Thomas J. Dodd Research Center, University of Connecticut Libraries: Letter from Robert Duncan to Charles Olson, August 19, 1954, Charles Olson Research Collection.

Department of Special Collections, University Libraries, Stanford University: Letter from Robert Duncan to Robert Creeley, January–February 1956, Robert Creeley Papers. Letter from Robert

Duncan to Robert Creeley, March 28, 1959, Robert Creeley Papers. Letter from Robert Duncan to Robert Creeley, February 19, 1964, Robert Creeley Papers. Letter from Robert Duncan to Robert Creeley, December 12, 1978, Robert Creeley Papers. Letter from Robert Duncan to Robert Creeley, June 4, 1979, Robert Creeley Papers. "Interview with L. S. Dembo," typescript included in letter to Denise Levertov, July 14, 1967, Denise Levertov Papers.

Poetry Collection of the University Libraries, State University of New York at Buffalo: Robert Duncan, Black Mountain College Notebook, Robert Duncan Papers. Excerpts from the "Preface," "A Man at the Crossroads," "I heard a demon in the air," "The Grue of Mandrake Park," "Thomas the Rhymer" of *Homage to Coleridge*, Robert Duncan Papers. "Interview with Mary Emma Harris," Robert Duncan Papers.

Lilly Library, Indiana University, Bloomington. Letter from Robert Duncan to Henry Rago, July 15, 1964, *Poetry* Manuscripts.

For published work by Denise Levertov: The following material by Denise Levertov is reprinted by permission of New Directions Publishing Corp.:

"A Common Ground," by Denise Levertov, from *Poems 1960–1967*, copyright ©1961 by Denise Levertov. "A Silence," by Denise Levertov, from *Collected Earlier Poems 1940–1960*, copyright ©1957, 1958, 1959, 1960, 1961, 1979 by Denise Levertov. "Biafra" and excerpts from "Staying Alive, Parts I, II, III, IV," "Staying Alive, Prologue: An Interim," by Denise Levertov, from *Poems 1968–1972*, copyright ©1970 by Denise Levertov. Excerpts, by Denise Levertov, from *Poems 1968–1972*, copyright ©1965, 1966, 1967, 1968, 1970, 1971 by Denise Levertov. Excerpts, "Greeting to the Vietnamese Delegates to the U.N.," by Denise Levertov, from *Life in the Forest*, copyright ©1978 by Denise Levertov. Excerpts by Denise Levertov, from *Light Up the Cave*, copyright ©1981 by Denise Levertov. Excerpt from "El Salvador: Requiem and Invocation," by Denise Levertov, from *A Door in the Hive*, copyright ©1989 by Denise Levertov.

The following material by Denise Levertov is reprinted by permission of New Directions Publishing Corp. and Pollinger Ltd.: excerpts from "A Speech: For Antidraft Rally, D.C., March 22, 1980,"

"Candles in Babylon," "Concurrence," "Desolate Light," "Her Destiny," "Her Judgment," "Her Secret," "Her Sister," "Her Vision," "In Memory of Muriel Rukeyser," "Mass for the Day of St. Thomas Didymus, i. Kyrie, ii. Gloria, iv. Sanctus, vi. Agnus Dei," "The Art of the Octopus," "The Bride," "The Soothsayer," by Denise Levertov, from *Candles in Babylon*, copyright ©1982 by Denise Levertov.

For unpublished work by Denise Levertov: "The Poem as Counterforce," typescript, by Denise Levertov, William Carlos Williams Papers, Beinecke Rare Book and Manuscript Library, Yale University. Published by permission of the Denise Levertov Literary Trust, Valerie Trueblood and Paul A. Lacey, Co-Trustees.

For excerpts from letters by Robert Duncan and Denise Levertov: Excerpts from letters by Robert Duncan and Denise Levertov published in Duncan, Robert, and Denise Levertov, *The Letters of Robert Duncan and Denise Levertov*, edited by Robert J. Bertholf and Albert Gelpi, Stanford: Stanford University Press, 2004; by the Literary Estate of Robert Duncan and the Jess Collins Trust; and by the Denise Levertov Literary Trust, Valerie Trueblood and Paul A. Lacey, Co-Trustees, respectively.

For published work by Charles Olson: The following material by Charles Olson is reprinted by permission of the University of California Press: "The Motion," *Collected Poems of Charles Olson: Excluding the* Maximus Poems (paper) by Charles Olson, copyright ©1987, 1997, 2007 by University of California Press—Books; excerpts from *Maximus Poems* by Charles Olson, copyright ©1987, 2007 by University of California Press—Books; excerpts from "a 3rd morning it's beautiful," "I, Maximus of Gloucester, to You," "Imbued / with the light, . . ." "Letter 2, May, 1959," "Main Street," "Maximus to Gloucester, Letter 27," "not the intaglio method . . . ," "Peloria . . . ," "The Cow of Dogtown," from the *Maximus Poems* by Charles Olson, copyright ©2007 by University of California Press—Books.

For unpublished work by Charles Olson: Permission to reprint excerpts from the following unpublished works by Charles Olson is granted by the Archives and Special Collections at the Thomas J. Dodd Research Center, University of Connecticut, as copyright holder and as the archive at which the material is housed:

"RIME, or notes on Verse pre-Chaucer and post-Pound,"

original typed [mss., c. 1953], Robert Creeley's Olson Materials, Charles Olson Research Collection.

   "The Mystery of What Happens When It Happens (A Communication, from Charles Olson)," original typed mss. With proofreader marks [January 1950?], Folder 1638, Charles Olson Research Collection.

For published work by Ezra Pound: Excerpts from Cantos LI, LXX, LXXII, XCIX, XXXV by Ezra Pound, from *The Cantos of Ezra Pound*, copyright © 1932, 1934, 1937, 1940, 1948, 1956, 1959, 1962, 1966, 1968 by Ezra Pound. Reprinted by permission of New Directions Publishing Corp. and Faber and Faber Limited.

For published work by Louis Zukofsky: Excerpts from *"A"* by Louis Zukofsky, copyright ©1978 (Berkeley: University of California Press, 1978) are reprinted by permission of Paul Zukofsky. The lines may not be reproduced, quoted, or used in any manner whatsoever without the explicit and specific permission of the copyright holder.

BEYOND MAXIMUS

Introduction

The term *Black Mountain* hovers uneasily on the horizon of recent literary history. The diversity of poets to whom it has been applied and the divergence of their careers after the late 1960s call into question what once seemed a meaningful grouping within the counterculture of post–World War II poetry. Historically, Black Mountain poetry has been associated with the publication of Charles Olson's 1950 essay "Projective Verse" and the little poetry magazines *Origin* (first series, April 1951–Winter 1957) and *Black Mountain Review* (1954–57), which were inspired at least in part by Olson's conception of "composition by field." In the preface to his 1960 anthology *The New American Poetry*, Donald Allen named the Black Mountain poets as one of five communities composing the counterculture of his "New American Poetry" and included poets "originally closely identified with the two important magazines of the period, *Origin* and *Black Mountain Review*" in the Black Mountain grouping: Paul Blackburn, Paul Carroll, Robert Creeley, Ed Dorn, Robert Duncan, Larry Eigner, Denise Levertov, Charles Olson, Jonathan Williams, and Joel Oppenheimer.[1] Allen's communities have become to some extent canonical in understanding the period. As with other poetry subcultures of the 1950s and 1960s, however, much of the common ground that united these poets had eroded by the early 1970s. The countercultural movements that gained momentum in the 1960s, especially protest against the Vietnam War, transformed American culture, representing a critical threshold to a different configuration of literary communities. From the perspective of 2007, we must ask whether the designation *Black Mountain* continues to be useful and from what vantage point to view poets associated with it.

Olson's "Projective Verse," with its poetics of "composition by field," proved tremendously important as a catalyst to innovation in poetry after World War II. While it did not produce a unified school of experimental poetics, "composition by field" provided poets as diverse as Amiri Baraka (then LeRoi Jones), Kathleen Fraser, Susan Howe, and Michael McClure with a crucial impetus to break with conventions and generate new poetic forms. Field poetics proposed an alternative to what Olson and others perceived as the bankruptcy of New Critical emphasis on the poet's craft and traditional forms and meter. In "Projective Verse," Olson argues the need for escape from what he perceives as the idealism of Western culture, which for him had imposed the forms of the human mind on the natural world, thereby alienating human beings from their existence as part of nature. Olson advocates eliminating the "lyric interference of the individual as ego" by rejecting the hierarchy of spirit over matter. For him, poetic composition becomes an open-ended tracing of environmental forces as they influence the poet, and poetic form should be an immediate translation of bodily experience (through breath and spoken language) onto the page.[2] Taken from physics' understanding of the world as an interaction of electromagnetic forces, the force field provides a model of reality in which all elements interact on the same level, each exerting force on the other. Rather than gaining meaning through an ideal order perceived and imposed by the poet, each element defines the other through resonance of similarity and difference that preserve its particularity. Poetic form should thus emerge not from a totalizing humanistic perception but from the interaction of independent things in the poem.

"Projective Verse" inspired impassioned discussion and drew poets and editors together in a strong sense of common purpose. The communities that developed around the magazines nurtured strong friendships influential in the individual development of many poets during the 1950s and 1960s as well as the growth of the larger poetic counterculture. Although Olson was directly involved only in *Origin* and *Black Mountain Review*, other little magazines (e.g., *Yugen, Floating Bear, The Evergreen Review*) drew on or praised field poetics. Thus while some poets claimed close allegiance to field or Black Mountain poetry or were associated with them, an even wider range of poets invoked Olson in formulating their poetics. Poets from three of the five groups that Allen's anthology identifies (Black Mountain, Beat, and younger poets) mention "Projective Verse" and its ideas explicitly. Frank O'Hara, associated with the "New York" poets, parodies "Projective Verse" in his influential essay "Personism." The widespread reception of the term *field* attests to its significance not only in the maturation of a small group of so-called Black Mountain poets but also as a term that expressed widespread desire for innovation among the New American poets. Field poetics was thus both influential and representative of its time.

The historical Black Mountain community and its critical reception require some explanation, for in the context of the arts "Black Mountain" evokes diverse meanings. While all of these meanings trace their origin to the small, experimental college in existence near Asheville, North Carolina, from 1933 to 1956,[3] the communities and esthetic principles associated with the college vary widely. Mary Emma Harris's documentary survey *The Arts at Black Mountain* divides the college's history into three periods: the college and farm founded by John Andrew Rice to implement John Dewey's pragmatic educational philosophy, the haven for Bauhaus émigrés from Europe dominated by Josef Albers in the 1940s, and the poetic-painterly community of experimental artists that formed during Charles Olson's rectorship in the early 1950s.[4] Although writers came to dominate the college community while Olson was rector, this community also included figures as diverse as painters Franz Kline and Robert Rauschenberg, composer John Cage, dancer-choreographer Merce Cunningham, mathematician Buckminster Fuller, and weaver Anni Albers.

The term *Black Mountain poetry* invokes a somewhat different community. Historically, the Black Mountain poets were associated not only with Black Mountain College but also with the little poetry magazines *Origin* and *Black Mountain Review*. Other poets and scholars define other combinations of poets, however, including for example John Wieners and Jonathan Williams.[5] Olson, Creeley, and Duncan taught at Black Mountain College, whereas Oppenheimer, Wieners, and Dorn were students. Perhaps due to generational differences, the students' emphasis on ironic and often humorous entrapment in cultural forms contrasts with their teachers' embrace of the poet's visionary role as shaper of culture and language. Levertov and Blackburn were never at the college but published in

Black Mountain Review, with which Dorn and Wieners had relatively little association.

Not only was the Black Mountain arts community esthetically diverse, but the Black Mountain poets sustained friendships of comparative intensity with other New American poets—for example, Duncan with Helen Adam, Creeley with John Ashbery, Dorn with LeRoi Jones, and Levertov with Adrienne Rich. The poetry and critical discussion in the magazines vary considerably, at times representing conflicting poetics. Alan Golding's study of the correspondence between *Origin* editor Cid Corman and contributors Olson, Creeley, and Duncan reveals the arguments and differences that shaped what may appear to be poetic consensus published in *Origin*.[6] Blackburn noted a difference between the first four issues of *Black Mountain Review* and the next three, and a change in the interests of the core group: "the range of critical prose widens, as does the general contents. The ring of contacts spread far beyond *Origin* people, the Black Mountain [College] contacts were taking over the center."[7] As late as 1968, Olson denied the existence of a Black Mountain school of poetry,[8] and Creeley refused to state a unifying poetics.[9]

Critical reception has perpetuated but further complicated the term. Due to the influence of Olson's "Projective Verse," Black Mountain poetry was initially associated with field and open form poetry. Both were seen as influential and typical in inspiring shifting local structures in poetic form, one critical rubric formulated to define a metaphysics or epistemology underlying Postmodern poetics. Such reception frequently elides "Black Mountain" with "composition by field," due both to assumptions of Olson's influence at Black Mountain and to the powerful influence of the idea of the force field on some of these poets' work. Noting the frequent reference to Olson's image of the force field and "Projective Verse" in the poetics statements of contributors to his anthology, Allen writes that "composition by field" is "the dominant new concept."[10] In 1974, Don Byrd wrote that "[t]he analogy of the field [for poetic structure] has begun to appear as suggestive of the twentieth century poets as the analogy of organism was for the Romantics."[11] Critics and poets of this first generation of interpretation were often concerned with defining the poetics of "composition by field" or "open form" as a significant formal innovation, sometimes reproducing the territoriality characteristic of the marginalized avant-garde movement.[12]

During the 1970s and 1980s, field poetics became a key element of Postmodern poetics, but critical reception reinterpreted field poetics, moving away from the communities that grew up around Black Mountain College or the little magazines *Origin* and *Black Mountain Review*. Critics such as Sherman Paul, Ekbert Faas, Stephen Fredman, Robert Von Hallberg, and Lynn Keller followed Olson in interpreting surrender to the physical force field as the way to free language from a restrictive intellectual tradition, but they broadened the range of poets that they associated with this new poetics beyond the historical Black Mountain College or *Review* communities. Faas emphasizes "physio-linguistic empathy" or body-based rather than "intellectual organization" of language that can fuse an "original language with the flow of creation." Fredman shifts focus from "composition by field" to a cluster of practices "grounding" poetics that Olson adapted from Emersonian and Modernist traditions and transmitted to other "projectivist" poets.[13] Von Hallberg argues that the theory of the force field erodes the world of sense objects, encouraging poets to challenge conventional structures of being implicit in closed syntax. Keller identifies ways the poem seeks to reflect the shifting nature of being and truth in the flux of the force field by tracking the open-ended flow of consciousness.[14] For these critics, field poetics is related to and representative of post–World War II poetry.

More recent studies have further attenuated this focus. By reading the poets' works from hindsight, often through their different affiliations since the 1970s, studies like Peter Quartermain's *Disjunctive Poetics* (1992), Sandra Kumamoto Stanley's *Louis Zukofsky and the Transformation of a Modern American Poetics* (1994), and Michael Davidson's *Ghostlier Demarcations* (1997) trace significant differences blurred by the earlier solidarity of these poets within the New American Poetry's counterculture. They place field poetry in an experimental tradition of twentieth-century American writing from Stein, Williams, and Pound through Zukofsky to some Black Mountain poets and finally the Language poets of the 1970s and 1980s.[15] Literary history has also complicated definition of a Black Mountain poetic community. Recent historical and archival research questions the delineation of the period's poetry into geographical or esthetic groupings widely accepted since *The New American Poetry* by demonstrating the fluidity of these groups.[16]

In focusing on the physical force field as a metaphysical or natural model for experimental poetics, critics have interpreted Olson and the first generation of writers he influenced primarily on their own terms. Field poetry sought to eliminate traditional symbols and meter to render the poem as visual scoring of the rhythm of body and breath. The poet, conceived not as order-imposing artificer but as transmitter of environmental forces, provided a new, nonsubjective view of the world whose decentering of the subject may be aligned with other Postmodern or poststructuralist projects. Such interpretations tend to focus on early work by Olson, Creeley, and Duncan and to include a range of other poets—among them, Zukofsky, George Oppen, Blackburn, Robert Bly, and Gary Snyder—while omitting poets whose careers later departed from this model of nature or took a more explicitly political turn in the 1960s, like Levertov and Dorn, and a "second generation" of Black Mountain College students such as Oppenheimer or Wieners.

Building on this combination of literary history and critical reception, I would locate the term *Black Mountain* somewhere between Rachel Blau DuPlessis and Peter Quartermain's interpretive "nexus" and Benedict Anderson's "imagined community." DuPlessis and Quartermain use the word *nexus* to describe the relation among the Objectivist poets. They define "nexus" as a group of poets who share a historical association (for DuPlessis and Quartermain's Objectivists, a community of predominantly but not exclusively New York City Jewish writers), sense of common interest, and varying reception of a central statement of poetics, all of which taken collectively constitute an important influence on literary tradition.[17] This concept describes quite well the relation between writers who gathered around *Origin* and *Black Mountain Review*, poets who shared an interest in field poetics, and the recovery of a Modernist tradition based on the experimentation of Pound, Williams, and in some cases H. D. and Zukofsky. The term *nexus* may fit so well because it reflects institutional structures shaping the publication of poetry, particularly avant-garde poetry, in the twentieth century. Both the Objectivist and the Black Mountain communities formed around little magazines professing a new poetics as influential vehicles of publication.

Although "nexus" describes many features of Black Mountain poetry, this historical focus requires the added dimension of Benedict Anderson's "imagined community," a collective identity formed through imaginative participation in or identification with common symbols that unite people beyond local community.[18] The poetic community that emerged around the little magazines *Origin* and *Black Mountain Review* was less homogeneous geographically and ethnically than the Objectivists, to whose New York City Jewish majority DuPlessis and Quartermain attribute some of their common concerns. The writers associated with Black Mountain poetry came from different regions and were rarely in the same place at the same time. Their intensive interaction was carried out predominantly in one-to-one interaction through visits and letters. As with Anderson's imagined community, commitment to "composition by field" bound both poets and critics through feelings of solidarity beyond local allegiance. "Composition by field" also played a significant role in the poets' work, as attested by their concern with its definition in *Origin* and *Black Mountain Review*, their loyalty to other little magazines supportive of field poetics, and their publication of mutually enthusiastic reviews and statements of influence and shared poetics. The dynamic of an "imagined community" has generated critical debate as well, for literary critics and historians continue to invoke the common term *Black Mountain* while ascribing it different meanings locally.

The poets often expressed their sense of shared purpose and concern for maintaining it more powerfully in published texts than on the local level, where tensions in individual interpretations and face-to-face social relations challenged solidarity felt from a distance. This imagined dimension of solidarity stimulated intense epistolary discussions of the nature of field poetics as well as individual interaction between the poets. Alan Golding has traced the concern Corman, Olson, and Creeley expressed about the form of *Origin* as an embodiment of their interpretation of field poetics and various Black Mountain poets' concern about the company in which Allen's anthology would publish them.[19] Libbie Rifkin observes that Olson's and Creeley's ideas of the "polis" "appeared to function most ideally on the epistolary page where it began."[20] The poets' sudden, unexpectedly explosive responses when they realize their differences of opinion (in Olson's and Creeley's irascibility in letters despite their mutual enthusiasm, Olson's and Duncan's sparring over the nature of "wisdom" in the mid-1950s, Duncan's and Levertov's intense debate about political poetry during the Vietnam War, and Creeley's and Duncan's discussion of what they see as Dorn's departure from field poetics in *Gunslinger*) erupted because of this implicit sense of shared purpose.

Imagined community also becomes evident in group loyalty and jockeying for distinction among poets who identified with other poetic subcultures. As leader in his Berkeley coterie, Jack Spicer expressed face-to-face hostility to poets he praised in other contexts. He chose, for example, to read his misogynistic "For Joe" at a party honoring Helen Adam and Levertov on the occasion of the latter's 1958 visit to San Francisco. Michael Davidson reads Spicer's act as a test of his community's loyalty against the perceived threat of a figure from the growing national avant garde.[21] Creeley, Duncan, and Levertov criticized "Beat" fame and the satiric urbanity of the New York scene in letters, strengthening their feeling of solidarity through contradistinction from different local scenes, however vaguely defined the sense of scene or difference. Despite the poets' feeling, especially after the 1960 publication of Allen's anthology, that they were part of a national avant garde, their identities remained strongly grounded in these local, if shifting, subcultures. They often corresponded enthusiastically with the very writers they criticized to others. Rifkin's analysis of Olson's frenetic all-night speech at the 1965 Berkeley Poetry Conference shows how his need to address a gathering of writers from different geographical and literary scenes brought these tensions to a head. She argues persuasively that Olson, in his alternately grandiose, domineering, and self-deprecating filibuster, attempted to negotiate his role as "boss poet" of this wider counterculture while fully aware that its diverse members expected different styles from him.[22]

The sense of a common project inspired by "composition by field" fueled intensive correspondence that remains a fruitful resource for understanding the extremely widespread and varied reception of field poetics and its significance, both to the work of individual poets and to the period. Within current multiple, fluid understandings of Black Mountain and field poetry, I will analyze a grouping significant yet increasingly obscured by recent criticism: poets who developed the social significance of the force field as a model of historical and cultural force.[23] This focus is intended to complement, not displace, the excellent critical work on the force field as a natural/scientific and metaphysical model of agency. While "Projective Verse" inspired much poetry with a natural and metaphysical focus, field poetics also drew writers into socially committed positions and shaped their approach to political poetry. My intent is not to define Black Mountain or field poetics narrowly or exclusively, but rather to trace a significant strand of the reception of this tremendously fertile image. Interpreting the physical force field as a model of social force complements attention to the philosophical and visual-metrical experimentation of field poetry. Field poetics helped poets to articulate and respond to changing conceptions of poetic subject and agency by providing a model of social force to explore the social agents that they perceived as influencing the poem. Field poetics thus illuminates social pressures motivating not only field poetry's innovations but also the public sphere shaping poetic production and reception—to use Christopher Beach's term, the "poetic culture"[24]—of the New American Poetry.

Among the many poets who develop or invoke the force field at some point in their careers, Olson, Creeley, Duncan, Levertov, and Dorn constitute a significant grouping in the reception of field poetics as a model of social force for reasons both formal and historical. These five poets engaged "composition by field" more intensely and consistently throughout their careers than most of their contemporaries. Olson's "Projective Verse" influenced profoundly the poetic maturity of the other four. Also influenced by Pound and Williams and in some cases H. D. and Zukofsky, these poets incorporated field poetics into a Modernist view of the poet's calling as seer and critic of his or her culture. They adapt the legacy of this tradition to the mass culture emerging in the United States in the 1950s and 1960s and explore poetry's potential as a force for social change within this culture. Their work transforms the Modernist legacy of the poet as crafter of cultural forms to acknowledge a richer spectrum of social agents as factors determining poetic structure in mass culture and confronts the problem of poetic authority in this culture head-on. Within this grouping, Creeley, Duncan, and Levertov share a distinctive core of beliefs about the social role of experimental poetry in the varied New American counterculture, whereas Olson's and Dorn's adaptations of the force field establish links to earlier and later generations, respectively. While the poets adapted field poetics to increasing political engagement in the 1960s, the Vietnam War brought a poetic crisis that destroyed both friendships and a sense of poetic affiliation. In seeking to make poetry a force in the growing counterculture, these poets reveal their belief in poetry's potential to work political change and their experience of the perils of their generation's political engagement.

Focus on the reception of the force field as a model of social force provides a significant revision of these five poets' full careers. It helps not only to recover the common ground that once united them but also to explain the reasons for their divergence from one another and current association with different poetic communities: Creeley with Language poets, Duncan with some Language poets and some poets who share his mystical vision of literature, Levertov with Christian poetry and ecocriticism, and Dorn with Western regionalism and controversial political poets. Nature-based interpretations of the force field describe well the similarities of these poets' early experiments, but they do not explain each poet's subsequent divergence or the emergence of their new affiliations after the 1970s. Poetic reception of the force field as a model of social agency reveals the intense responsiveness of poetry to public language informing many of the period's formal innovations. By recovering the social and esthetic discussion in which Black Mountain poetry emerged and the issues that divided the poets in the late 1960s, we can understand the attempts at a difficult alliance between experimental poetics and public voice that made Black Mountain poetry a crucial element—and the force field a significant element—in the New American Poetry's artistic and political struggle.

My analysis of the social reception of the force field builds on recent studies of American poetry since World War II that focus on constructions of voice and authority in relation to projected audience. Edward Brunner's *Cold War Poetry* traces the demands that the expanding audience of GI Bill students and Creative Writing/MFA programs made on 1950s poetry. Rifkin shows how avant-garde poets bidding for membership in the canon constructed "professional" identities. For Terrell Scott Herring, Frank O'Hara's intimate yet impersonal "personal poem" creates a homosexual public sphere within mass culture.[25] Michael Davidson's *Guys Like Us* theorizes that poetry of the Cold War period implicitly forges alliances of homosocial community to counteract poetry's marginality.

The reception of the force field as a model of social force from the 1950s through the early 1970s adds a valuable dimension to this discussion of multiple public spheres.[26] By using the poem to register social forces acting on the imagination, the poets articulated changing perceptions of cultural media and thus of the space and role of poetry as a social institution. Theoretical discussion of the force field and innovative poetic forms reveal the hopes and fears for the social and political role of poetry within the rapidly changing public sphere of mass culture. Whereas other New

American poets (O'Hara and the Beats, as Herring and Davidson have shown) "work strategically *within*" (Davidson's phrase)[27] this mass public sphere, Black Mountain poets who develop the force field as a model of social force reveal the radical, often violent transformation of poetic and political subjectivity accompanying participation in this new public sphere.

Such studies recontextualize James Breslin's influential argument that Olson's "Projective Verse" was a crucial element in the New American poets' rebellion against the traditional critical decorum praised by figures of the New Critical literary establishment.[28] For Breslin, Olson's call to eliminate the "lyric interference of the individual as ego"[29] by rejecting the hierarchy of spirit over matter inspired many writers to abandon the New Critics' emphasis on traditional forms. Such an interpretation fits the sense of shared purpose among poets attracted to *Origin* and *Black Mountain Review*. These poets had little faith that traditional forms would confer value or dignity on human experience.[30] Many of the pieces they published treat the breakdown and transgression of social norms through themes like adultery and madness.[31] Poems by Richard Eberhart and William Bronk voice the alienation and dislocation of human beings in a meaningless universe.[32] Special issues on the "New German" and "New French" writing, particularly writing by Gottfried Benn and Antonin Artaud, communicate the European struggle against nihilism and irony in the wake of the war.[33]

The sea becomes a pervasive image for this experience of chaos and power, as in Theodore Enslin's "seaview," "penetrable by so many winds that charts / of probability are useless."[34] Poets frequently expressed their disorientation in imagery of the wanderer, whose quest for an ordering principle in the cosmos structures their early work.[35] Contributors to *Origin* and *Black Mountain Review* rejected traditional forms as signs of the culture's lack of vitality and sought forms that emerged more directly from the rhythms of their contemporary experience and speech. Reviews by Martin Seymour-Smith and Corman criticize Theodore Roethke and Karl Shapiro, then editor of *Poetry*, for their "self-effacing" style, "using old rhythms and imposing no sign of personal diction." For Seymour-Smith and Corman, these poems do nothing but translate philosophical or psychological platitudes into meter.[36]

However much this counterculture conceived itself as rejecting mainstream forms, research on American culture in the 1950s and 1960s

has begun to find continuity as well as difference between Cold War con-
servatism and subsequent liberal and radical protest movements. Field poetics' focus on tracking "force," particularly new or unacknowledged
agents influencing the imagination, reflected and provided a way for writers to explore widespread social anxieties of the Cold War period and the
emerging mass and global culture. Tom Engelhardt's *The End of Victory
Culture* argues that after World War II confidence in the United States'
ethical superiority and in clear national boundaries gave way to fear of the
invisible yet immediately threatening forces of the atomic bomb and communism, with their power to invade from afar. Engelhardt traces this feeling from the 1940s aftermath of nuclear holocaust and the beginning of
the Cold War through the Vietnam War, with its elusive guerrilla enemy,
and the United States' increasing embroilment in global politics.[37] Terence
Ball and Sean McCann identify similar concern with new agents and social
forces in postwar political science paradigms. Both academic/theoretical
and practical/activist theories de-emphasize the agency of individuals and
the political state in favor of more diffuse "systems" or power flows that
render agency and accountability impersonal and invisible.[38]

The feeling of heightened vulnerability from abroad was intensified
by perceived threat from forces at home. Widespread surveillance and in-
terrogation in the McCarthy era and Johnson's welfare state extended the
arm of the government farther into private life. Deborah Nelson's study of
legal and literary constructions of privacy 1959–73 describes the "death of
privacy" as "a topological crisis in which bounded spaces of all kinds
seemed to exhibit a frightening permeability."[39] The growth of mass culture that magnified celebrities to superhuman proportions and entered the
home in the vivid media of radio and television further blurred the boundary between public and private. Timothy Melley's *Empire of Conspiracy* reveals the intense pressure that the political culture of mass media exerted
on conventional conceptions of selfhood. Melley traces the pervasive paranoia or "agency panic" in many areas of popular culture, the fear that the
media could erode "a long-standing model of personhood."[40]

From this perspective, both the New Critical attempt to contain self
and literary tradition by insulating them from historical forces[41] and field
poetics' concern with tracking these forces, albeit at first in natural settings, emerged as different responses to a similar consciousness of public
forces intruding on the private individual. Both responded to a deep con-

cern with environmental influences that seemed to render the individual a mere node within or vehicle for transfer of social force. Both New Critical standards of taste and the Black Mountain adaptation of the Modernist image of the poet as social visionary seek to uphold the poet's authority and social role in the political and poetic cultures of the 1950s and 1960s. The force field provides a significant topos for studying changing conceptions of poetic agency in what Habermas calls the transition from the "bourgeois" public sphere of rational, autonomous individuals to one in which individual debate and alliance formation are mediated by other systems. The reconfiguration of the poetic subject around newly acknowledged social forces makes visible what Wendy Brown calls "post-liberal" subjectivities emerging from a crisis of faith in the liberal democratic subject and the new public sphere composed of these post-liberal subjects.[42]

In articulating new modes of poetic agency for a changing public sphere, the five Black Mountain poets that form the subject of this book both exemplify and influence the transition from the mainstream 1950s poetic culture that Brunner traces in *Cold War Poetry* to the greater political reach of poetry in the 1960s counterculture. Their early work was shaped by the ideologies informing the Cold War poetry that Brunner describes, particularly the depoliticization of poetic culture and an ideology associating poetry with the domestic sphere. While tensions in Olson's *Maximus Poems* reveal the shrinking public and "monumental" dimension of poetry since the Modernist period and the difficulty of the poet's role as epic bard, Creeley, Duncan, and Levertov are typical of their generation in initially developing their experimental poetics in domestic contexts. In an era that severed poetry from politics so effectively that for many poets "there was no model for political action," these three poets adopted the stance of Brunner's exemplary "citizen poet,"[43] whose ethically responsible actions in the private sphere address public tensions obliquely. Like the mainstream culture Brunner describes, they believed that poetry should act as an "improving" antidote to emerging mass culture.[44]

As Creeley, Duncan, Levertov, and Dorn attempted to forge a socially engaged poetry for the growing counterculture of the early 1960s, they also registered the changing authority of language and other cultural media and developed new poetic forms to respond to them. By focusing attention on the poem as a transfer of energy from the environment through the poet to the poem, "composition by field" encourages the poet to articulate influences other than consciousness shaping the poem. Tracking the public forces encroaching on the poetic subject allowed these poets to voice ways that private self is eroded and to seek new ways of preserving imaginative autonomy to resist such invasion. Their constructions of self and agency transformed what Marianne DeKoven, in her analysis of 1960s cultural texts, has termed a modern faith in the individual as an agent of social change into a Postmodern view of the individual as embedded in subterranean or individual systems of power. They reflect what DeKoven terms the "modern/postmodern Möbius strip," the simultaneity and entwining of these positions characteristic of a wide range of 1960s cultural production, from experimental theater and poetry to political treatises and sociology.[45] Their crises and innovations reveal the profound reorientation of poetic subjectivity this shift requires and the accompanying unique openness of self to public sphere that inspires the period's idiosyncratic forms.

After tracing the changing reception of the physical force field as a model of social force from the Modernists to Olson in Chapter 1, I will analyze the Black Mountain poets' conceptualization of this field as a model of social force and interpret their poetry as a response to their perceived social context. Each chapter will focus on a key issue in the poets' correspondence to reveal their changing conceptions of field poetics. Chapter 2 discusses early adaptations of field poetics that depart from Romantic and Modernist conceptions of culture grounded in natural order to define self through culturally defined place. In the 1950s, Olson's and Creeley's intense discussion of place and their experiments with colloquial speech, popular myth, and social convention reveal the growing authority of collective over natural and personal voice.

Chapter 3 traces Creeley's and Duncan's shift in the late 1950s and early 1960s away from exploring the expressive possibilities of colloquial speech that they and many of their contemporaries embraced as more authentic than literary diction. For Creeley and Duncan, colloquial language lost its authenticity and could no longer provide a safe experimental space in which to renovate their impoverished culture. Seeking to expand linguistic meaning through literary transformation of everyday speech, Creeley, Duncan, and Levertov developed strategies to separate poetic language from popular culture and colloquial idiom. The close bonds of friendship and mutual admiration that united Creeley, Duncan, and Levertov from the late 1950s through the mid-1960s were nourished by their shared conception of the poem as a linguistic field where imagination can act on these social forces, re-creating ordinary language to enrich collective language and perception.

While Creeley and Duncan's discussion of abstract form theorizes this changing perception of field poetics, Duncan and Levertov's correspondence, particularly their discussion of Vietnam War poetry, articulates the social role of the poet and the perception of the public sphere to which this abstraction responded. Experiencing the power of political rhetoric during the Vietnam War shook the poets' belief that the poetic imagination could transform other social forces. Like many of their contemporaries, Duncan and Levertov engaged a popular or mass audience and modes of communication in the attempt to challenge the authority of public rhetoric. Chapter 4 analyzes the dramatic changes in their Vietnam War writing to expose the different constructions of authority each believed would give poetry force in the public arena. The strain this attempt produced led Duncan and Levertov to conceive the polis and thus the poet-audience relation as situations in which social and individual agency, public and private voice seemed radically different, so different that the model of the force field could no longer hold them in productive interaction.

If the idea of the poet as renovator of communal language united the Black Mountain poets during their period of greatest solidarity, Dorn's perspective from a younger generation departs from the Modernist high calling of the poet to express the critical distance of a changing poetic climate. Duncan's and Levertov's troubled wartime poetry and the increasingly dominant agency Dorn attributes to popular culture rather than poetic imagination signal the difficulty of balancing social forces in the field of the poem and the declining use of the force field as a model of poetic structure in such a public arena. Chapter 5 shows how the divergence between Levertov's and Dorn's work of the 1970s illustrates the erosion of field poetics as the common ground of Black Mountain poetry and forecasts the emergence of different conceptions of poetic agency and poetic forms.

Together, the five poets initially expressed surprising optimism and innocence about the power of popular and emergent mass culture to disseminate their ideas and make art a significant force for social change.

In so doing, they expressed beliefs about the social potential of poetry shared by the little magazines and larger counterculture of which they were a part.[46] This confidence led them to imitate new forms and media of massified popular culture in the attempt to exploit its authority and reach. While initial optimism nurtured powerful friendships and collaboration, the ways each poet adapted "composition by field" to register the social (especially linguistic) forces acting on the poet and thus the forms each poet develops imply different conceptions of the public arena. The divergence of their later writing stems from their different conceptions of the cultural forces competing with the poet's craft to influence poetic form. The poets' discussion of these cultural forces in their letters provides a valuable framework for interpreting the development of their careers as a response to the changing status of language and poetry in the United States' emergent mass culture. Their spectrum of responses—comprehension, adaptation, and resistance—to this social context helps to distinguish them from each other and to provide a framework for relating their formal innovations to those of their contemporaries. These Black Mountain poets' eventual divergence helps to explain the tensions that motivated younger poets' rejection or transformation of field poetics and the emergence of the new, more fragmented and local poetic cultures of the 1980s and 1990s, from ecopoetics to Language poetry.

1

History as Force Field in Pound, Zukofsky, and Olson

The significance of the force field as a model of social force for the Black Mountain poets has its origins in Modernism. The physical theory of the force field has frequently been used to explain the breakdown of representational form in Modernist art and the emergence of Postmodern "open form." In dissolving the world of discrete objects into a flux of atoms shaped by invisible forces, this model of nature challenges both the distinction between individual and environment and the belief in individual autonomy. Many critics interpret Modernist fragmentation as a response to this seemingly chaotic natural world.[1] The analogy between the structures of art and nature explains well the absence of traditional forms of order in the fragmented structure of Modernist art. However, the force field also serves to represent social forces that began to subvert the Modernist poet's confidence in such traditional forms and in his or her ability to forge order from experience. Analyzing the social reception of the force field thus reveals the forces that begin to break down the conception of artistic agency as autonomous craft and form new conceptions of poetic subjectivity.

Since the nineteenth century, writers have used the scientific model of the force field to describe collective economic, political, and ethnic forces as the dominant agents of history. As practiced by the "scientific historians,"[2] this model of social change interpreted history less as the deeds of individuals than as the evolution and interaction of trade networks, monetary systems, and institutions that structure the social environment. While the Naturalist novel constitutes one major strand of reception for this model of force field, it was also engaged by some twentieth-century poets with political aspirations—Ezra Pound, Louis Zukofsky, and Charles Olson. For them, the force field provided a way of describing the artist's role in society.[3] All three poets were active in politics, and the relation between poet and polis became the subject of their lifelong projects, *The Cantos*, *"A,"* and *The Maximus Poems*. As a materialist model of force, the field allowed each poet to conceive a direct, material connection between art and history that reflected his political experience. While art thus becomes a social force, this immediate connection to historical process also renders the poet vulnerable to social forces beyond individual control. In developing a poetics based on the force field, each poet addressed this problem of the unstable relation between the individual poet and the social forces structuring his poetry. Although Pound, Zukofsky, and Olson began with a belief that social change is a direct extension of individual action, they also perceived a widening gap between individual creativity and an independent, impersonal momentum of social forces. In imagining the relation between poet and polis, each attempted to bridge this gap in different ways. Their solutions reveal a shift from individual to social agents as the predominant forces shaping the imagination and the emergence of a poetic subjectivity no longer autonomous but yoked to or embedded in a wider circulation of social force. Each poet responded differently to this perceived invasion or reshaping of the individual, revealing the growing authority of social forces and media shaping artistic imagination.[4]

The social problems of the 1930s and early 1940s, with the Depression and the spread of fascism, raised crucial questions about the relation of individual action to social change. For Pound, esthetic creation could no longer be imagined as an expression of economic energy, and he rejected the influence of economic forces on the artist. He came to see economic and esthetic value as antithetical, true art as originating in a neo-Platonic world of ideal forms outside history. Believing that desire for profit and production for market demand corrupt morality and taste, Pound advocated social reform through fascism. The absolute power of a fascist philosopher-ruler possessing superior comprehension of these ideal forms would enable their realization in the construction of an ideal society. In contrast to Pound's increasing insulation of art and statecraft from economics, Zukofsky's embrace of communism during the Depression led him to see artistic and social production as inseparable and thus to accept the force field as a valid image of the power Marx attributes to capital. While the artist for Zukofsky was materially conditioned by social forces, his or her very embeddedness in society enabled art to transform these conditions. In its transformation of language, poetic creation became a form of social action. Where the communist Zukofsky affirmed the power of language to influence history, Olson saw in the spread of fascism, the explosion of the atomic bomb, and the demise of the New Deal a declining ability of the individual to effect social change.[5] The power of the masses and of technology seemed to Olson to possess a momentum beyond individual control. In embracing the force field as the source of individual energy rather than a force antithetical to it, Olson's "composition by field" subordinates individual agency to impersonal forces in the environment. The *Maximus Poems* represent the city as a social organism and the individual as a part of this greater being. Perceiving the destructive power of such large historical processes, Olson embraced local popular or folk culture as a response to immediate natural environment to oppose mass culture. It is this shift from individual to social agency that renders "composition by field" a manifesto for so many Postmoderns and helps to explain the diverse poetic voices that develop from its influence as hybrids of personal and public voice.

1

The writings of Brooks and Henry Adams were important sources and points of reference for Pound, Zukofsky, and Olson. The Adams brothers' efforts to apply the physical theory of force fields to the human sciences defined this theory's implications for the concept of individual agency as an issue with which each of the poets struggled. Attempting to explain the rise of a monied class that displaced their family and the intellectual elite with which they identify, the two Adams brothers defined the role of the intellectual differently in a society driven by the circulation of wealth. Although both felt a tension between capital's impersonal and the individual's personal agency, their different conceptions of how the tensions between these agents affected history provide the framework within which to understand Pound's, Zukofsky's, and Olson's conceptions of the force field and its influence on their poetry.

In his theory of history, Brooks Adams identified "Nature" or "energy" as the primary agent of social change. Individual action is not self-motivated but occurs "in obedience to an impulse as automatic as is the impulse of gravitation."[6] Defined as the energy of the dominant class, this energy is primarily economic: "Capital is autocratic, and energy vents itself through those organisms best fitted to give expression of the power of capital."[7] Brooks Adams's *The Law of Civilization and Decay* (1896) and *The Theory of Social Revolutions* (1913) trace the concentration and dispersion of wealth in different civilizations, interpreting politics and culture as products of worldwide patterns of the distribution of wealth. They combine images from biology and physics to present both the dominant class and the nation as beings with their own lives. Just as individuals are merely parts of a greater social organism, dependent on its life, so nations grow and decay in response to forces in the international context. From the perspective of physics, the biological organism is merely a system of atoms and molecules seeking equilibrium with its environment.[8] When applied to social organisms, this theory renders even national identity vulnerable to the international circulation of capital. In writing history, Brooks Adams thus derived social and political institutions from remote forces whose laws differ radically from the political ones individuals construct for themselves. This view of history as the product of impersonal forces rather than of individuals acting to shape their environment alters the task of the historian as well. History becomes a discovery of the "natural" and therefore predetermined laws governing the circulation of capital. Individual action is remarkable only insofar as it works with or against the inevitable momentum of class and nation.

Although unable to dismiss Brooks Adams's theory that capital, not the individual, drives history, Henry Adams criticized Brooks's methodology, questioning the validity of applying scientific law to history. In *The Degradation of the Democratic Dogma* (1919), Henry Adams interpreted a society's conception of creative or active force in the universe as an image of perfection toward which individuals shape their lives. In this respect, he viewed the "multiplicity" of modern science as a destructive image, one of chaos through which individuals "can only develop into that chaos of which [they form] a part."[9] Further, by identifying social organisms with

natural ones, scientific history subjects them to the second law of thermodynamics, the tendency to increased entropy or disorder. Such a perspective erodes any optimistic teleology of human development: "if the second
law of thermodynamics controlled all history . . . , man became the most
advanced type of physical decadence."[10]

Henry Adams struggled against this worldview. As an alternative to
the impersonal, chaotic "multiplicity" of modern science, he presented the
neo-Platonic order of medieval Christianity. By assuming a personal prime
mover, the Medievals imagined the force driving the world as anthropomorphic and thus anthropocentric, in harmony with human ideals.

We deal with Multiplicity and call it God. After the Virgin has redeemed by her
personal Force as Love all that is redeemable in man, the Schools embrace the real
and give it Form, Unity, and Motive. . . . [T]he thirteenth century supposed mind
to be a mode of force directly derived from the intelligent prime motor, and the
cause of all form and sequence in the universe—therefore the only proof of unity.
Without thought in the unit, there could be no unit, without unity no orderly
sequence or ordered society. Thought alone was form.[11]

Henry Adams's thirteenth-century Scholastics perceived the material world
in terms of ideal categories of the mind. This view not only rendered the
activities and ideals of the intellect real but inspired involvement in historical process to realize these ideals in the material world. Henry Adams's effort to interpret his own life as the product of intellectual rather than social
force was only partially successful, for he was unable to dismiss the power
of the new economic elite that excluded him from politics.[12] In recounting
his own life in *The Education of Henry Adams* (1918), he vacillates between
personal voice and the scientist's detached analysis of social influences characteristic of Brooks Adams's histories. Each perspective undercuts the other
ironically, revealing the unresolved tension between the two.

In their experiments with scientific history, the Adams brothers explore the tension between personal and impersonal, individual and social
agency. Henry's choice of the intellect and Brooks's of wealth as the primary agents in history generate different images of society, as composed
of either groups or individuals, and of the role of intellectuals, as active subjects working for change or as detached analysts identifying predetermined
patterns. Pound and Zukofsky confront a similar tension between individual and social agency, between self as a product of original artistic vision

and invisible social force. For the Modernists, the force field provided an image for social forces to whose influence the artist was especially sensitive. In the 1910s, the sculptor Henri Gaudier-Brzeska and Pound, among others, ground their esthetic theory of Vorticism in the physics of the force field. Ostensibly a manifesto proclaiming the principles of Vorticism,[13] Pound's *Gaudier-Brzeska: A Memoir* (1916) describes the artistic image as the artist's crystallization of a "vortex" or force field of social energy.[14] With the social and economic upheaval of the 1930s, however, this union of esthetic and social energy became increasingly difficult to achieve. Although the Vorticists were initially optimistic about a harmony between individual and social energy, the economic and political upheavals of fascism and the Depression in the 1920s and 1930s rendered such vulnerability to social force threatening. Pound's forays into economic theory and the long break between the first and second halves of Zukofsky's *"A"*-9 (1938–48) are signs of the difficulties of sustaining such a close connection between social and esthetic order. While both poets came to feel the vulnerability of self and imagination to social change, they responded to this threat differently in their poetry. Pound attempted to realize an ideal order like that of Henry Adams's thirteenth-century neo-Platonism, whereas Zukofsky explored the connection between self and a cultural tradition that, like Brooks Adams's capital, actively shapes individual identity.

When, writing in 1918, Pound affirmed Gaudier-Brzeska's belief in the influence of the social vortex on the artist, he conceived of this vortex as ordered by the mathematical harmony of geometrical forms. In his later essay "Cavalcanti" (1934), this assurance of an ordered source of energy is gone. Pound laments the emergence of the physics of the force field as chaotic and therefore threatening to artistic form:

We appear to have lost the radiant world where one thought cuts through another with clean edge, a world of moving energies . . . , magnetisms that take form, that are seen, or that border the visible, the matter of Dante's paradiso, the glass under water. . . .

For the modern scientist energy has no borders, it is a shapeless "mass" of force. . . . The rose that his magnet makes in the iron filings, does not lead him to think of force in botanic terms, or wish to visualize that force as floral and extant. . . . The medieval philosopher would probably have been unable to think of the medieval world, and *not* think of it as a world of forms.[15]

Although he wrote briefly and negatively of Henry Adams,[16] Pound wished to return to a similar medieval neo-Platonism in which the intellect imposes form on inert matter and thought is the "magnetic" force creating physical form. Matter conforms to idea with the transparency of glass in water. The rose's beauty indicates the correspondence between natural harmony and ideal creator. By contrast, the world of modern science is chaotic, for the material world possesses energy independent of the mind. Because this energy is a "shapeless 'mass' of force," Pound struggles to counter its seeming formlessness and inability to create. Where ideal forms rule, this force would lack essence and thus be ineffective as a generative power.

As with Brooks and Henry Adams, natural comes to stand for social energy. Implicit in Pound's, as in Henry Adams's, rejection of modern science for medieval art is nostalgia for a hierarchical society ruled by an intellectual elite. In radio broadcasts and essays during World War II, Pound praised Brooks Adams as an "analyzer of mercantilist materialist process" who interpreted the history of his time accurately, including the "real reasons" for intellectuals' disenfranchisement from politics.[17] His criticism of intellectuals' inability to understand modern economic and political processes paved the way for his own poetic-political project. While Pound accepted Brooks Adams's materialist understanding of history, he believed that Adams misunderstood the distinction between economic process and accounting as the representation of wealth, with its potential for distortion and deception. Such distortion, "the wangles of accountancy or the money wangles that corrode both the system of production and the processes of exchange,"[18] enables departure from a single (e.g., gold) standard and the manipulation of paper money that make usury possible. Pound criticizes Brooks Adams for attributing agency to money, the "concept . . . of money as an accumulation of energy."[19] For Pound, "[m]oney does not create energy," and the belief that it does creates the usurious capitalism that destroys contemporary art. Pound attacks usury in the same terms in which he attacked modern science in the "Cavalcanti" essay. Denying the possibility of any creative agent except the intellect, Pound perceives the acceptance of money as the lifeblood of society as a "satanic transubstantiation, [a] Black Mass of money"[20] violating the authority of God as sole creator. Like matter, money must remain an inert medium given form and agency only by the will and intellect.

For Peter Nicholls, Pound's fundamental hatred of usury lies in the fact that it allows money to increase and thus to create value from itself.[21] Such powers render money master rather than servant of its possessor, a force that governs individual creativity by the impersonal circulation of the wealth that creates market value. *The Cantos* present the productive power of money as perverted creativity or decreation against the artist's incarnation of divine form in matter. In Canto 14, "money-lust" produces a false elite of politicians and financiers whose productivity is often described in scatological terms.[22] Usury is the "[f]ifth element; mud," whose formlessness prevents the realization of divine form in art. "With usury has no man a good house / made of stone, no paradise on his church wall / . . . . It destroys the craftsman, destroying craft; . . . Under usury no stone is cut smooth."[23] Pound's ideal society is one in which artist and philosopher create forms that inculcate social order. Usury destroys this clarity of form by seducing the artist to create for profit, according to the demands of the market rather than to absolute standards of beauty or truth. As maker of the structures people inhabit, both physically and spiritually, Pound's artist has the power to instill the knowledge of divine order that fosters social harmony. In his search for a model of such an ideal social order, Pound moves from an idealized European Renaissance in the *Malatesta Cantos* (1930) to an ideal or paradisal natural order outside history.

The circulation of capital that for Brooks Adams obeys a regular set of laws is for Pound an invisible and chaotic historical force subverting the true reality of eternal forms. In his insistence on the individual's power to shape history, he does not explore or articulate specific ways in which social agents undermine or shape the individual, but rather denies these agents form and ultimately reality. Pound resists the chaotic force of usury he perceives in contemporary society by advocating a medieval neo-Platonism in which a harmony of ideal forms constitutes the true earthly order. Rather than reconfiguring his "poem including history" to the usurious social forces he observes in contemporary society, Pound asserts his alternative vision of an order that transcends history. Beginning with the *Pisan Cantos* (1948), Pound portrays history as a turbulent current or heap of rubble that has fragmented paradise into momentary occurrences for the living, "who have passed over Lethe."[24] In so doing, he abandons the effort to create a sustained vision of paradise like that in Canto 17 (1930).

His new awareness of his position in history prevents a return to Canto 17's transmutation of the natural world into the eternal "marble," "silver," and "gold" of art in a writing so natural that "the vines burst from my fingers."[25] The *Pisan Cantos* arrange the fragments of history into patterns significant of totality.[26] Whereas the earlier *Malatesta Cantos* present the temple commissioned by the wealthy merchant Malatesta as the flowering of Renaissance economic prosperity and trade in a monument both physical and spiritual, the temple Pound builds in the later cantos exists in the mind and outside history. A product of Pound's "constructive imagination," its walls are of law, its foundations of "*sagetrieb*,"[27] the drive to speak.

In response to the historical forces shattering poetic vision, the *Pisan Cantos* introduce a new, selective method of arranging fragments of history that reveals underlying patterns or "ideograms" of cosmic order. Pound understands the Chinese characters for Confucian ethical virtues as embodiments of a sacred natural order implicit in their concrete etymologies.[28] His poetic ideograms provide a similar model for social harmony through the interplay of imagistic and syntactical elements in the poem.

> What you depart from is not the way
> and olive tree blown white in the wind
> washed in the Kiang and Han
> what whiteness will you add to this whiteness,
> what candor?
> "the great periplum brings in the stars to our shore."[29]

Although each line presents an image made fragmentary by the absence of concrete or syntactical context, the correspondence between the white olive blossoms and the light of the stars establishes a harmony between earthly and heavenly orders. By allowing the lines to remain fragments, Pound projects a world in which they would be completed, the ideal forms implicit in their correspondences realized "as light into water compenetrans."[30] Now imagined as a "periplum" or sea journey navigated by the stars, the poem orients itself in history by reference to the unchanging order of the heavens, thereby realizing this divine order in the earthly. In positing an ideal world informing history, Pound asserts the priority and autonomy of art in creating meaning, the imagination's power to rearrange history according to its own forms of totality. Although he presents his vision as the discovery of eternal forms in the process of nature, Pound's departure from his earlier understanding of history as *Kulturmorphologie* in the *Malatesta Cantos* allows him to reconstruct the world and continue the imaginative transformation of his subject matter by excluding as inessential the disruptive, chaotic forces of usury.

2

Like Pound, Zukofsky used the image of the force field to represent social forces independent of individual agency. However, Zukofsky's adherence to Marxism into the late 1930s reflected his belief that economic conditions have a strong influence on individual consciousness. Unlike Pound, therefore, and despite his nostalgia for Henry Adams's thirteenth-century world governed by ideal forms of thought, Zukofsky's poetry does not exclude social forces as formless and destructive of poetic form. While embracing Communist politics, Zukofsky does not dismiss economic history as a usurious aberration from ideal form as Pound does, but attempts to represent human identity in terms and as a product of such economic conditions. His position can thus be characterized as "between" those of Brooks and Henry Adams in that he recognizes both the influence of social forces on the imagination and the power of artifice to create the poetic self in and against history. *"A"*-9 (1938–48), Zukofsky's fullest development of the force field as an image of social forces, contrasts the dissolution of human integrity as a function of exchange value in modern capitalism with the anthropomorphic forces governing the neo-Platonist's image of reality. Opposing medieval art to modern science like Pound's "Cavalcanti" essay and Henry Adams's *Education*,[31] Zukofsky's *"A"*-9 explores the thirteenth and twentieth centuries' different understandings of labor and thus of human agency. Presenting both orders in essentially the same vocabulary, Zukofsky reveals the meaning of words as relative, dependent on syntactic position, thus opposing Pound's view that they participate in and serve as ideograms of a divine logos. Rather, the meaning of words and the subjectivity they construct emerges from the material conditions of labor in each culture. Zukofsky's relativism creates a discontinuity of meaning between the first and second halves of the poem that renders past and present mutually exclusive, history a process of change that undermines the integrity of individual voice.

The first half of *"A"*-9 portrays Marx's analysis of industrial capitalism through the imagery of the force field. The poet has no discrete identity but rather is presented as a disembodied

> impulse to action [that] sings of a semblance
> Of things related as equated values,
> The measure all use is time congealed labor
> In which abstraction things keep no resemblance
> To goods created. . . .[32]

Many critics have traced Zukofsky's distinction between "semblance" and "goods created" to Marx's distinction between exchange and use value from which the capitalist gains profit. Before discussing how Zukofsky's Marxism influences his concept of poetic creativity, I will trace the different understandings of agency in human history and their implications for human nature as presented in each half of the poem. For Marx, alienation prevents the worker from recognizing the product of his or her labor and thus from understanding labor as self-expression. Unlike Pound, who rejects social force as subversive of true being and form, Zukofsky presents the invisible "abstraction" of labor time as more fundamental than the "semblance" of material objects detached from their origin in industrial production. Whereas for Pound individual voice and selected fragments of history achieve their value from an order that transcends history, Zukofsky translates human being into the terms of the economic system of production. For Zukofsky, the force field represents not the false economic concerns that cloud vision of reality but the system of social forces that defines labor as the realization of self. Just as electromagnetic forces energize atoms, social forces animate individuals within this system.

> Values in a series taking on as real
> We affect ready gold a steady token
> Flows in unbroken circuit and induces
> Our being, wearies of us as ideal
> Equals that heady crises eddy.[33]

As for Brooks Adams, "gold" or wealth is the lifeblood of the society. Individuals are subordinate to the larger social organism. Zukofsky defines human nature in industrial capitalism as impersonal, determined by the laws measuring the flow of wealth. Like the "goods" in the first stanza, the "value" of human beings is stripped of ethical or esthetic meaning, indicating instead quantity or position in a system. "Affect" and "being" likewise become mere impulses, "induced" like electrical current by the autonomous circulation of wealth. Driven by the desire to maximize profit and thus efficiency, this system's "division / Of labor" renders individuals mere "foci of production,"[34] eliminating the ideal dimension of human labor as creation of a self.

The second half of *"A"*-9 wrenches the same words out of their meaning for contemporary Marxism to recover a past vision of the world as the creation of a personal divinity constructed by conscious intelligence. Like Pound's, Zukofsky's divine order defines the ideals according to which people labor to transform their world:

> An eye to action sees love bear the semblance
> Of things, related is equated,—values
> The measure all use who conceive love, labor
> Men see, abstraction they feel, the resemblance
> (Part, self-created, integrated) all hues
> Show to natural use. . . .[35]

Describing simultaneously the love by which the medieval Christian God produces the "semblance" or image of the material world and the human desire for perfection, which interprets the material world as significant of something more perfect, these lines present an incarnation of the ideal as the force animating matter. Equated directly through the love sensual beauty arouses rather than in the third terms of labor time and capital as in the first half of the poem, ideal and real are "integrated" through the belief that material reality is part of and thus participates in the form of ideal perfection that would make it whole. This interrelation of individual mind and body rather than of social forces as the source of creativity provides the basis for labor as a realization of the ideal. Words that previously referred to a system of mechanical or chemical impulses—"bear," "value," "conception," and "labor"—now refer to the fruitful intercourse of ideas and things, outlining human labor as natural use rather than commercial usury.

Critics have interpreted *"A"*-9 as an affirmation of the imagination's power to transform history.[36] While I agree that Zukofsky's virtuosic rewriting of the materials of his cultural tradition is such an affirmation, I see Zukofsky's poetic form as a hybrid of individual and historical agency that transforms both the poet and inherited cultural tradition. Although *"A"*-9 shows nostalgia for the incarnation of the ideal in the real, the poem does not follow such a poetics. If the discontinuous meaning of the words in different contexts highlights their meaning as relative, Zukofsky's compositional techniques reinforce this absence of essential or absolute identity. By constraining *"A"*-9 to the rhyme scheme of Cavalcanti's "Donna mi Prega," the vocabulary of Marx's *Capital* and phonetic patterns in the mathematical proportion of the formula of a conic section, Zukofsky renders poetic creativity a hybrid of individual vision and the intellectual artifacts of history, admitting both as creative agents.[37] Whereas Pound's translation of Cavalcanti's "Donna mi Prega" in Canto 36 invokes neo-Platonism to oppose modern science, Zukofsky treats Cavalcanti's poem as a formal rather than metaphysical structure that shapes the poet's imagination. Zukofsky forces his own imagination to bend to the forms of pre-existing cultural artifacts, admitting cultural tradition as an unavoidable presence shaping the imagination.

Zukofsky's essay "Modern Times" (1936), on Charlie Chaplin's film of the same name, reiterates the belief implicit in *"A"*-9 of the power of material culture to structure subjectivity. The essay focuses on Chaplin's character as inseparable from the machinery of modern industrial capitalism with which he works. Zukofsky observes that "Charlie in the past yoked himself to the world, and now lives and works in this age of gears."[38] This existence creates the "terror of Charlie's face brushed by a mechanical wiper, and the later cumulative terror of Charlie lovingly wiping the face of a machinist caught in a machine."[39] "Yoked" incongruously together, machine and person take on each other's attributes, the machine transforming its human maker through a mechanical momentum alien to human activity. Under these conditions, traditional affect is misguided, for it reverts to individual sympathy, ignoring the subject's real identity and needs as subordinate to a larger material process of production. All products of human labor, whether machines or poems, have for Zukofsky such transformative power, and this power lies in a seemingly incidental, artificial structure separate from the meaning or function that the creator may have intended. Against Pound's cultural tradition as a body of material from which to derive a universal standard for human achievement,[40]

Zukofsky emphasizes form or artifice as concrete historical forces independent of the vision or order its creator intended it to embody. His poetry explores how artifacts preserved by tradition create a social fabric influencing the individual in the course of history.

Zukofsky's conception of the artist as embedded in rather than infusing personal meaning into a cultural tradition generates a different conception of creativity from Pound's. Whereas Pound forges historical particulars into an epiphany that transcends them, Zukofsky accentuates the material conditions from which the epiphany arises. *The Cantos* begin with a descent into the underworld of history in order to ascend to paradise, fusing Odysseus's *nostos* with this ascent to define divinity as the true "home" of humanity. In contrast, *"A"* begins by performing an immediate resurrection in a concert of Bach's St. Matthew Passion, which then disperses with the crowd into the flow of everyday life.[41] The intensity of the concert-inspired vision is diluted by subsequent daily events. Initially a powerful presence that frames the narrator's response to subsequent events, the epiphany fades, displaced by the more vivid events of recent memory. As the poem develops, facts seemingly incidental to the internal meaning of the work, such as the letters of Bach's name or the rehearsal conditions of musicians in the eighteenth century, emerge as structuring forces in the poem. The poem traces not the participation of historical occurrences in a unified cosmology but a history of shifting structures that transform the narrator as well. It is not, therefore, the epiphany that reveals the order informing or underlying history; rather seemingly accidental cultural products become active forces shaping the imagination as it structures its contemporary world.

In defining "Objectivist" poetry in the *Objectivist Anthology* (1932), Zukofsky defines the object (physical or emotional) not through some integrity presumed to be inherent in the object but through the process of naming. He extends Pound's understanding of the ideogram as a concept abstracted from concrete particulars to view "each word [as] an arrangement"; "it may be said that each word possesses objectification to a powerful degree." Language in its varied and changing forms constitutes objects. Likewise, Zukofsky's definition of the poem's development as "inextricably the direction of historical and contemporary particulars"[42] incorporates the independent movement of history into the poem. Pound's eternal ideograms give way to local and changing constellations of order, *"A"* mirroring instead the process of historical transmission that destroys absolute form.

The imagination is thus for Zukofsky not the organ through which to perceive an original, forgotten totality but rather a hybrid of cultural memory and contemporary particulars whose structure changes continually. Zukofsky's image of the temple in *"A"*-6 and *"A"*-8 develops these differences in creative agency. Zukofsky's temple represents the original community of a religion whose members are now scattered, an idealized cultural order transformed beyond recognition through its transportation to different places.

> If this world, the sources,
> Fathers, wherever they put their hats,
> Spiralled with tessellation as sands of the sea,
> The Speech no longer spoken and not even a Wall to worship,
> Holy, laundered into a blank and washed over
> Tradition's pebbles, the mouth full . . .[43]

Like Pound's temple, the original edifice of Zukofsky's "Fathers" is fragmented in the rubble of history. But whereas Pound reconstructs the fragments into ideograms that represent a transcendent order, Zukofsky adds an impersonal force, that of the sea, which shapes the rubble into new patterns, spirals perhaps alluding to a social force like that of the vortex. Further, the fragments themselves are transformed, eroded into pebbles and sand, which must lead to new combinations. Like Demosthenes, the poet learns to speak beautifully not through knowledge of the world these ideograms impart but by accommodating speech to these autonomous presences within his personal voice. Nature and labor are simultaneously "creator" and "created," shaped by the impersonal force of cultural tradition and shaping it in their own efforts to speak.

The artist becomes a changing moment in the fabric of cultural tradition. "He who creates / Is a mode of these inertial systems— / The flower— leaf around leaf wrapped / around the center leaf."[44] Zukofsky invokes the Romantic notion of the artist as the medium of God or Nature. However, the creator is no universal being but a rather local intersection of specific natural processes. The flower has no essence, but gains form from a coincidental pattern of particulars; even its center is somewhat arbitrary, a "leaf" no different from the other leaves. This flower develops an earlier image of a flower pattern formed by the moon's reflection in the sea in *"A"*-2. Here too, the flower has no discrete identity but emerges only from the inter-action of independent processes. In representing the creator by such an im-age, Zukofsky dissolves not only being but also creative agency into separate and autonomous processes beyond the scope of individual control or intent.

Although Zukofsky does not define the sea that moves the discon-nected pebbles of cultural tradition, *"A"*-7 develops this image as the envi-ronment for the process of creativity. In the course of the poem, the sea emerges as a dense network of correspondences generated by the sediment of artifacts, which interact in the poetic imagination with the contingen-cies of history. *"A"*-7 traces such a network, its images of horses linked obliquely by the pun on "see" and later in *"A"* by Zukofsky's more ex-tended association of the sea with horses. Beginning with a manic series of associations, the poem promises to transform sawhorses into living horses.

> Horses: who will do it? out of manes? Words
> Will do it, out of manes, out of airs, but
> They have no manes, so there are no airs, birds
> Of words, from me to them no singing gut.
> For they have no eyes, for their legs are wood,
> For their stomachs are logs with print on them;
> Blood red, red lamps hang from necks or where could
> Be necks, two legs stand A, four together M.[45]

The first stanza generates the horses' missing parts from incongruous asso-ciative chains of words and images: ears from the common elements in "airs" (songs) and birds; manes etymologically via *manes*, Latin for ghosts; and vitality from the blood-red lamps. Created almost "out of air," Zukof-sky's horses are the products of melopoeia, phanopoeia, and logopoeia, the musical, visual, and idiomatic registers of language that convey meaning, according to Pound in *The ABC of Reading* (1934). Although both Pound and Zukofsky write of these structuring devices as able to "charge words with meaning" and therefore as subordinate to the overall meaning of the poem,[46] Zukofsky here makes them independent agents that generate new creatures characterized by presence and absence. He uses these techniques to generate networks of association from language as a medium in itself. The incongruous verbal patterns that emerge throughout the poem are products of correspondences that depart from conventional reference.

Apparently the most abstract word play and therefore an exercise of the imagination as it departs from its concrete setting, *"A"*-7 establishes the cultural structures of neighborhood and language as the lines along which the imagination develops. Zukofsky retains belief in the power of artistic imagination to construct self through virtuosic manipulation of concrete particulars. The final "A" and "M" represent self ("am"), however, as inseparable from the concrete object of the imagination, signifying the poet's being not in a transcendent "I" or self but the unique combination with and immanence in place that emerges in the letter patterns seen in the sawhorses. Self is made from the intersection of collectively constructed place and language. Although the poem celebrates word play, it also indicates the physical structures of language and neighborhood, not individual psychology, as the lines of force along which the imagination develops. Just as the flower formed from individual "leaves" has no identity apart from the pattern of leaves, the horses—and ultimately the self—are hybrids of historical particulars, sawhorses and language, with its systems of phonetic and etymological correspondences.

Later in *"A"*-7, Zukofsky links the horses with the sea, developing further the significance of the sea from *"A"*-6 as the image of historical change first suggested in *"A"*-6. The resulting "[s]ea of horses that once were wood, / Green and, and leaf on leaf, and dancing bucks . . ."[47] identifies the sea of history that moves the fragments of the temple as the cultural fabric, whose currents or lines of force influence the imagination. Like elements of the temple reformed as mosaic, the units within Zukofsky's lines have little significance in themselves but add up to the larger image of horses. Individual particulars have no meaning in themselves, but through coincidence with others they generate patterns often logically remote from their own identity. The poem thus does not reveal an ideal form of horse but rather illuminates the network of associations in the structure of cultural artifacts themselves and explores the patterns possible within this network. An inchoate sea or node in this network, the horses become a part of the poem's fabric in later sections of *"A."* They persist as a structure from the past that branches into a variety of other areas, from the sea horses in *"A"*-7 to horsepower as the transformed significance of horses in industrial civilization in *"A"*-8.[48] This pattern of oblique emergence, dispersion, and return of poetic elements, perhaps transformed by a new context, throughout *"A"* imitates the process by which individuals

interact with tradition to produce history. The seemingly oblique correspondences from which patterns emerge reveal the unpredictable agency
of a cultural fabric that renders impossible the endurance of any thing
unchanged by history.

3

For both Pound and Zukofsky, the close connection between individual and social forms of production limited the extent of individual creativity. Whereas Pound rejected history as the principle structuring the
poem, Zukofsky's bending of his imagination to formal structures from
cultural tradition generated an incongruous hybrid of human and inhuman. Olson, in contrast, worked to renovate culture by invoking a nonanthropomorphic divinity that reflects a "multiple vitality" of human beings.
Both inhumanly depersonalizing and constructively nonhumanistic, this
divinity reflects forces that erode the individual yet reveal a new collective
force through which to renovate culture. In the draft essay that developed
into "Projective Verse," entitled "The Mystery of What Happens When It
Happens" (1948–49), Olson coins the term *objectism* as an alternative to
"the anthropomorphic divine of Dante, Dostoevsky, Lawrence."[49] For Olson, these writers restrict religion to "dogma" and art to "automatic and artificial notions of the function of the creative man."[50] Their concept of
human nature, invented by Socrates and Christ as rational and spiritual,
represents a "death-in-life" based on the suppression of sensuality. Olson
rejects the spiritual for a "materialism" and "objectism" that define humanity in new terms, nonanthropomorphic "quantity as an expression of force,
and quantity as a birthplace of myth."[51]

Previous critics have either placed Olson's work in the tradition of
the Modernist epic "poem including history" or emphasized his break with
Modernism in the tendency of his poetics to ground an ideal cultural order in nature.[52] Although I focus here on Olson's break with the Modernists, I believe this break must be understood in the context of the
Modernists' notion of the force field. Most critics have taken Olson's naturalizing poetics at face value. They emphasize his repudiation of the
"subjectivism" of "western man" for an "objectism" that views "the artist's
act in the larger field of objects, [and thereby] . . . dimensions larger than

the man."[53] In so doing, they accept Olson's categories of subject and object, understanding the object as he does, as a natural entity defined by the rhetoric of natural science. They thus view Olson's objectification of the subject as a reduction of thought and language to an origin in physical existence. This objectifying impulse underlies Olson's utopian poetic project to reintegrate the self into nature but does not explain his choice of the polis as the framework for human thought. The polis as collective culture formed in response to local geography becomes the constellation of forces within whose context individuals must be reconceived.

Olson drew his language of physical vitality as quantity and force from Simone Weil's essay "The *Iliad*, or The Poem of Force."[54] For Weil, "[t]he true hero, the true subject, the centre of the *Iliad* is force. . . . To define force—it is that *x* that turns anybody who is subjected to it into a *thing*."[55] In Weil's analysis, war unleashes violent, impersonal energy that creates dehumanizing extremes of power and vulnerability. These extremes destroy the "armor" of ethical and metaphysical or religious idealism by which Western metaphysics would obscure human bondage to physicality, mortality, and time:

The Occident, however, has lost it [a concept of the "geometrical rigor" of retribution against those who wield force], and no longer even has a word to express it in any of its languages; conceptions of limit, measure, equilibrium, which ought to determine the conduct of life are, in the West, restricted to a servile function in the vocabulary of technics.[56]

Like Zukofsky's flow of "gold" in *"A"*-9, Weil's "force" strips life of its ethical dimension and measures it in the nonanthropomorphic terms of physical quantity. For Weil, however, the nonhuman material environment presents a positive rather than negative measure of humanity. Her essay ends with a new interpretation of Christ's crucifixion in order to recover its origin in physical experience. Weil sees the crucifixion not as an event unique to Christian culture but as an extension of a characteristically Greek heroic confrontation with physical existence and mortality like that in *The Iliad*.[57] Although Weil does not identify force as either social or natural but presents it as a condition of human fate, her writings on war, agricultural and factory work, and politics (works with which Olson was familiar[58]) explore the dimensions these concrete social conditions add to human life, particularly their influence on spirituality.

The mutual informing of spiritual and physical in Weil's thought provided Olson with an alternative to the hierarchy of spiritual or subjective over physical being that he sees as predominant in Christian and Western poetic traditions and in Pound's poetics. As with the Adams brothers, Pound, and Zukofsky, Olson's understanding of nature was implicitly one of society. The draft essay on objectism frames the discussion of objectism's return to sensuous experience in an argument for a return to popular myth and story. Olson views the shared cultural understanding of texts such as the Hebrew Bible as "essentially primordial,"[59] expressing the immediate natural vitality in human beings. Whereas for Pound the image of nature emerges from the artist's vision, a vision that Pound sees as superior to that of other human beings, Olson sees popular myth as the true basis for the poet's understanding of nature. Arguing against the "too literary and professional" "eliotic" notion of the writer, he presents a new image of the poet as "folk-maker" and "mythographer." This role is modeled on writers like Melville and Homer, who for Olson take their materials from myth, "the one common cloth the culture—the writers and the people both—possessed."[60]

Olson rejects Pound's idealization of wealthy Renaissance merchants whose patronage of the arts represented an elite's effort to influence social order by commissioning art that "carried in it graces and perceptions which were of use to people."[61] Instead of this aristocratic view of the artist's role in society, Olson praises the writer who draws on popular myth to represent popular consciousness. "Homer . . . gave the gods and legends of Greece their prime circulation, yet . . . he himself, like Melville, was only giving reality a mythic extension, was himself, in fact, using inherited and available story and personage, as Melville did, to accomplish that extension."[62] Olson refers to Henri Bérard's interpretation of the *Odyssey* as a compilation of sailors' accounts of natural phenomena they encountered in the Mediterranean. Olson, with Bérard, interprets Homer's poems as the record of a culture's common imaginative understanding of its natural environment. This collective imagination, not the individual's experience of nature in itself, moves the artist to express vitality beyond that of traditional individual subjectivity.[63] Olson seems originally to have conceived the natural context of art in "Projective Verse" as social. The published essay's "the field of larger objects, dimensions larger than the man" by which "the artist's act"[64] is to be measured begins as the field of popular culture.

The essay on objectism thus articulates the context greater than the individual as "that extension which we call the mythic,"[65] a collective cultural rather than natural vitality.

Olson understands the poet's contact with nature as mediated through popular culture. Although "Projective Verse" in its final form grounds "composition by field" in rhetoric of nature and natural science, the direction that Olson's poetry took reflects his continued interest in the processes by which collective culture develops. In the mid-1950s, he began a series of poems cast as letters from the narrator Maximus to the city of Gloucester, which both criticize contemporary culture and seek to describe the structure of the city. Although Maximus speaks from "off-shore"[66] in the first poem, his subjectivity is a product of social place throughout the *Maximus Poems*.[67] Although he challenges mass culture by affirming as more authentic a local popular or folk culture that reflects collective response to local geography, he consistently perceives the artistic imagination as formed by collective culture.

The first volume of the *Maximus Poems* (1960) represents Olson's immediate response to the natural landscape of his native Gloucester as part of a collective tradition. "On first Looking Out through Juan de la Cosa's Eyes" juxtaposes Olson's reply to the first impressions of other travelers—Juan de la Cosa, Odysseus, Columbus, John Lloyd. Olson seeks similarities and differences among these impressions to determine the common structure of human response to nature.[68] As in Zukofsky's poetry, individual identity is embedded in preexisting structures of cultural tradition. Rather than asserting the power of individual imagination through virtuosic negotiation between these structures as Zukofsky does, Olson dissolves individuality into them, presenting reality as the interaction of these structures and individuals as functions of these interactions. The social forces Pound sought to counteract thus become inseparable from the process of individual thought presented in the poem. This shift from the primacy of individual identity to that of the community, with its division of labor and patterns of trade, renders social forces prior to individual ones and individual being a derivative of social.

As he begins to explore how to express the mythic in his poetry, Olson traces the origins of both individual and collective consciousness to the economic conditions that define human interaction with nature. For Olson, the individual is embedded in the social network of division of labor.

As he writes in a letter to Robert Creeley, "each one of us each day is to his or her degree an act of trade. . . . The minuteness and absoluteness of trade as daily fact of any one of us is such a familiar, peculiarly lost sight of in the present mountainous economies." In language reminiscent of Weil's suggestion that this "armor" of metaphysical and religious idealism denies mortality, Olson argues that trade thus deprives the individual of "the permission of maintaining the armor of his distance,"[69] the fiction of the self's integrity. If the "armor" of idealism protects against massified trade, it also perpetuates illusion. With his awareness of the social quality of individual experience, Olson structures the world of the *Maximus Poems* around collective rather than individual being and consciousness. In announcing the project of the *Maximus Poems* in the first poem as an effort to define the root of human experience, Olson again conflates nature and culture: "the underpart is, though stemmed, uncertain / is, as sex is, as moneys [*sic*] are, facts! / facts to be dealt with, as the sea is."[70] Sexual and economic production, as well as the vast power of the sea, affirms material rather than spiritual and collective and interpersonal rather than individual sources of human energy.

Olson's uncertainty about the identity of his root led him to explore various methods of structuring the social organism of the city. From his reading of Brooks Adams, he decides that it was not "puritanism" but "fish," natural resources that determined the character of the early community.[71] In following Brooks Adams's concentration on geography and trade as the primary forces shaping the community,[72] Olson began to measure and experiment with ways to represent the economic forces that Pound excluded from *The Cantos* as chaotic and inessential. Many poems in the first volume of the *Maximus Poems* map the economic and collective features of his community: population statistics; the growth of the fishing industry and technology; tables of a community's total production and consumption; maps of places, property boundaries, streets; and the stories of mythical figures and history that constitute landmarks of a popular culture. These aspects of the town's collective life become the primary structuring forces in the poem, delineating the polis as a structure of experience shared by its citizens. "Letter, May 2, 1959," for example, configures the lines and words on the page to the town's geographical and property boundaries. "14 MEN STAGE HEAD WINTER 1624/5" lists the resources required to support the early settlement for a year in the community's history, attempting to quantify the relation between nature and culture and the material basis of culture in its use of natural resources.[73] Olson departs from Pound's view of the imagination as an individual vision that imposes meaning on the particulars of its world. He focuses instead on the structuring devices independent of personal meaning that define the social being of the polis.

As the *Maximus Poems* developed, Olson became increasingly conscious of the difficulty of achieving an unmediated response to nature. The poems turn to tracing the origin of the cultural categories informing his perception and that of his community. As he incorporated Alfred North Whitehead's philosophy into his poetics from 1952 onward, Olson came to see categories of perception (such as color, softness, and even fact—etymologically "made thing") as products of public consensus. Although Whitehead emphasizes that these categories are humanly made rather than inherent in the physical world, he assigns them a reality at least equal to that of the material world, terming them "eternal objects."[74] Throughout the three volumes of the *Maximus Poems*, Olson reconstructs historical events that create the local landmarks of a community's shared landscape. However, as he explores the confluence of various strands of cultural tradition composing particular moments of his experience, his poems reach beyond three-dimensional mapping to create a dynamic representation of the cultural organism.

An early poem in the second volume of the *Maximus Poems* announces this change in Olson's conception of polis from geographical to historical construct. In "Maximus to Gloucester, Letter 27," Olson presents geography as shaped by personal memory. He opens the poem with a description of a particular part of the Gloucester landscape through his memory of summer picnics there. The recognition that not only this particular memory but also the act of investigating the past at all, the genre of history,[75] has its origins in the past initiates the poem's explicit statement of this new historical representation of Gloucester:

> This, is no bare incoming
> of novel abstract form, this
> . . .
>   It is the imposing
> of all those antecedent predecessions, the precessions

of me, the generation of those facts
which are my words, . . .[76]

The speaker does not claim special insight into an ideal city and its relation to nature, but recognizes his identity as a product of those who have gone before. As in Zukofsky's poetry, the self is an interaction of individual experience of place with language as a social product. The concrete terms of "generation" and "fact" now indicate psychological rather than physical structures and a reality of collective tradition and common language analogous to that of the material world.

The power of environment is stronger for Olson than for Zukofsky, however. Although the speaker asserts that he is "one / with [his] skin" and therefore in immediate contact with his environment, "incoming" and "imposing" indicate that energy and form flow from society to the individual, displacing any fiction of discrete individual identity. One gains autonomy only by giving oneself over to this influence of tradition, admitting experience of place as a product of the temporal forces of history:

> Plus this—plus this:
>
> that forever the geography
>
> which leans in
>
> on me I compell
>
> backwards I compell Gloucester
>
> to yield, to
>
> change
>
>   Polis
>
> is this[77]

The speaker fights the influx of place by assertively seeking to discover the history that formed him. However, individuation both creates a self by severing culture from nature and blurs the distinction between the individual and the flow of history. The absence of clear syntactical units and resulting multiple constructions of meaning in the lineation characteristic of Olson's poetry present speaker and city as inseparable yet indeterminately related. The act of self-definition as a compelling of self as well as of Gloucester suggests exploration of the temporal polis within the self, examination of the influence of collective tradition on consciousness. Although Olson compels Gloucester "to yield" to this new definition of polis as a cultural inheritance formed by time rather than by a spatial geography, he must also accept change. No longer standing as an exemplum for the Ur-city defining the universal human response to nature, Gloucester—and with it the poet—becomes the product of history. This poem introduces Olson's explicit focus on place, the making of the city and self as products of a cultural tradition as well as natural process.

Although he includes verbatim the voices of inhabitants of Gloucester and their experience of the city, Olson places these voices in the impersonal framework of the city as a social organism, interspersing poems of individual testimony with poems that attempt to represent this impersonal structure. In addition, the common elements of the individuals' experience of their environment build throughout the *Maximus Poems* to represent the city's collective culture as it has evolved from the first inhabitants. Individual voices are thus presented as embedded in cultural traditions, segments of the strands of culture that make up the city whose greater form emerges through history.

Olson's presentation of his own experience involves it even more completely in the collective processes of the polis as these emerge throughout the *Maximus Poems*. "The Twist" exemplifies the centrifugal direction of consciousness as an interaction of forces independent of the poet. Epiphany emerges not from poetic craft but from the contingencies of everyday life. Beginning with an analogy between nature and culture, inscape and landscape—"Trolley-cars / are my inland waters"[78]—the poem diverges into rambling anecdotes from Olson's past. These anecdotes reveal, however, the role of two fixtures of popular culture, Gloucester's trolley lines and the fairy tale "Hansel and Gretel," shaping Olson's experience of nature. The motion of the crowds dispersing from the trolley and of the tidal river Annisquam, on whose shore Gloucester lies, combine to form an image of consciousness as an offshoot of larger forces in the environment. The poem ends with a vision of a flower that expresses the interrelation of these forces in a harmonious cosmology.

the tide roars over

    some curves off,
when it's the river's turn, shoots
calyx and corolla by the dog
                        (August,
the flowers break off

    but the anther,
the filament of now, the mass
drives on,

    the whole of it
coming,
to this pin-point[79]

Although image "blooms" unexpectedly from Olson's contemplation of the waves, the rest of the poem contextualizes this cosmic vision as it emerges from the contingencies of history. As with Zukofsky's flower in *"A"*-2, the beautiful form emerges from an interaction of unrelated processes rather than a universal harmony coordinating all things. Whereas Zukofsky chooses this natural object as an image for the formation of the self in time, Olson presents even this choice as a product of history. Insofar as each aspect of the image has concrete precedent in the poem, the cosmology is a product of the particular associative forms of his experience as structured by Gloucester. The order Olson perceives is merely a pattern within these larger forces, from which the I disappears. Against Zukofsky's consistent signaling of the self's presence, however epiphenomenal, Olson denies an articulate ego that would achieve such distance. Although the outflowing river and the flowers suggest force and form initiated by the individual, the course of the poem abandons these individual formations, which "break off," and follows instead the enduringly generative process of "the mass." The third volume of the *Maximus Poems* traces the flower's significance as image of processual cosmos in different traditions of myth, locating the origin of Olson's epiphany in patterns of deeper cultural imagination.

The underlying structures of the *Maximus Poems* are the collectively formed structures of popular myth and tradition. Olson's effort to represent the polis changes the poem's focus from the expression of individual voice to representation of the life of the group. He thus completes the shift from the authority of individual to that of social agency begun in Pound's retreat from the pressure of history and developed further in Zukofsky's partial embrace of history as an active structuring force in the imagination. The difficulty that Olson encountered in trying to root cultural order in natural place makes his work significant for the subsequent development of "composition by field." Although Olson's general effort to present these cultural structures as emerging from natural order provides some synthetic framework in the *Maximus Poems,* however inconsistently observed, the absence of orientation and hierarchical order among these structures frees them for isolation as independent forces developing in time with a dynamic independent of a universal natural order. The pieces of Olson's epic that experiment with new, public structures—his emphasis on language as a sediment of collective thought, his investigation of comparative mythology and of the transformation of deities through time, and his effort to analyze the many strands of tradition that compose individual consciousness—identify some of the cultural artifacts that take on lives of their own and become structuring agents in the work of the other Black Mountain poets as they explore the social implications of field poetics.

2

From Natural to Social Place in Olson and Creeley

The focus on place in Olson's and Creeley's early writing emerged from the ghost of a Romantic natural supernaturalism in the Black Mountain poets' early work. The disaffection with traditional forms that Olson, Creeley, Duncan, and Levertov shared focused on the failure of Romantic epiphany associated with a Christian poetics that "incarnates" spirit in matter. (I do not discuss Dorn here because, while he shared some of these concerns, his early work shows Olson's influence.) Even before they became friends, these four shared the feeling that neither nature nor language could provide a form that corresponded to the imagination's desire for spiritual beauty or truth. Their poems written before the influence of "Projective Verse" frequently express the inability of language to articulate spiritual meaning in nature. Creeley uses Christian imagery to describe the dullness of the material world unreceptive to his mind. "Hélas! Or Christus fails. / The day is the indefinite."[1] Levertov finds it "Too Easy: to Write of Miracles," to "haunt" her world with spirits rather than to face the facts of "innocent and cold" day.[2] In his early poems, Duncan disciplines his imagination to the cosmology and language of Christian tradition but represents it as a violent spiritual order antagonistic to natural life. *The Years As Catches: First Poems (1939–1946)* portrays the destruction of the body as necessary for spiritual salvation. "Sun will overcome his beasts; . . . / the brief burnd breast to rise." The speaker finds no language to describe the "[m]ute world: in my original dark wondering flesh"[3] and likens traditional poetic form based on harmony between nature and spirit to inhumane war strategy. "An Essay At War" prefers imperfect form, "the clear immutable pitcher / flawd by our rage," to "the responsible traind military technician's art / without rage . . . / planning campaigns / organizing, ordering, giving orders until the blood flows red from each page."[4] Traditional poetic order does violence to a more chaotically vital reality.

Without the security of some traditional realm of spirit to define meaning, the relation of thought to material reality and the purpose of each remain undefined. Levertov's neo-Romantic spirit world has a gothic cast, its landscapes peopled with ghosts of the past and fantasies of death as a richly dressed bridegroom.[5] The speaker becomes "a half-contented guest among my ghosts," asking whether she "can now take root in life."[6] Whereas Creeley and Levertov emphasized the shadowy unreality of inherited concepts against "cold fact," Olson and Duncan criticized the tyranny of Western culture, particularly Christianity, for valuing the spiritual over the material and inculcating ideals of the hero and law that deny the body and mortality. Culture no longer seemed to articulate meaning inherent in the world but had become a system of beliefs manipulated for interested purpose.

Before their contact in the early 1950s and the influence of "Projective Verse," each of these Black Mountain poets pursued different possibilities for grounding new poetic form that constituted important steps in their development. In a 1949 letter to Jacob Leed, Creeley praised the moral framework of the existentialist act as the basis of self-definition. He also found new ways to "realize" self in D. H. Lawrence's ability to make passion concrete through the interaction of his characters.[7] These insights remained confined to letters, however, for Creeley found no poetic form through which to realize them until his contact with Olson. Duncan, Olson, and Creeley experimented with but could not accept the exuberant escape of Stevens's linguistic imagination. For Creeley, a Stevensian southern climate of the imagination "suggested by language, / a world of inner warmth" cannot persuade the listener to shed his gray coat.[8] Other poems characterize those who dream of escaping from a dreary reality as an "honest thief" and a "gangster" who must eventually return to the "reckoning" of "a wife and two kids."[9] Duncan represented this conflict as one of imagination and responsibility in the game of dice between King Haydn of Miami Beach, who "never abandons / the never come true" and "Mr. Responsible Person."[10]

Like the creative imagination, poetic form needed more direct grounding in everyday life. In their reading, the poets searched for principles of poetic form to replace traditional metrics. Duncan meditated on Pound's ideogram as a way of relating images without recourse to abstract essence. He imitated Stein to explore patterns of sound rather than meaning and to free words of the political and religious values acquired through history. Dissociation of sound and meaning fails to engage reality for Duncan, however. Sound alone remains "the beautiful senseless tone in the language crippling the sentence."[11] Nature provided no viable alternative to linguistic order. If the escape into beautiful language seemed insufficient, physicality appeared to offer only dissolution into a material world without order, symbolized for Olson and Creeley by Hart Crane's suicide. Although Olson wrote several poems on death as a return to nature, mere physical decomposition yielded no place for the active imagination.[12] Levertov's apprenticeship to William Carlos Williams helped her to shift from vague lyric emotion to the concrete particular, but the ten-year gap between *The Double Image* (1947) and her subsequent books indicates the depth of change this reorientation required.[13]

"Projective Verse" and the poets' early contact brought dramatic changes in the work of each. Olson's conception of the poem as a force field produced remarkably uniform early experiments among the Black Mountain poets, defining a common ground from which all five developed their innovations. Creeley's "Still Life Or" exemplifies the early Black Mountain reception of "composition by field," in its focus on breaking Romantic epiphany into constituent elements seen anew. Whereas the Romantic poets tried to harmonize thought and natural form, the Black Mountain poets articulated an interaction of independent forces in the field of experience, defining each as particular through the interplay of similarity and difference between them. They questioned the metaphysical foundations of Romantic belief in the correspondence between human being and natural and attempted to identify essential elements of experience free of such assumptions.

Still Life Or

mobiles:
           that the wind can catch at,
      against itself,
                 a leaf or a contrivance of wires,

in the stairwell,
to be looked at from below.

We have arranged the form of a formula here,
have taken the heart out
                 & the wind
is vague emotion.

To count on these aspirants
these contenders for the to-be-looked-at part
of these actions
           these most hopeful movements
needs
a strong & constant wind.
        That will not rise above the speed
which we have calculated,
        that the leaf
remain
     that the wires
be not too much shaken.[14]

Creeley engages a Romantic tradition of inspiration, "tak[ing] the heart out" or eliminating the pathetic fallacy and leaving the wind as a "vague emotion" that resists human sympathy. He objectifies poetic or personal stance to place the mental and physical elements of experience on equal footing as actions, invoking no shared spirit to explain the conjunction of these facts in artistic form. Separate from his artistic intent yet also active, not inert, the concrete elements form "the to-be-looked-at part / of these actions." Language too becomes an independent element. The "that" clauses composing the final sentence fragment identify grammatically the nature of the mind as wish, the hopeful search for a correspondent form in the external world. These grammatical fragments and the partial, wryly tentative personification in "vague emotion" and "aspirants" define the mind as both analogous to and different from material things. The fragmented syntax and spatial organization isolate both material and mental facts. Eliminating the bridges of regular syntax that would harmonize the facts, this isolation reflects the presence of the concrete world in thought and the interpenetration of the two as very different kinds of being. The poem thus articulates the nature of thought in its relative power to act on the external world. Its form reinforces the separation through visual scoring that isolates units of thought or breath against the grain of conventional syntax, a strategy that other Black Mountain poets adopt in their early experiments with field poetics.

The resemblance between "Still Life Or" and poems of this period by Olson, Duncan, and Levertov is striking. Olson's "The Motion" divides his perception of the flash of a newt, an experience he might have rendered as a Romantic epiphany, into separate elements. Analysis of the moment yields knowledge of self and poetic imagination as different from rather than in harmony with the natural order.

> the motion
> not verbal
>
>   the newt
>   less active
>
>   than I: the fire pink
>   not me
>
>   (the words
>   not me
>
>   not my nature
>   I[15]

The steps trace a progression of thought from the perceived phenomenon to a moment of self-consciousness. The pairings, the second term negating the first, show thought proceeding by conscious difference rather than similarity. The implicit parallel between animal action as motion and human as speech breaks down as the speaker recognizes their different rhythms. Language fails to define the individual, however. Christian Moraru observes that Olson communicates the problem of verbal correlatives of thought in the poem's spatial descent, which "parallels, if not symbolizes, the passage from identity to alterity" and ultimately the fragile ego alienated from words.[16] Self becomes increasingly remote from language as words form images distinct from self and object. Olson distinguishes poetic image, "the fire pink," as verbal construct and thus as a departure from rather than clearer expression of newt or self. Finally, even the speaker's "nature" is different from the verbal construct "I." Like Creeley, Olson isolates self, natural object, and words as structured by different orders. The poem emphasizes each term in its particularity rather than attempting to synthesize them. In the spatial scheme, poetic image emerges from the difference between animal and human, and autonomous language increases the distance between them.

Levertov's "A Silence" also dissects the fusion of spiritual stillness and natural image in Keats's "Ode on a Grecian Urn" to emphasize the accidental, fleeting conjunction of elements that compose the epiphanic moment.

A Silence

Among its petals the rose
still holds
          a few tears of the morning rain that
broke it from its stem.
               In each
shines a speck of
               red light, darker even
than the rose. Phoenix-tailed
slateblue martins pursue
     one   another, spaced out
in hopeless hope, circling
          the porous clay vase, dark from
the water in it. Silence
surrounds the facts. A language
still unspoken.[17]

Levertov's urn unites perishable flowers still wet with rain, the wet porous clay of the vase, and the speaker's impression of the decorations on it. The eternal stillness Keats's poem finds embodied in the urn remains distinct from these disparate elements in Levertov's as a "silence" that merely "surrounds the facts." Levertov's line breaks place linguistic or perceptual units in counterpoint with the objective image, isolating the actions of holding, breaking, and shining as perceptions rather than allowing linear and spatial units to correspond to subject and object. Ultimately, language does not fuse with thing, nor the urn's message with the poem's. Instead, the poem contrasts what each element—perception, language, and concrete particular— can and cannot communicate. Levertov's *Here and Now* (1957), in which "A Silence" was published, abandons the image of the artist as visionary dreamer to develop a new conception of the artist as the artisan or scavenger who chooses, arranges, and shapes the given elements of reality.

Although Duncan may have been temperamentally unlikely to take a concrete object or still life as the subject of his poem, his analysis of language in "FOR A MUSE MEANT" dissects Romantic epiphany in a way similar to that of the other poets' representations of nature. Duncan focuses on the process of perceiving each element of the epiphanic moment—interplay of spirit, body, and language—in its unresolved specificity, abandoning the conceptual given of the epiphany to identify new elements that compose reality. The poem articulates these elements through a visual scoring of experience typical of the early Black Mountain experiments. Duncan echoes Creeley's revision of inspiration as the physical word coexisting with and aspiring beyond the concrete fact yet not partaking of any transcendent spiritual order.

FOR A MUSE MEANT

in
s p i r e d /the aspirate
the aspirant almost

without breath

it is a breath out
breathed—an aspiration
pictured as the familiar spirit
however
above
each loved each

a word giving up its ghost   *hesitate (as if the*
memorized as the flavor   *bone-cranium-helmet*
from the vowels (the bowels)   *in-bearing); clearing*
of meaning   *old greym attar.*
(BE STILL THY BRATHE AND HEAR THEM SPEAK:)
voices?   images?   essences[18]

Duncan unmasks the familiar conception of language as logos to reveal the actual discrepancy between spiritual concept—divine truth or abstract meaning—and the sensual form of language. For him, spoken or breathed words hover "above each loved, / each," merely associated with rather than embodying the things they represent. The line breaks create ambiguity. "[G]iving up its ghost" may yield the sheer "flavor" or physical sensation of pronunciation in the absence of meaning, but it also suggests the opposite, that attending to meaning "kills" awareness of the aural and visual form of words, that the "flavor" of the word's ghost independent of sensual form emerges from the vowels/bowels of *meaning*. When breath is "still," meanings independent of the sound of words emerge, among them "voices" of others' usage distinct from the speaker's voice, "images" as reference to concrete things, and "essence" as abstract concept. In isolating these different elements of language, Duncan unsettles the origin and location of verbal meaning. He reveals the physical and historical processes shaping language to break away from the traditional conception of poetic language as embodiment of spiritual meaning in natural symbol. The poem accentuates the discrepancy between "sign" and "design," "breaking up / All melodic lines (the lyr- / ick strain)" to sever the naturalizing connection of etymology, meaning, and aural and visual form. Form and meaning diverge in the puns, phoneticizations, and misspellings to contradict the poetic illusion of harmony between linguistic meaning and the sensual forms of language.

Like the early poems in which Olson, Creeley, and Levertov incorporate "composition by field," "For a Muse Meant" juxtaposes thought, language, and body to accentuate the particularity and independent rhythm of each as forces interacting in the field. "Composition by field" inspired each poet to track the particular force of mind, nature, and language in openended process, resisting the Romantic closure that would harmonize cultural and natural form. In adopting the force field as a model of agency, the poets identified the forces disrupting the drive toward Romantic epiphany as the rhythms of cultural constructs such as self and language, rhythms different enough from those of natural objects to achieve independence from them.

Although the drive toward epiphany in the poem gave way to open-ended exploration of the forces shaping consciousness, place emerged as an essential focus in the early field composition of Olson and Creeley. As both poets began to redefine subjectivity by recording the interaction between thought and physical process, investigation of place provided a focus by which to render the ongoing and potentially aimless flux of experience coherent and to provide a basis for closure. As the totality of environmental forces, place represents the ground against which the self's form emerges. For Olson, Mayan petroglyphs express the relation between individual and environment. "[T]hose gestures [the glyphs] must be read against the sky as silhouette, into the confines of the human body for background."[19] The *Maximus Poems* explore this relation in terms of his local Gloucester as "root person in root place."[20] Olson's expansion into geographical place, extending from Gloucester to the entire globe, contrasts with Creeley's intensely introspective one. For Creeley, self-understanding emerges only in distinction from place. "[T]his 'I,' comes to life only, only when some THING in the story throws back at, on, this 'I' to so place him . . . where the reader has access to things of sufficient force to PLACE narrator's apprehension of them."[21] As I argue in Chapter 1, Olson's "root" is difficult to define, indicating as it did in "The Twist" several different cultural and natural forces. Creeley also encountered other agents—particularly language—as obstacles when he attempted to represent his self-conscious thought patterns thrown into relief by place. In their efforts to track these new agents as forces within self, Olson and Creeley expressed self as yoked to social forces in ways that hybridize or dissolve its integrity, typifying and forecasting loss of imaginative autonomy in other poets' social adaptations of the force field.

Place as the ground of poetic form focused Olson and Creeley's dialogue and their admiration for each other's work. In a review of Creeley's *For Love* (1958) in 1962, Olson praised Creeley's "symbiosis of self and landscape."[22] Creeley's first draft of the "Introduction" to Olson's *Selected Writings* focused almost entirely on Olson's conception of place, beginning from "geography, the complex of place . . . the complement of all human condition."[23] Following Olson's objectification of the subject as a material being receptive to the physical stimuli of environment, Creeley quotes Olson's emphasis on body and breath as formed in response to environment in "The Resistance." "It is body that is his answer, his body intact and fought for, the absolute of his organism in its simplest terms, this structure evolved by nature."[24] For both poets, place threw the self into relief to enable identification and synthesis of thought's temporal flow. Physical environment provided a foil for recognizable identity in the flux of the force field. While they perceived the body as a discrete, limited identity, its formation was so entwined with nature that individual integrity must be "fought for," indicating its difficult isolation as an entity separate from the rest of nature.

While "Projective Verse" drew on a Modernist tradition of force as both natural and social, Olson and Creeley departed gradually from a conception of place as composed of natural forces to construct place as primarily social. Their early attempts to articulate mind in relation to environment strained toward the harmony or coincidence of mental with natural structures that they have inherited from Romanticism. In the early 1950s, influenced by Williams's *In the American Grain* and D. H. Lawrence's *The Plumed Serpent*, both poets imagined nature as maternal and sexual. They imagined fulfillment of desire and self as reunion with place. In a letter to Creeley, Olson admired Lawrence's attempt "by way of woman . . . [to push] nature back into shape," to achieve a primordial essence of "formalization *beneath* both the human & the natural."[25] The conceptual alienation from nature he perceived as characteristic of Western culture made all things "bitter, words even / . . . to taste like paper." *In Cold Hell, In Thicket* (1953) attempts to recover original unity with deified place. Olson's question, "How shall he who is not happy . . . turn this unbidden place / how trace the necessary goddess," introduces the "arched" sky goddess of Egyptian religion as an ideal heavenly realm beneath which male earth is "at ease as any monarch or / a happy man," her "awkward stars drawn for teats to pleasure him."[26] Communion with place provides the harmony and completeness that fulfills the individual.

Natural place provided similar nourishment and completion of self for Creeley. He wrote enthusiastically to Olson of Hölderlin's statement that human beings are the navel of the earth.[27] Although Creeley's focus on the moment of separation, or individuation, intensified in his subsequent work, the writing inspired by his early contact with Olson strives for original unity with a maternal nature as the source and context of human activity implicit in Hölderlin's image. Reading Malinowski, Creeley became interested in myth as immediate response to nature rather than etiological story and planned a poem on the "Primordial Child" that would recover such innocence of perception.[28] Discussing Lawrence's "The Escaped Cock," Creeley described "geography" as a "metapsyche" of whose force "we are the living instruments & examples." He praised "identity" and "resonance" between personal psyche and metapsyche as "comparable only to the finest speech."[29]

Even as they projected an ideal harmony of human and natural shape, Olson and Creeley identified local forces whose influence on thought resisted harmonization of mind and nature. Both struggled to synthesize the divergent Modernist legacies of Williams's concrete and Pound's idealist foundations of form.[30] In so doing, they came to perceive cultural order and process as fundamentally different from biological. Although Pound and Williams fragmented traditional form, both retained poetic control by selecting facts in the attempt to reveal correspondences between nature and culture. In contrast, Olson and Creeley recognized the organic self and poetic form of the Romantics as an artificial framework inadequate to their experience.

Whereas Olson retained belief in the harmony between nature and culture, continuing a Modernist tradition that Albert Gelpi describes as the truth if not the perception of an organic whole,[31] Creeley ironized and then broke with an organic model of form. Olson's *Maximus Poems* gather encyclopedic data in the attempt to map the correspondence between nature and the laws governing collective institutions such as monetary currency and myth. While he affirmed the harmony of nature and culture as sources of form, his desire to trace patterns of history accurately drove him to study cultural processes as they differ from as well as conform to those of nature. His omnivorous gathering of fact grew from his confidence that all facts signify a natural order in which cultural as well as biological forms originate. Olson's search for the natural ground of cultural forms prevented him, however, from articulating positively the new forces that displace cultural subject and natural object as centers of agency driving contemporary history. The *Maximus Poems* continue to seek harmony between nature and culture and represent departures from this harmony as dismemberment or disintegration of form. In contrast to Olson's sprawling poems, Creeley's slender early lyrics, surrounded by white space on the page, express the isolation and smallness of self once nature is eliminated. As they abandon the effort to define natural place, Creeley's poems begin to explore the social and psychological agents shaping poetic subjectivity and form.

1

As he attempted to map Gloucester, Olson found agents other than nature and individual thought to be the primary forces shaping place. Although the *Maximus Poems* work to reconstellate polis around new agents informing subject and object, they remained deeply influenced by the poles of subjective and objective order that structure Olson's models in Modernist epic. Robert Von Hallberg traces Olson's effort to integrate *Paterson*'s objective grounding of form in geographical place with *The Cantos*' subjective or ideal order of the ideogram.[32] Williams and Pound synthesized their found material, *Paterson* in the metaphor of city as man and nature as woman and *The Cantos* in the attribution of natural harmony to an ideal realm of neo-Platonic forms. This correspondence, already so strained as to prevent closure in these Modernist long poems,[33] becomes even more attenuated in Olson's epic.

Critics tend to read the *Maximus Poems* either as radical integration of these Modernist poles that levels the hierarchy of subject over object or as disintegration into disparate subjective and objective elements indicating the difficulty of synthesis.[34] I argue that Olson's epic explores both a greater range of correspondences between his subjects and objects and the differences that prevent him from forging a single order from them. The parataxis many critics consider characteristic of the *Maximus Poems*[35] places subjective and objective facts in a relation of contiguity, simultaneously suggesting their relation and intensifying difference through the absence of logical connection. Olson's straining of the Modernist epic form used by Pound and Williams unsettles conceptions of culture and self modeled on biological form, forecasting the emergence of new conceptions of cosmos and identity based on social centers of form and agency as Olson comes to perceive subject and object as subordinate to social forces he cannot identify.

Olson's departure in the *Maximus Poems* from the unifying devices used by Williams and Pound dissolves the individual and cosmic order into interacting processes in which form becomes local and changing rather than universal. Olson's reception of Alfred North Whitehead's philosophy of organism helped him to articulate this departure from his Modernist predecessors. Whitehead imagined the cosmos as an organism in which physical and mental processes collaborate and adapt to each other like the organs of an animal. Individual form emerges from the "concrescence" or growing together of life processes rather than from discrete being. Whitehead's model of being is not the discrete particle in absolute Newtonian time-space coordinates. It is the point defined as a convergence of forces and known as a pattern or consistent process rather than as a single entity, as in the case of the electron subject to force in the electromagnetic field. In *Science and the Modern World*, Whitehead constructs "a system of thought basing nature upon the concept of organism, not upon the concept of matter."[36] Not only is the individual being a "social order" or "nexus" of processes, but society is a single organism whose members contribute to the life of the whole. Bruce Holsapple summarizes this interconnection of things: "[t]he problem with taking . . . the perceiver (subject) or the perceived (object), as independent or absolute is that, in doing so, one ignores the fact that both 'events' occur within a larger event, which united them."[37] Whitehead thus shifted philosophical conceptions of being away from "[t]he mechanism of God and the mechanism of matter [as] monstrous issues of a limited metaphysics and clear logical intellect"[38] to explore forms produced by the interaction of natural and cultural processes. Like Olson's "Projective Verse," Whitehead levels the traditional hierarchies and undoes the dichotomies of traditional Western metaphysics, such as mental and physical, organic and inorganic.

Olson's early poems are rich in images whose concrete sensuality echoes Williams's work. However, Olson embeds and develops these images differently than Williams in the fabric of the poem. Williams's counterpoint of concrete description and lineation articulates the distinct processes of thought and material being to confirm subject and object as fundamental elements shaping reality. Olson, in contrast, blurs rather than sharpens these boundaries. By presenting elements of the local landscape such as diorite stone or sea serpent as hybrids deriving significance from geology, biology, myth, and local history, Olson dissolves Williams's concrete object into shifting systems of knowledge or natural process and begins to trace identity as a composite of forces whose identity and origin are ambiguous or ultimately unknown.

Olson also undermines Pound's eternal neo-Platonic forms as inappropriate to an evolving universe like Whitehead's. Citing Duns Scotus's "all things that are are lights"[39] to indicate the unity of being as an emanation of the neo-Platonic One, Pound traced all being to an origin in ideal form. Although the sun is the source of life in the *Maximus Poems*, Olson presents its creative power primarily as illumination of each object in its difference from others. We know each thing not by returning to its ideal source but through the interplay of similarity and difference in concrete appearance. Against Pound's paradisal realm of Platonic forms, Olson's universe incorporates destruction and conflict into changing systems rather than eternal ideals.

Olson's conception of changing cosmic and poetic structure also yields an understanding of poetic creation different from Pound's. Pound's image of poetic creation as *intaglio*, the imprint of form on an inert surface, draws on Dante's Christian universe, in which matter is passive, identity imprinted by ideal form.[40] Olson offers "not the intaglio method or skating / on the luxurious indoor rink / but Saint Sophia herself our / lady of bon voyage."[41] For Olson, the fixity of Pound's image of nature is superficial and artificially maintained, like the climate control of an indoor rink. Olson finds matter too fluid to hold the mind's form. Physical process actively alters human creativity, making artistic creation a journey or navigation of the unknown. Pound's nature cannot bear the test of reality, the open sea and elements to which Olson exposes himself in search of wisdom. Physical processes involve cultural as well as natural forces that alter the poet's role, local collective belief shaping the poetic imagination. Representing wisdom as a saint like Gloucester's St. Sophia, to whom the sailors pray for safe return, Olson shows how wisdom and spirituality acquire forms specific to a community's labor. Individuals imagine the spirit world in local, not universal, forms. As poet, his "method" is not a separate force acting on nature but part of the popular imagination informed by physical labor.

Like Whitehead, Olson represents social reality as evolving like the biological organism to develop new structures yet inconceivable to the conscious imagination.[42] Drawing on Hesiod's *Theogony*, he presents history and cosmology as changing, driven by the forces of *eros* and *eris* that lead each generation to create a new cosmic order. Modernized as the migration of centers of civilization that Brooks Adams proposes in *The Law of Civilization and Decay*, Olson's theory of history informs the evolving, inconsistent structure of the *Maximus Poems*. Rejecting Pound's and Williams's organization of their long poems into sequential numbered sections,[43] he presents some *Maximus Poems* as letters ordered by specific place or date but assigns others numbers, and places the "proem" in the middle of the second volume.[44] His poem, like the world it represents, emerges from the interaction of processes and ordering systems that cannot be synthesized into a coherent whole.

No longer subordinate to a single, unifying order in nature, place and poetic form in the *Maximus Poems* dissolve into a dense network of associations and forces. Olson's "a 3rd morning and it's beautiful" grounds poetic form in the local intersection of natural and cultural processes, emphasizing both the particularity of the individual thing and its vulnerability to these processes. Beauty emerges from the mutual illumination of local particulars, whether concrete or abstract, and changes with time and position. Opening with the precise scientific placement of the speaker measured in terms of date, hour, and tide level, the poem explores the mutual attraction of the landscape's elements like that of moon and tide. While each object is illuminated as though newly created by the sun, light is not incarnate in the thing. The "stiffness" of Shag Rock, the shine of port and island, and the white and gray of buildings and water[45] emphasize the differentiating quality of each thing—rigidity, texture, and color. Since the landscape is formed by the tide level as well as the sun's light, the moon constitutes a second center of agency. Its gravitational force, like its changing reflection of the sun's light, suggests multiple and indirect influences that challenge the sun's power as sole creative source.

Since being does not emanate from a single source, part is not concentric with whole. Individual beings exert their character and influence on the local scene, and beauty emerges from mutual reflection among particulars.

> and out ahead   pointing out the Harbor <u>west</u>ward from
> the Island (like its 'sleek head'
> the verse he sd in his work emerges
> like Shag Rock—like the 'head' of the
> Sea-Serpent (its 'first-fold'
>   And the Island
>   carrying on
> behind [like the <u>Queen Mary</u> a thin
> cup of tea   a thin
> <u>Queen Mary</u> going forever
>   just in her own place
>   in this Harbor   floated up
> like the 'tie' she <u>must</u> have
> to the 'Land' Below: a <u>aglaia</u> of
> this Port ["Gloucester-Port"]
>   with this <u>Jewel</u>
> in her Eye . . . [Square brackets within the quotation are Olson's][46]

While articulating the mind's response to nature much as Williams does, the poem departs from imagistic representation of place. Linguistic and literary associations rather than concrete description generate forms. The adverb "ahead" suggests the form of a head for the island. Butterick traces "sleek head" to Joyce's praise for the "sleek head" of Pound's verse and to the local lore of the Gloucester sea serpent sighted offshore in the nineteenth century.[47] With Olson's unexpected comparison of the island to a thin cup of tea, perhaps inspired by the New England association of the boat with traditionally English tea, analogy achieves centrifugal momentum that disperses form in increasingly remote associations. "Thin" refers grammatically to the cup but more logically to tea, rendering the island either a fragile form and vessel different from the surrounding water or a fluid medium like the sea from which it emerges. The image of island as jewel retains the independent elements of sea and island, while relating them through "aglaia" (ancient Greek for splendor), again blurring the boundaries between fluid sea and solid island. The cumulative effect of these very different images of island as serpent's head, ship, cup of tea, and jewel is difficult to resolve, for each image seems to displace the other metonymically rather than to cohere around a single metaphoric center.

Although conscious that this displacement is the product of poetic description, Olson cannot ground imagination and poetic form in a natural order. The chain of similes renders the relation between the images unclear. By making head and rock similes of each other, Olson creates an infinite regress in which each is known only through its correspondence with the other. Like the phrases in open parentheses, the similes elaborate what they modify but do not subordinate description to the thing described, leaving the relation between the elements unresolved. Creative agency shifts between sun and ocean. As a ground to which the island is "tied," the ocean suggests both umbilical cord and humanly cast rope and anchor, an ambiguous natural origin that may indicate maternal nature or human projection. Although Olson attempts to establish one source generating these forms, he remains unable to define them except through the shifting associations.

Olson's phrase "The 'Land' Below," which takes its title from a poem by Dorn, uses the metaphor of Heinrich Schliemann's ancient Troy to explore the cultural past preserved in the land. Olson's allusion reinforces this ambiguity of origin. While Dorn's poem excavates the geological and cultural history informing the American landscape, Olson's leaves the sea's depths unexplored, asserting but not demonstrating "the 'tie' she <u>must</u> have." The addition of quotation marks around "land" to Dorn's original title further qualifies the substance of the land that Olson seeks. The absence of identifiable agents in local processes renders the relation between matter and spirit contingent on context, subordinating discrete identity to these processes, which emerge with greater prominence than individual elements of the landscape and dissolve these objects into their flow. Although Olson later associates the specific phenomenon of "<u>aglaia</u>" with a goddess Aglaia, he does not describe her further. In the same way, he sees the grace Eurynome in the sprawling form of Black Rock covered by cormorants and gulls, which resembles a head and hair. Divinity exists only "epiphanically" as a pattern of coexistence between many beings, beauty emerging coincidentally in this diversity.[48] While Olson explores the interpenetration of mental and geographical forms throughout the poem, the syntax is disjoint, each phrase connecting to those before and after it but not cohering into a full, grammatical sentence that would fix their relation. As with the branching associations and allusions throughout the poem, each possible combination projects a mutually exclusive perspective. What sounds like a continuous flow is in fact a "composite nature" whose sequence of shifting relations forms a paradox of unity and disunity.

Like "a 3rd morning," the *Maximus Poems* as a whole appear to be individual poems merging in local process, but their discontinuity draws attention to Olson's inability to identify the source or agent driving these processes. While "a 3rd morning" presents a high degree of correspondence between human and natural forms, other *Maximus Poems* accentuate the disparate, conglomerate character of form and instability of being subordinate to and originating in forces beyond the individual. "Main Street / is deserted" defines both natural and cultural beings as hybrids without identifying the forces that have produced these conglomerate forms. Set at "the Polls [Poles]," a region of porphyrious rock that seems to have formed from the contact between two originally distinct kinds of rock, the poem represents landscape as the indeterminate conjunction of different concrete things. The boundaries between the original rocks blur in the observed form and, like the sea "tied" vaguely to natural creation in "a 3rd morning," hidden "subglacial streams" yield no clues to the forms they have produced. The poem ends uncertainly, quoting Shaler's "Geology of Cape Ann," which presents two possible but incompatible theories for the Polls' formation: "[T]he diorite / is included in the granitite / the granitite has burst up around / the diorite, / leaving it as an undivided mass."[49] Nature remains unreadable, and science as mere theory or interpretation undermines nature as the ground of cultural form.

Like science, physical and mental labor change natural form. The "rocks are soft / from the scales" of fish cleaned there by the fishing industry.[50] Names reflect human history as well as nature, the nearby cellar known popularly as "Widow Day's kame" blending history and geology. Again Olson records the interaction of separate forces, not emanations from a common source. In "Main Street," Olson links himself to the Phoenician myth of the Diorite Man, a blue stone in human form that grew from the bottom of the sea. While the Diorite Man unites blue sky, sea, earth, and animate organism, his growth is so rapid that the gods destroy him, suggesting his threat to cosmic order. Although the poem presents Olson growing like the Diorite Man from the rock on which he sits, Olson's scrutiny of the rock reveals an unbridgeable gap between the discrete, static visible forms of the landscape and the dynamic but invisible forces that have created it. His humanity seems to be not a harmonious fusion of forces but an unpredictable aberrance in nature.

Olson's confidence in his power to reconstruct the invisible forces that have created physical and mental landscape declined in the course of the *Maximus Poems*. "Main Street," for example, contains nearly all the Shaler passages quoted in an earlier poem entitled "The Cow of Dogtown" and is set in the same geographic location but provides much less connection than the earlier poem. "The Cow of Dogtown" moves from the geological and historical specifics of Gloucester to a mythical vision of the Egyptian deities Nut and Ptah to suggest the universal ground of myth born immediately from nature. Beginning "Shaler says," the earlier poem distinguishes Olson's voice from that of his sources. Poetic craft synthesizes science, history, personal experience, and ancient religion to recover a single vision of original humanity. Olson's placement of himself as individual in this geological and cultural tradition culminates in a vision of nature like that of the ancient Egyptians. "Nut is over you / Ptah has replaced the Earth / the Primeval Hill / has gone directly / from the waters / and the mud / to the Cow of Heaven / the Hill stands / free / . . . Nut is in the world / (Monday February 11th, / 1963."[51] Gloucester and the speaker share a mythic vision that unites them through a universal human origin in nature. In contrast, the later "Main Street" blends Shaler's voice into Olson's without distinction, signaling the dissolution of Olson's poetic autonomy into other cultural voices. Past and present, earth and human being, individual and collective, ideal and real coexist without definite or fixed relation in an evolving landscape.

Elsewhere in the late *Maximus Poems*, Olson's narrator attempts to create images of cosmic unity. The untitled poem that follows "Main Street" introduces a seemingly incongruous organic rather than geological image as the model for cosmic evolution: "Imbued / with the light / the flower / grows down / the air / of heaven."[52] As the *Maximus Poems* progress, images of world harmony like the flower of creation become increasingly general,[53] remote from the specifics of history and landscape. Olson's epic persona changes accordingly. Olson initially wrote from the prophetic persona of the *homo maximus*, an alchemical and Jungian archetype of human perfection. This early "off-shore" persona "obeys the figures of / the present dance"[54] responsive to the sea and exhorts his city to follow. In the early poems, the many hybrid monsters (the Lernean hydra, Hesiod's Typhon "terrible and proud / And lawless,"[55] the Phoenician king Cecrops with a serpent's tail, the Diorite Man, and the stone-eyebrowed Algonquin child of a woman and a mountain) construct human nature on a larger scale by tapping its roots in natural power. These poems integrate political and scientific knowledge, frequently invoking Jane Harrison's theory that both the natural symbol and the hero's appropriation of natural power across cultures express a universal human derivation of power from nature.

The second and third volumes of the *Maximus Poems* emphasize not the *homo maximus*'s virile identification with nature but the poet-hero's tragic dismemberment in history. The later *Maximus Poems* represent world process only at the cost of violence to the individual. The Hesiodic image of intergenerational strife, in which the child destroys the parent, dominates. "Maximus is a whelping mother, giving birth / with the crunch of his own pelvis."[56] Later hybrids express the relation between the hero and figures of cosmic process as painful. Self is "Odin or Christ stretched on that Living Tree / pure Flayed Skin all that's left / when one has given or it has been stolen or one is All Loss."[57] The body, whose organic integrity should provide a clue to cosmic form, has disintegrated into mere surface so torn as to reveal only the absence of form. In contrast to the early anagrammatic "Dog of Dogtown" signifying a God immanent in the physical creature, Volume Three presents the dog as the savage wolf Fenris of Norse mythology, which the hero Tyr captures only by sacrificing his hand as bait. The hand with which Olson writes is wrenched violently into the service of this greater power: "Space and Time the saliva / in the mouth / your own living hand amputated living on / in the mouth / of the Dog."[58] A *Maximus* poem not included in the published volumes, "Maximus at the Reach of Himself," develops this image of violent interconnection as "so many . . . gobbled up, . . . lost / on the insides of the world animal."[59] Individual hero and poet lose agency as they are consumed by larger forces that Olson represents mythically, in terms of popular imagination of history.

The late *Maximus Poems* suggest that this cosmic myth emerges in a collective production of culture alien to the local processes accessible to the individual. Human beings become tiny figures on the body of the elephant deity Ganesh, "wrapped in the elephant's / skin, all the outside of / all above deadly / destructive which the species now craves / wrapping itself in impenetrable garments / & chasing the little cars motion / of a receding / universe."[60] Invoking de Sitter's model for the expansion of space as the two-dimensional surface of a ball being inflated, Olson's modern Ganesh is not the Hindu fusion of animal and god but rather the limited version of reality available to human perception. Exiled to the outside of nature's "impenetrable garment," human beings spin obscuring myths. Their "little cars" suggest a misguided inorganic, mechanical production of culture that pursues but holds no clue to the "receding universe."

Conscious of his invasion by or inseparability from these collective cultural forces, Olson seems to have lost confidence in the individual's ability to create myth that would unify human and natural being.[61] Neither political leader nor poet can wrest control of evolution from the collective species. "Stevens Song" contrasts the American colonial visionary and rebel William Stevens's escape from England to found a new law with the unsuccessful attempt of Olson's father to reform the national postal service. "Stevens ran off / My father / stayed / & was ground down."[62] The poem expresses nostalgia for a world in which law is not savagely predatory. Olson attributes to ancient Egyptian and Greek rulers the power to impose a social order in harmony with nature on their subjects.

Kheops's solar barge, which carried the sun through the Underworld, preserves light's vitality and order against chaos and darkness. The Greek ruler achieved similar power to control the collective, the "prince" having been "instructed / to have in his mouth / the ability to lend / aid / to the bewildered / mob."[63]

For Olson, the contemporary poet and hero have no such autonomy but are embedded in collective processes. Volume Three replaces the persona of *homo maximus* with images of the hero in violent conflict with the collective. Olson represents this loss of independent vision as the disruption of existing identity rather than the emergence of new agents replacing poetic vision. The mythical-historic hero Enyalion, who wars with the "Imago Mundi,"[64] embodies a conflict between society and its ideal or emblematic individual. The violence of this collective identity also affects poets. The later *Maximus Poems* link poetic creation to social and familial violence in the story of Gassire's lute, which sings only after being soaked in the blood of the king's family. Abandoning the figure of the mythopoeic ruler whose vision harmonizes culture with nature, Olson came to imagine the epic poet as the voice of a collective humanity whose erring self-production destroys it.[65]

2

Although Olson seems increasingly to have despaired of discovering a natural order grounding all branches of knowledge, he continued to treat his material as if such an order existed, to gather facts in the hope of discovering their significance. "[E]ach bit can be brought together and / gone over until as though it were the secrets of a universum."[66] Olson's vacillation between "until" and "as though" suggests that this universal significance might be projected rather than real, and even his early writings recognize the potential for misinterpretation. Despite these doubts about human ability to understand meaning, he conceived poetic language throughout his career as a natural rather than human creation. An early letter to Creeley asserts that Indo-European language must represent an original unity of culture as it emerged directly from nature.[67] The sensual materiality of language—pun, etymology, and phonetic similarity—reveals constellations of meaning in nature. The phonetic similarity between *topos* (place), *tropos* (figure of speech), and *typos* (type or general form), for example, indicates the correspondence between forms in nature, language, and intellect.[68] While the "duplicity" of language causes "sounds [to] slide into each other, melt, and thus lose their structures, and the structure of saying," Olson attributes this agency of language as material medium to its "genius" as a part of nature. Words "can be used to speak the 'rhein' or Heraclitean flow any maker is obedient to." Although the *Maximus Poems* do not realize this ideal, Olson maintains faith in the potential of natural language as a cosmic rather than a specifically human agent.[69]

Whereas Olson persisted in seeking the origin of human place in nature, Creeley experienced human meaning as alien to nature. In a poem dedicated to Olson, Creeley admires Olson's ability to expand into nature as the form of self but cannot emulate it.

> He feels small as he awakens,
> but in the stream's sudden mirror,
> a pool of darkening water,
> sees his size with his own two eyes.

> The trees are taller here,
> fall off to no field or clearing,
> and depend on the inswept air
> for the place in which he finds himself thus lost.[70]

In Creeley's view, Olson sees nature as a mirror that reveals the self through reflection and mutual recognition. Olson's gaze lends stature to the trees, whose size seems to be enhanced through conscious reflection. Unlike Olson's "place," in whose union of human and natural the self awakens to consciousness as part of the larger cosmos, Creeley's identification with place increases self-consciousness but threatens loss. Whereas Olson views etymology as the key to cosmic order, Creeley perceives thought and language as so different from nature that they provide no clue to natural order. Place becomes subjective. "The local is not a place but a place in a given man."[71]

Creeley's early reading and writing about poetry focused on placing human beings in nature. In the 1950s, he read Prescott, Parkman, and Malinowski as well as Williams and Lawrence as he searched for an epic American theme. Although Creeley wrote of body and breath as the basis of meter in the naturalizing terms of "Projective Verse," his early writing

traced the eccentricity of individual mind and word. Before his acquaintance with Olson, Creeley was immersed in Sartrean existentialism, exploring its emphasis on the independent act as self-definition. In a letter
to his friend Jacob Leed in the late 1940s, Creeley rejects the "pseudo-
religion" of Romanticism that "breathes spirit into nature" for Sartre's
"act," "because we are to define ourselves through what we choose to
act."[72] His early poetry separates this act from the external world to define
self in art as "the destruction of reference."[73] Early stories like "The Gold
Diggers" isolate the "web of emotion which of course is available beyond
'place' or 'incident.' "[74] In articulating emotional or psychological place as
distinct from natural, Creeley shifted the emphasis of his field poetics to
identifying the cultural, particularly linguistic, agents structuring self.
Whereas Olson's hybrids unsettle the Romantic subordination of nature
to culture but fail to suggest alternatives, Creeley begins to identify new
cultural agents as the forces structuring place and poetic form.

When Olson read Whitehead, he envisioned the individual as a locus
or node in interacting cultural systems that form the "organism" of the cosmos. Creeley, in contrast, was inspired to isolate the single strand or line of
force within this organism that constitutes the individual. Although place
was crucial to defining the individual for both poets, Creeley emphasized
difference from nature over origin in or union with it. Of Whitehead, he
wrote, "How can I argue against it, these particulars [trees]: hard / fixed / and
not to be cajoled. I wd isolate, my phrase, & I wd, perhaps, want it thrown
into form, as, the mud strikes, splatters, to shape, on the ground. It is that?
It is that form, I am after. . . ."[75] Although the common substance of mud
and ground implied that language originates in and is made of the same
stuff as the object to which it refers, Creeley emphasized their resistance to
each other and attempted to grasp the contours of language shaped by nature's resistance.

For Love plays on conventions of romantic love that associate it with
natural harmony and define nature as the home in which the self finds
wholeness. Although place plays a central role as desired fulfillment of self
through participation in natural harmony, the failure of place to ensure
a home leads Creeley to construct linguistic alternatives to such illusory security. "Wherever it is one stumbles (to get to wherever) at least some way
will exist. . . . Insofar as these poems are such places, always they were
ones stumbled into: warmth for a night perhaps, the misdirected intention

come right; and too, a sudden instance of love, and the being loved, wherewith a man also contrives a world (of his own mind)."[76] The structures of world and self built from such "stumbling" contact are accidental and transitory, and the world discovered may be psychological projection. However, Creeley's search for the structures that express the individual's originality led him to focus on cultural agents that disrupt or shape the individual's use of language.

For Love begins by recognizing the failure of Romantic conventions to integrate self into nature through language. Much like the revision of Romantic inspiration in "Still Life Or," Creeley's "Hart Crane" satirizes the Romantic poet's attempt to achieve sublime experience through the trope of the bird.

> He had been stuttering, by the edge
> of the street, one foot still
> on the sidewalk, and the other
> in the gutter . . .
>
> like a bird, say, wired to flight, the
> wings, pinned to their motion, stuffed.[77]

For Creeley, Crane expresses the inadequacy of name to embody nature. Linguistic structure, like a stuffed bird, provides only a crude, rigid reproduction of natural beauty. Longinus's image of the sublime as sudden, suspended flight becomes grotesquely static, indicating not access to a realm that transcends time but the unnatural fixity of language as distinct from natural process. Such an effort stretches animal form painfully on an artificial frame. Captured only as dead trophy, nature confirms self through the conventional masculinity of the hunter, as brutal mastery of nature. Creeley's conversational "say" makes explicit the performative and constructed quality of simile and accentuates the way seemingly transparent rhythms of colloquial speech depart from reference, fragmenting culture and nature into separate realities, as in Creeley's citation of Crane: "*And so it was I entered the broken world.*"[78] The contrast between the seeming naturalness of culture conveyed in colloquial speech and the awkward unnaturalness of language restricted to concrete reference undercuts the Romantics' conception of language as a medium linking nature and spirit. In analyzing Creeley's debt to Crane, Alice Entwhistle analyzes both poets' "push" of sound beyond meaning to create a disrupting ineffability of language.[79] The Romantic effort to heal human alienation through return to nature is hindered by cultural, especially linguistic, structures that obstruct body consciousness, rendering nature alien and inaccessible.

For Creeley, Crane's awkward speech and gait result less from his body (as in the case of the bird) than from his position. Like the man at the edge of the street, Crane is neither comfortably inside the common paths of convention nor freely outside them. Unlike the Romantic poet on country footpaths, Crane straddles two artificial, socially constructed roads, the street for vehicles and the sidewalk for bodies. Creeley seems to distinguish two courses in language, one for mechanized transport in vehicles, the other a body-based motion. That both are public thoroughfares suggests, however, that the language of the individual body, as well as the impersonal ready-made vehicle, are socially determined. Positioning the poet in the poem awkwardly between the two, Creeley reveals multiple linguistic agents influencing self, which can only be expressed in the stutter that deforms these dominant paths.

Recognizing the failure of Romantic convention is easier than moving beyond it. Throughout *For Love*, union with nature haunts Creeley's poems as a structure of desire that the poem should fulfill. "The Place" exemplifies *For Love*'s ironic conflation and subversion of conventions of romantic love and Romantic nature poetry.

> What is the form is the gro-
> tesquerie—the accident
> of the moon's light
> on your face.
>
> Oh love, an empty table!
> An empty bottle also.
> But no trick will go
> so far but not further.
>
> . . . .
>
> Agh, form is what happens?
> Form is an accompaniment.
> I to love, you to love:
> syntactic accident.[80]

Although describing love as the harmony of natural and human beauty in the moonlight on his beloved's face, Creeley accentuates the arbitrary ground of this feeling, born of the accidental details of moon, furniture, and wine. The empty bottle parodies Romantic intoxication from nature's beauty and calls attention to the empty form. Although the speaker wishes to adhere to his poetic goals of tracing experience ("form is what happens"), his mind leaps beyond the moment-by-moment perception of table and bottle to an intuition of cosmic harmony. In discussing this poem, Creeley described its form as "grotesquerie because it intervenes between the literal reality and his understanding of it."[81] As he is unable to dissociate projected feeling from concrete perception of particulars, his impulse to poetic form suggests underlying unity in the shared music of "I to love, you to love." Awareness of poetic convention as an agent influencing the imagination reduces words' power to incarnate truth to "syntactic accident." Although the poem parodies romantic love as a feeling of unity with the world in no way supported by nature, it reveals the power of this convention as a force shaping the speaker's experience and creation of form.

Although the speaker's persona does not measure up to literary ideals, the poems explore the power of these ideals as the primary forces substantiating self. In "The Bed," the social recognition these ideals confer commands individual emotion and desire.

> She walks in beauty like a lake
> and eats her steak
> with fork and knife
> and proves a proper wife.
>
> Her room and board
> he can afford, he has made friends
> of common pains
> and meets his ends.
>
> Oh god, decry
> such common finery as puts the need
> before the bed, makes true what is
> the lie indeed.[82]

Satisfaction in the marriage comes from each partner's fulfillment, however piecemeal, of social and literary types, the wife's of sexual and domestic roles and the husband's of the financial solvency and sociality essential to a New England ethic of masculinity and integrity. Although they have no concrete content, the set phrases "proves a proper wife" and "meets his ends" (echoing both "to make ends meet" and "to meet one's end") signify adherence to social formulas.

By playing with the range of literal and colloquial meanings, however, the poem reveals the precarious multivalence of such language, whose clarity often depends on unquestioned cliché. Just as "meets his ends" may imply meeting one's doom, the ominous undertone of "friends of common pains" suggests both friendship formed in shared suffering and a more literal and troubling friendship with pain that threatens the surface tone of normalcy and respectability. The unstable meaning of cliché reveals the arbitrary character of colloquial idiom, destroying its power to substantiate identity. Yet Creeley cannot free himself from these idioms. Even poems that seem to focus on intimately personal emotions are structured by convention. For example, "Goodbye," a painfully self-conscious account of emotion in a lovers' quarrel typical of Creeley's early work, places the woman in the traditional position of the muse. Framed by the open window and blocking the man's view, she thwarts the Romantic poet's conventional view of women as mediators of natural inspiration. Her resistance so threatens the lover's identity as man and poet that it halts the poem.[83]

Apparently sincere personal expression yields irony and consciousness of entrapment as social conventions maintain their power to define individual self. The final stanza of "The Bed" affirms "common" symbols as attributes more fulfilling than the physical and emotional intimacy conveyed by the shared bed of the title. The poet's desire for security in these symbols confirms the "lie" of convention as more substantial than individuality. Just as symbols seem to make the marriage, rhyme props up his unpoetic sentences, as if rhyme were sufficient to make any words poetic. Yet like the literal meaning that threatens to invade the familiar meaning of the clichés, the displaced rhymes, sometimes within and sometimes at the end of a line, disrupt conventional poetic forms. Whether these rhymes express a personal music struggling to emerge within convention or the disharmony of different conventions, their interference in the fabric of colloquial and poetic cliché is minor, sufficient to unsettle but not to replace its authority.

Creeley's writing reproduces colloquial speech rhythms with wonderful sensitivity. Lynn Keller has shown how Williams's poetic adaptation of the vernacular helps Creeley to establish a personal voice in his early po-etry.[84] However, this idiom does not convey Williams's effect of gritty, local authenticity. When Creeley identifies language rather than nature as the medium in which self is defined, he encounters colloquial and literary idiom as artificial forces shaping his own experience and creativity. Although it recognizes that conventional Romantic form is arbitrary, *For Love* cannot free itself from the authority of tradition. Creeley's severing of natural reference "frees" him not to personal style but to a language of social conventions. Most of the poems of *For Love* are intensely allusive, grounded in conventional forms and themes. Many express entrapment in traditional poetic and local New England conceptions of self. So thor-oughly do conventional topoi pervade Creeley's imagination that he cannot write his experience except in these forms. The self remains inaccessible behind the rigid, increasingly estranged conventions that structure both colloquial and literary language.

As Creeley's awareness that he cannot fulfill Romantic ideals grows throughout *For Love*, the poems become frenetic in their attempt to break through entrapment to achieve authentic voice. Later poems adopt and then exhaust clichés one after the other as each fails to provide adequate expres-sion of self. "Can I eat / what you give me. I / have not earned it. Must / I think of everything / as earned. Now love also / becomes a reward so / re-mote from me I have / only made it with my mind."[85] Dissatisfied with the traditional image of love as the soul's nourishment, the poem shifts to an-other convention of self-worth, the Protestant reckoning of debits and credits. Uppermost in the speaker's meditation on love, these conventions isolate him from his beloved, cliché alienating him from an original lan-guage of emotion. Other poems move rapidly from nature to an idealized beloved or the purely musical "airs" of Campion in desperate pursuit of an ever-receding source of inspiration. The final plea to his lady, "Catbird, catbird. / O lady hear me. I have no / other / voice left,"[86] expresses the exhaustion and futility of borrowed voices that lack the power and origi-nality he desires.

Recognizing the power of linguistic conventions as agents defining meaning, Creeley begins to trace self as indirect expression, as the defor-mation of the meanings and emotions conventionally associated with set images and phrases. Rather than using such images to evoke the social val-ues or cosmic order they might imply, he allows them to become vehicles to express the strong but ineffable force of his psyche through distortion. "The Flower" transforms a Romantic image of natural order and beauty into an idiosyncratically associative image of his pain.

> I think I grow tensions
> like flowers
> in a wood where
> nobody goes.
>
> Each wound is perfect,
> encloses itself in a tiny
> imperceptible blossom,
> making pain.
>
> Pain is a flower like that one,
> like this one,
> like that one,
> like this one.[87]

The speaker's obsessive projections replace universal nature with an imagined landscape of isolation. Perhaps alluding to the philosophical problem of whether a tree that falls in the forest makes noise, Creeley wryly suggests that his self may not exist because no one can witness its feelings. Language is unable to express original feeling, to take others to this private "wood." Yet the obsessive elaboration on the speaker's "tensions" confirms their power to generate a poem, however opaque. Radically different from the wound yet metaphorically related to it, the blossoming words take a different, unsettling direction as Creeley invests these phrases with emotion but cannot render them expressive of his individual situation. The pain remains private, inaccessible behind the set phrases of colloquial expression to which thought gravitates. Deformed by private emotion, these expressions give the speaker's wounds a perverse perfection or consistency of individual character even when devoted to painful rather than healthy growth. The final stanza, reminiscent of plucking the petals to the rhyme "he loves me, he loves me not" suggests that poetry is deliberate mutilation, not nurture, of the self, the need to nurse pain as all that the self has. Yet the simile's reference to other flowers indicates the arbitrariness of the object of comparison and the gravitation of language into familiar patterns regardless of words' meaning. "For Fear" describes the need to cling to such pain, "to make myself again / under the thumb / of old love, old time / subservience / and pain, bent / into a nail that will / not come out."[88] Love, even if "old," painfully constricting, or wounding, affords security.

Creeley's adoption of a charged nursery rhyme singsong later in *For Love* develops further the self's eccentric relation to language. Whereas the Romantic poet turns to children and other "innocents" to find a purer, more poetic language of nature, Creeley explores the mysterious life of language in the child's psyche. Here too, colloquial expressions loom, charged with emotions for which the young speaker has no vocabulary. Creeley's "The Cracks" moves from an inversion of the magical-illogical "Step on a crack, break your mother's back" to Little Jack Horner's "What a good boy am I" as all that remains of a "nightmare" memory of the speaker's mother. Although Creeley cannot recall his original experience, these fragments of nursery rhyme remain fixed in memory, returning obsessively to evoke the emotion he cannot comprehend. The experience itself remains "a memory / or an insinuation or two / of cracks in a pavement."[89] Hidden beneath the "pavement" or common thoroughfare of language, personal experience is visible only in cracks as unsettling evidence of unknown forces below the surface.

Because conventional language is composed of ready-made structures, emotion adheres somewhat randomly to it, achieving expression only as it warps the conventional surface. "The Ball Game" falls into obsessive repetition in its effort to grasp the significance of a defining, perhaps traumatic childhood experience. "The one damn time (7th inning) / standing up to get a hot dog someone spills / mustard all over me."[90] Locked in the continual present of a participial phrase, the experience remains vivid but undigested. The speaker has interpreted the experience as a metaphor for life, a sudden formative awakening "out of the park / of our own indifferent vulgarity" into new awareness of self shaped by the collision of "particulars [that] need / no further impetus."[91] While this intrusion of external influence reveals the power of environment to shape self, its effect seems arbitrary, opaque. Representing self in baseball metaphors attributes character to the formative local scene of the all-American baseball field, but the assertion that "[e]arly in life the line is straight / made straight / against the grain" undercuts Williams's mutual influence of person and place in *In the American Grain*. For Creeley, local images influence but provide no clue to character. Identity seems inscrutable to both reader and speaker. The final stanza returns to the event but merely repeats the words in which Creeley first described it. Unable to provide further elucidation, the poem can only track the obsessive path of the mind back to this moment, grasped in an alien language, as its unfathomable center.

Unable to transform public language into a vehicle that conveys personal emotion or constructs individual self, Creeley isolates the absurd and often inappropriate images, phrases, and rhythms to which emotion adheres. *For Love* increasingly tracks illogical, opaque inner speech as the individual's most intimate relation to language, the most private and authoritative mode of expression. "On that horse I see so high,"[92] for example, may relate to the speaker's birth and mother, yet the poem does not provide enough information to determine the nature of this psychological bond. In the same way, "Saturday afternoon" is a beloved "monster," "furry" and "wooden eyed."[93] The image patterns express the speaker's feeling but remain incomprehensible without the concrete situation in which they emerge. While recognizing language as the only medium of self-expression, Creeley is caught between extremes of authoritative but empty convention and the vivid but eccentric, lonely life of language in the individual imagination. The possibility of bridging this gap by representing the concrete situation or rendering conventional language malleable to personal experience erodes in the course of *For Love*, reflecting the increasing authority of and alienation from conventional language.

Both Olson and Creeley were fascinated by the collective consciousness expressed in language and struggle to give it form. Their poems depart from harmonizing cultural with natural place to view culture as evolving by mechanisms different from those of nature. Olson's many hybrid creatures reveal the inadequacy of conventional categories of being yet do not identify new ones. Because he continues to believe that nature is the ground of culture, he tends to leave the problem of form's origin unresolved and rarely imagines new agents in positive terms. The later *Maximus Poems* represent increasingly hybrid forms whose formative principles are indecipherable; images of the agents shaping creation, particularly human evolution, become increasingly general, remote from Olson's concrete facts. Like Olson, Creeley arrived at an understanding of human nature as defined collectively by community convention and language rather than by the individual. It is "as a whole consciousness which they, in their multiplicity, possess."[94] Collective human nature "lead[s] to a *whole* species totality."[95] As Creeley abandoned Olson's (and an earlier Modernist) view of language as structured by natural reference, his poetry began to explore the structure of language in isolation and its role as an independent agent forming self.

Both Olson and Creeley came to view language as a multivalent system shaped in part by literal and individual reference but also by colloquial idiom and traditional forms. As concrete reference became unstable, Olson's and Creeley's double consciousness of individual and collective voice grew deeply alienating, disrupting the autonomy and transformative power of the poetic imagination. The poem as force field provided a place in which to explore these collective agents' interaction with personal voice. As awareness of the breach between individual and collective voice grew in their work, the colloquial language and popular culture that seemed powerfully authentic to both authors in the early 1950s came to seem more restrictive. While Olson's roots in Modernist beliefs about language led him to continue to seek a universal natural order, Creeley, Duncan, Levertov, and Dorn began to explore the ways in which individual imagination interacts with these cultural agents and to preserve poetic originality by developing strategies to insulate the imagination from the influence of these external agents.

3

Creeley, Duncan, and the Uses of Abstraction

Although Olson continued his attempts to synthesize elements of popular culture and myth to discover a natural ground for the collective imagination, in the mid-1950s other Black Mountain poets ceased considering myth and popular speech the most authentic or interesting forms of expression. For Creeley, Duncan, Levertov, and Dorn, colloquial language came to represent not a rich local culture but a limiting mass mentality. The rejection of colloquial speech motivated their break with Cid Corman's *Origin* and the 1954 founding of *Black Mountain Review*, in which they had planned to promote a more rigorously unified poetics.[1] Corman's editorial statements in *Origin* advocate poetry that captures the rhythms of everyday speech modeled on concrete simplicity, and Duncan attributed the break to Corman's insistence on a "speech-based" poetics and to his endorsement of too "eclectic" a group of poets working from Williams's American Idiom.[2]

The disagreement between Creeley and Corman over Paul Blackburn's poetry exemplifies Creeley's growing distance from an esthetic based on colloquial language. Corman interpreted Olson's derivation of poetic rhythm from breath as a turn from unnatural traditional meter to the greater naturalness of spoken idiom[3] and objected to the richly literary description and pace of Blackburn's lines. When Corman comments that Blackburn does not compose "by ear," Creeley defended Blackburn as sounding language carefully. Citing Blackburn's "A swollen white spike on each / of the line of rotten piles stepping / out from shore," Creeley argued that "the deliberateness, the deliberately toned language, IS the extension, the variation, on a spoken, conversational rhythm."[4] While grounding his poetics in spoken language as the measure of body and breath, Creeley preferred enrichment of everyday speech to imitation for the more concentrated expression that the poet's creative use of common idiom allows. In *Black Mountain Review*, Olson and Creeley attempted to define a conception of poetic form distinct from their contemporaries' growing emphasis on any form of free verse that resembles colloquial diction. Although written later, Levertov's essay "Some Notes on Organic Form" (1965), which seeks to establish a psychological and metaphysical basis for form in free verse poetry, emerged from the same debate.

In viewing poetry as a civilizing antidote to mass culture, Creeley, Duncan, and Levertov echoed the social expectations for poetry that, as Edward Brunner has shown,[5] dominated mainstream culture during the 1950s. The friendships between the three as well as their influence on each other deepened. They expressed their sense of a common purpose in poetry in letters and poetics statements. A reading at the Guggenheim in 1963 became the occasion to recognize mutual influence and pay tribute to each other.[6] From the late 1950s to the mid-1960s, Creeley, Duncan, and Levertov came to share an understanding of the poet's role as creator of forms that renovate rather than reproduce colloquial idiom. They differed from their more mainstream contemporaries, however, in seeing original reworking of everyday speech rather than elevated diction and traditional forms as the means of resistance.

Although each poet distances poetic language from colloquial in different ways, all three transformed the Modernist image of poet as exceptional leader-hero whose knowledge of literary tradition and language enables him or her to provide society with esthetic forms. Rather than transcending colloquial speech, the writing of Creeley, Duncan, and Levertov is embedded in it. Reflecting in 1960 on the importance of Olson and Williams to his own poetry, Creeley valued not their politics but their emphasis on prosody and technical precision as crucial antidotes to 1930s "poets of 'content'" like Kenneth Fearing, content implying moral or political message. For Creeley, careful use of language was fundamental to social change, for the medium of communication positions the speaker. Precise use of language provides a needed distance from the "mass orientation" of colloquial language, "which says that everything is all right (when it is patently not all right) . . . , the 'walk don't run' character of current [1950s] political and social jargon."[7] Deemphasizing Williams's American Idiom, Creeley preferred the poetics of *The Wedge* (1944), which defines the poem in structural terms as "a small (or large) machine of words," whose selective transformation of everyday speech provides "revelation" in language.[8]

Like Creeley, Duncan and Levertov saw poetry's social function as enriching common speech. Both attempted to increase the reader's critical consciousness of everyday media of communication and their range of expression. Duncan reiterated the need to differentiate artistic language from colloquial idiom. He admired Frank O'Hara's ability to create language that sounds "almost like chatter on the telephone," thereby calling attention to the forms of everyday language "that nobody was going to pay attention to before." For Duncan, O'Hara's creation defamiliarizes common speech, heightening consciousness of this cultural material and making it new.[9] In his 1956 Guggenheim recommendation for Creeley, Duncan argued the social importance of such poetry, emphasizing that Creeley's work is valuable because it can "vitally influenc[e] the speech of others."[10] In "Kresch's Studio," a poem from the early 1950s, Levertov too defined the poem as a "counterforce," a more intense expression of human energy to oppose the "squandered energy" of the ordinary.[11] Her essay "The Poem as Counterforce: Responsibilities" argues that the poet must resist imitating both predecessors and the social "motions" of politicians and the masses.[12] While retaining Olson's vocation of writing poetry as a force for social change, Creeley, Duncan, and Levertov repeatedly articulate the poet's obligation to engage and transform rather than record collective usage. Because Creeley and Duncan theorize this poetics most explicitly in their correspondence, this chapter focuses on their discussion of experimentation from the late 1950s to the mid-1960s, in which they developed a concept of abstract poetic form to insulate poetic usage from limited everyday speech.[13] Chapter 4 delineates the changing conception of the public sphere and the poet's role within it that accompanies this move to abstraction and forms a significant focus for discussion in Duncan and Levertov's correspondence.

As they find that natural form fails to inspire poetic form, Creeley and Duncan depart from the emphasis on speech that Olson associated with the body and nature in "Projective Verse." They formulate principles of abstract creation to escape the limits of conventional language. For Olson, popular myth and spoken language were the resources by which to recover culture's origin in nature. The reform of Western culture that Olson advocated in "Projective Verse" would eliminate subjective accretions to language to make it a purer medium of access to human beings' original vitality in nature. The result would be a language in which "*all* parts of speech . . . spring up like unknown, unnamed vegetables in the patch," where line and word "lie clean as wood as it issues from the hand of nature."[14] For Creeley and Duncan, language neither emerged from nature nor possessed revitalizing natural force. Like the Creeley of *For Love*, Duncan rejected natural supernaturalism as projection of the mind's forms into the conventional imagery of Romanticism. The form of the artistic medium and the cultural and individual agents shaping it become the true context of art, insulating the mind from popular environment and increasing awareness of agents shaping the medium.

In freeing themselves of this Romantic legacy, both Creeley and Duncan gravitated toward Coleridge's more independent conception of spiritual form, in which the imagination dissolves and reforms the sensual world according to its ideal forms.[15] They attempted to free art of external reference in order to isolate the individual mind's forms more purely. Piecing together a new nonreferential or abstract poetics from the rhetoric of Coleridgean theory, painterly abstraction, and the later work of Zukofsky, they located poetic inspiration in the mind and in language as a medium in itself. To achieve imaginative freedom, they shifted focus from Olson's mapping of the anthropological force field of popular culture to a linguistic one in which words freed from referents, like paint in abstract painting, can express imaginative forms not subordinate to the representation of external objects or collective myth.

1

During the mid-1950s Duncan, like Creeley in *For Love*, turned away from seeking inspiration in nature. When he arrived at Black Mountain College in the summer of 1954, Duncan was working on "Homage to Coleridge" in the Romantic ballad tradition familiar from the work of San Francisco friend and gothic ballad writer Helen Adam. In "Homage to

Coleridge," nature is animated not by a transcendent spirit but by the soul's obsessions. The "Preface" dedicates the work "to Coleridge for his <u>Cristobel</u> [*sic*]."[16] In Coleridge's *Christabel*, the ballad of a love triangle between the maiden Christabel, her father, and the strange Lady Geraldine, what seem to be supernatural phenomena may originate either in enchantment or in the emotional tension between the characters. Like *Christabel*, Duncan's poem sequence represents nature's spiritual power as human projection, progressing from failure to discovery of renovating power in nature and finally renunciation of the green world as the source and object of poetry. Duncan may have chosen *Christabel* as a source because its sexual undertones permit him to attribute alienation from nature to anxiety about the body, especially homosexuality. However, Coleridge's suggestion that his characters' emotions cause supernatural phenomena also provides Duncan with a model for imagination that can alter perception of the natural world, enabling his breakthrough to the abstract style and celebration of domestic sexual love in *The Opening of the Field*.

As in *Christabel*, nature in "Homage to Coleridge" is possessed by psychological demons that seem to have destroyed its fertility. In the first poem, "A Man at the Crossroads," a wanderer seeks tranquility and freedom from past pain in the natural landscape but finds only a wasted pastoral of "old fields / ruining southward under the moon," "used girls" and "witherd babies." The wanderer's invocation of Christian grace brings no redemption but only consciousness of nature as possessed by other demons. "The Name passd through him / straight as lightning to the heathen ground," where it "disturbs the dead." Nature is not a redeeming power but a ghostly voice of the wanderer's own past. The moonlit landscape is a "looney path" animated by his madness, where regrets reproach him in the form of a "disguised crow by the roadside"; "<u>What you've not dared lasts forever</u>." "The Grue of Mandrake Park" and "I heard a demon in the air" record the failure of the speaker to free himself from the past, and the final poem, "Thomas the Rimer," rejects poetry's attempt to transform nature into a healing power as mere illusion. A son persuades his Romantic poet-father to abandon the "dream" of a beloved Lady Nature "with her green eyes and her leafy toe-slippers," who would invite him into her world through a door in a tree root. Although the son comes to regret this disenchantment of his natural world, reduced to " 'the sky / grey to the grass / and an old stone,' " he cannot embrace his father's vision.

Also turning to Coleridge, Creeley moved from natural form as the model of culture to the mind's projection of its own life into nature. Discussing Coleridge with Duncan in the early 1950s, Creeley began to focus on Coleridge's separation of the life of spirit from natural form. Although experimenting with various Romantic conceptions of form, Creeley preferred the dejected Coleridge, who doubts the mind's connection with nature and articulated the forms of the spirit in isolation. Like Duncan, Creeley was fascinated by Coleridge's definition of the imagination as the mind's animation of nature. In a review of Duncan's *Letters* in 1960, Creeley invoked the honesty of Coleridge's "Dejection: An Ode" in recognizing nature's failure to inspire the poet. Citing Coleridge's "O Lady! we receive but what we give, / And in our life alone does Nature live,"[17] he advocated tapping the imagination, not nature, for spiritual nourishment and creativity.

While Creeley and Duncan first interpreted Coleridge's demystification of natural spirituality as the mind's neurotic projection of its demons into nature, they gradually embraced Coleridge's secondary imagination as a means to liberation. For Coleridge, the "Primary Imagination" is "the living Power and prime Agent of all human Perception, and a repetition in the finite mind of the eternal act of creation in the infinite I AM." As the subject repeats the act of creation in thought, this act is not imitation but a reproduction of the world in the mind that constitutes self as part of the cosmic order. The "Secondary Imagination," an "echo" of the primary, develops the transformative implications of consciousness. "It dissolves, diffuses, dissipates, in order to recreate; or where this process is rendered impossible, yet still at all events it struggles to idealize and unify. It is essentially *vital*, even as all objects (*as* objects) are essentially fixed and dead."[18] While Coleridge's secondary imagination "dissolves" the object to reintegrate it in a higher understanding of nature, Creeley's and Duncan's writing explores the transformative power of this imagination as conscious creation of new "vital" forms of the mind.

The discussion among abstract painters of the canvas as a world apart from nature and society provided Creeley and Duncan with a site for adapting Coleridge's secondary imagination to their poetry. Interpreting abstraction as an extension of this secondary imagination, they developed a sort of Romanticism without nature that renders the blank page rather than the natural landscape the ground against which the poet articulates ideas.

Psychological form replaces natural place as the structuring force in the poem. Both poets associated this new impulse in their work with developments in experimental painting.[19] Creeley attributed his interest at least in part to his friendship with René Laubiès, whom he met in Europe in the early 1950s.[20] Duncan was influenced by the work of his partner, painter and collage artist Jess Collins. His "Notes on Poetics Regarding Olson's *Maximus*," published in *Black Mountain Review* 6, relate Olson's poetics to this new energy in American art.[21] Both Creeley and Duncan attended the Black Mountain College summer session of 1954, where they met early Abstract Expressionists and other painters experimenting with abstraction (Robert Rauschenberg, Franz Kline, Cy Twombly, and Robert Motherwell) as well as art critic Clement Greenberg. This language of painterly abstraction helped them to articulate their emerging sense of abstract form.

Creeley's and Duncan's choice of painting as the model for poetic form signaled their departure from Olson's view of language as natural sign. For them, Olson's logocentrism was the source of his impatience with painting. According to Duncan, Olson shared Robert Graves's view of poetry as "an old set of ideas," in which language holds the key to sacred knowledge of nature. "Graves really feels, again, painting's a medium not an intelligence. Well, now Charles, again felt poetry was the primary intelligence," whereas painting for Olson was "a kind of therapy for people who weren't very bright." For Duncan, in contrast, other artistic media represent a crucial diversity of modes of expression. He commented on Olson's "fundamental lack of imagination of what a primary language music was, or what a primary language painting was."[22] Following the popular psychoanalytic interpretation of Abstract Expressionist painting as an expression and, ideally, a processual integration of unconscious forces in the mind, Olson saw language as intelligence (implicitly, of something), as logos signifying a cosmic order, while he saw paint as a formless, arbitrary medium malleable to expressive energy. For Duncan, artistic media are "primary languages," their multiplicity necessary to understanding the full range of human imagination and communication. All media contribute to the evolution of culture, and no single medium is closer to nature than the others.

Although they no longer attributed linguistic structure to nature, Creeley and Duncan did not abandon reference completely. Duncan did

not privilege language as an artistic medium over others, but he emphasized verbal reference as a crucial element of language. "[O]ne thing that I
have, and I would have this in common certainly with Olson and Creeley,
is that I have absolutely no words that are not also meanings."[23] Duncan
and Creeley, however, did not attempt to recover original reference to natural order. Reference becomes merely one valence or dimension of language
as expression of the imaginative possibilities of a cultural and linguistic order. Language as a medium in itself with its own "materiality" or substance
is another such force. As part of a cultural fabric that interweaves material
and ideal, language is both distinct from and capable of intervening in
nature.

In contrast to the psychoanalytic interpretation of abstract painting
as an extension of psychological activity, Creeley and Duncan adopted a for-
malist perspective which, like that of critics Clement Greenberg and Harold
Rosenberg, emphasizes the canvas as a space apart from the everyday world,
a free space in which to imagine new forms. Greenberg's essay "The Avant-
Garde and Kitsch" argues that nonrepresentational art provides the only escape from kitsch, the commodification of the lowest common denominator
of representation, to render painting palatable to a mass audience.[24] For
Greenberg, the structure of the artistic medium, radically different from that
of the external world, insulates the artist from mass modes of perception.
The flatness of the canvas and texture of paint create an alien environment
in which the imagination may explore new forms.

In their correspondence, Creeley and Duncan focus on a similar independence of the medium. For them, abstraction accentuates art's autonomy
as solid object, allowing the mind to realize newly created forms as concrete
presences. Creeley echoes Greenberg's discussion of the estranging effects
of the medium to free the artist from conventional modes of perception,
among them realistic reference. Introducing Franz Kline's black and white
paintings in *Black Mountain Review* 4, Creeley compares them to photo-
graphic negatives. Whereas representational painting uses the material
world as the vehicle through which to structure and express the artist's feeling, Kline's work isolates this feeling in itself. Just as negatives reverse light
and dark, so the paintings reverse the usual subordination of mental to
physical form, articulating the mind's forms in their difference from those
of physical objects.[25] Like Greenberg, Creeley emphasizes that the unique
solidity of the work of art lies in its materials, "the application of paint or

ink to a given surface which shall affect a thing in itself significant, an autonomy." He envies painters the "immediacy" of "a nonverbal medium" and praises Cezanne's destruction of the actual Mount St. Victoire to recreate it in the mind's geometric forms.[26] The formal structures of the artistic medium can give substance to pure forms of the mind.

Creeley's "The Painters" is a first attempt to grasp the nature of such representation. Composed circa 1951–52 in France, the unpublished poem describes what might be a naive viewer's response to the vaguely representational, hieroglyphic forms of a Laubiès painting. The speaker reflects on the different responses evoked by the forms in the painting and by its object, real people.

> The shadows of the people.   Upon cloth
> stretched there,   on frames, in the
> street held there.
> 　　　　　　　　　　The grotesque & abnormal
> forms, to be offered
> to the gods!
>
> But we were talking, - of what.
> Laubiès!   the woman was more interesting
> to me at least
> than the pictures, -   it is
> a state of mind!
>
> But goddamn well not
> to stick there
> 　　　　　　　　　(She looks
> not on me, she
> wants me not
>
> Which is the difficulty.
> My own.
>
> You otherwise. This success
> is foremost in <u>my</u> mind. your
> own.
>
> Tell me what happened to those
> german expressionists,   those characters so bleak
> in their desires
> and so damn dismal.

(break)

What was wrong with them.
Not that gods come & go so simply
but that they do,   damnit –
the black water.

Or Lawrence said so, and I
believe him. I have always
believed him.

What was forgot? Destroyed
finally, by wish.   Or what
was willed to.

They tell me Cezanne used to walk
almost five miles to paint his pictures
of Mt. Saint Victoire.

I haven't seen one of them.   The
selfsame mountain looks, anyhow, at me
right here.

What about that? How to adjust to
the real thing, -   against the other
the greater
manifestation?
Even though unseen.

To ask a man, - help me
with my wife, my children
hate me.
Help me.

What else.

It is an art that enters into
pressures, the escaping steam, etc.
The heart.[27]

Foregrounding the independent texture and dimensions of canvas and paint in language reminiscent of Greenberg, Creeley emphasizes the distortion of the figures by the flat medium into which the artist has translated them. Mere shadow in comparison to living beings, they seem to transport the viewer to a different realm, either divine or inhuman. He is frustrated that a woman in the picture does not engage his look. Unable to assume the common ground of sympathy and desire on which he meets living people, the speaker experiences the picture's rendering of human forms in an alien light. The end of the poem voices nostalgia for the "bleak" but comfortably familiar "characters" and "desires" of the German Expressionists, whose shapes seem to follow familiar emotional forms. Creeley emphasizes the unsettling novelty of abstraction, which captures the "pressures" of emotion as they "escape" from physical form. The narrator's confusion about whom he addresses throughout the poem—artist, painting, another interlocutor, or a "they" of popular opinion—explores the ways in which art intrudes on and restructures the everyday. Its force or "pressure" exerts a palpable influence on environment, capable of alienating the viewer and altering his or her perception of it.

Duncan also finds the painting's autonomy as object a useful model for the poem. He echoes Harold Rosenberg, for whom abstraction represents the shift from outer to inner subject matter that (as also for Greenberg) may alter massified ways of seeing. For Rosenberg, social change begins in the individual. "[B]y pursuing his or her individuality, the modern artist destroyed mass culture and helped to create revolutionary circumstances for all."[28] Rosenberg preserves a view of art as activism inherited from the 1930s but turns it inward to encourage exploration and reform of the self: "Before Marx's internal pioneer opens a frontier without end."[29] In the same way, Duncan transforms Olson's quest for the origins of culture into an internal quest achieved on the edge of mind rather than nature. In a letter to Creeley, Duncan describes Olson as a pioneering "heroic" "backwoodsman" who "explores territory [of 'primitive cultures'] in order to remain at the frontier of the mind." For Duncan, the artist should rather explore "the wilderness of writing itself, there being no actual untamperd [*sic*] wilderness."[30]

Duncan thus shifts imagination from physical nature already colonized by conventional perception to language in itself as frontier. "From a Notebook" conflates Romanticism with art for art's sake to describe the blank page rather than nature as the "absolute and real" "privacy" in which mind realizes spiritual forms. "The persistent idea in these notes that form is Form, a spirit in itself, we owe to the Romantics. To Mallarmé the area of the page is a void of meaning upon which, into which, in which, the poem appears. This is very different from later expressionism with its emphasis on the poem as a psychological event." Although the page represents a private space, the creative spirit is not so much personal as impersonal, "art in search of itself "[31] in the autonomy of its formal medium. This spirit transcends the limitations of the individual to discover the mind's greater potential. In a 1959 letter to Creeley, Duncan writes of the need to transcend "[t]he insidious evil of the world-mind in this age [that] . . . incites us continually to rant." Poetry involves "the search for an indwelling in the poem, an undistracted (hence, formal) thingness of the poem to disappear myself into and thru correspondences and presence."[32] Correspondence and recontextualization become central to Duncan's transformative representation of worldly things. The solidity of the poem as object delineated by the formal medium lends substance to these new forms.

Like Creeley, Duncan embraced the transformative dimension of the canvas or page, but he imagined the transformative process somewhat differently. While Creeley emphasized the artistic medium as material alien to everyday reality, Duncan imagined art as a deliberate appropriation and rearrangement of the materials of the everyday in collage. Duncan's ideas concerning collage developed in conjunction with those of Jess. In the early 1950s, Jess shared Clyfford Still's view that painting must resist "Moloch, the Culture-State," "the collective/denomination of this time," through exercise of the "responsibilities of freedom, intrinsic and absolute" in the free space of the canvas.[33] Jess used canvas and paint to transform found objects by disrupting conventional associations of specific colors with specific themes or objects.[34] His series of "Translations" reproduces other artists' paintings or prints in different colors, radically changing the mood of the original.[35] His "paste-ups," collages made from magazine cuttings that develop "a poetics of materials," also renovate the found materials to create a new life independent of their conventional cultural meanings.[36]

Creeley's conception of poetic language as radically alien to the everyday world and Duncan's as capable of rearranging it foreshadow their different adaptations of painterly abstraction to their poetry. Zukofsky's poetry provides the model by which they translate the abstract painter's use of paint into an equivalent poetic "music" of words. Mark Scroggins and Sandra Kumamoto Stanley distinguish Pound's visual imagism from Zukofsky's musical form (e.g., fugue) and Pound's cosmic from Zukofsky's historical order.[37] The increasingly independent agency Zukofsky attributes to artistic form makes his work a useful model for Creeley and Duncan. Zukofsky's definition of the poem as autonomous object, a "poetic object," "a job, a piece of work"[38] defines art as a product of labor fitting for Depression times, but it also establishes art's unique integrity, the autonomy and solidity Creeley and Duncan seek against mass culture's increasing encroachment on linguistic usage and imaginative autonomy. They adapt Zukofsky's postwar writings, particularly *"A"*-11 and *"A"*-12 and *Bottom: On Shakespeare* (1963) to insulate language from social influences threatening imagination.[39]

Zukofsky's early political poems blend Modernist avant-garde techniques and those of proletarian poetry, but with unstable effects.[40] When he renounced Marxism, however, Zukofsky's distrust of the masses and popular rhetoric led him to abandon belief in the power of the individual artist's usage to transform public discourse and by extension economic relations. When he resumed *"A"* in 1948 after a ten-year hiatus, he opened *"A"*-10 with skepticism about the Catholic mass as a collective ritual of spiritual incarnation. In contrast to the performance of Bach's St. Matthew Passion and its dispersal into history as an agent of form at the beginning of *"A"*-1, *"A"*-10 presents the destructive incarnation of shattered culture and the carnage of "mass death"[41] during World War II. "Mass, massed refugees on the roads / Go to mass with the air / and the shrapnel for a church." "Incarnate / Carcass smiles."[42] The resonance of mass as ritual with mass as formless displaced crowd and of "incarnation" with "carcass" expresses history's destruction of beauty. Sadistic, chaotic fascism, not idealized communism, has become the expression of the people's will.[43] Language as the material of history threatens poetic inspiration, corrupting the poet's vision with destructive meanings.

Zukofsky insulates poetic language from history by turning it into music. Earlier, *"A"*-7 and *"A"*-8 yoked the self to history by restricting the imagination to play on the forms at hand. These poems spin associations from the sawhorses barricading a street in the collective space of a neighborhood. Zukofsky's virtuosic word play explores the social and technological networks of power associated with the horse in mechanized horsepower and the Trojan horse. Whereas imaginative association in these early poems follows economic and political forces driving history, later poems in *"A"* develop the philosophical and literary associations of horses. *"A"*-12 alludes to Plato's horses as figures of desire in the *Timaeus*, as forces the individual

must guide to pursue either sensual or ideal objects, and to Pegasus as figure of poetry's flight beyond the earth.[44] Zukofsky seeks transcendence by
using language like music, freeing words from the referential meaning that
burdens them with history. "Song, my song, raise grief to music, / Light as
my loves' thought."[45] Guided by the formal tension between discord and
harmony rather than by reference to the external world, music can project
the fulfillment of desire analogous to formal resolution of discord into
harmony. *Bottom* expresses faith in intellectual desire as a sense groping
toward an object it cannot grasp. Zukofsky searches for a "[v]oice without
scurf of gray matter, / For the eyes of the mind are proofs."[46] Paul, Louis's
son, provided Zukofsky with a model for new, private construction of
sound-based meaning. Paul's mis-hearing as a child learning to speak (e.g.,
"bloodshy" for "bloodshot") demonstrates the child's initial acquisition of
language as at least partially innocent of consensual and historically received meaning.

Although he longs to recover innocence like the child Paul's, Louis
cannot embrace it wholeheartedly. He presents himself as suspended between idealized past and future, between Paul's innocence and Louis's father Pinchos's connection to a Jewish visionary tradition. Born in America,
far from the Russian Jewish community that inspired his father, Louis
does not believe in the ritual forms that sustained such vision.[47] Nor is innocence a possibility for the adult. However liberating, language errors like
Paul's lose their charm in the mouth of the poorly educated soldier Fred-
die, whose letters Zukofsky quotes. Although Zukofsky is aware that the
poet's mature transformation of materials requires consciousness of their
history, he finally turns to the ordered play of music as the means by
which to establish new meanings. The artisan deforming biological form
to create musical instruments emerges throughout *"A"*-11 and *"A"*-12 as an
image of innocent use of language in art. Like the violin-maker sounding
wood to see whether it will make a good violin,[48] Zukofsky sounds the language for its potential beyond the limits of everyday communication.

Bottom theorizes Zukofsky's transformative procedure in *"A"*-11 and
"A"-12 in a philosophically grounded poetics. Tracing the relation between
sight and knowledge in Shakespeare's works, Zukofsky presents modern
thought as a scarring of sense perception. Thought does not produce conceptual categories that conform perfectly to sense perception but damages
immediate experience in bringing it to consciousness. Although necessary

as an architecture creating home and shelter for human beings, thought severs them from a nourishing nature. Seemingly transparent, the "glass wall of the modern architect" cannot obscure the fact that "all invention headed off by thought in late cultures has this wound."[49]

For Zukofsky, this scheme of knowledge drives a wedge between words and things, producing a "double self" " 'compounded' to return time after time, page after page of the total natural activity of words to judge its thought by the 'simple': *All eyes!*"[50] The discrepancy between sense perception and knowledge, "eye" and "I," divides the subject from the world and produces incompatible modes of knowing. "*Looking* has its own logic, but (it may be inferred from Wittgenstein's *looking* logic) he who *looks* is still the Philosophical *I*, the metaphysical subject, the limit—not a part of the world." "[N]or can the eyes *know*, i.e. conceive of the nature of things."[51] Visual experience, lacking form and thus inaccessible to the intellect, is only ineffable feeling that thought strives continually to grasp in concept. For Zukofsky, love alone mediates between things and thoughts, impelling the mind toward fuller knowledge but simultaneously opening the possibility of deception. Motivated by love, poetry uses vision and music to charge language with feeling and push it beyond established intellectual categories.

Zukofsky's anatomy of sensory and conceptual knowledge structures Creeley's and Duncan's initial explorations of nonreferential language.[52] Their discussion of poetics and their poetry of the late 1950s and early 1960s are steeped in his imagery. In a letter to Creeley, Duncan praises Zukofsky's innocent language, his ability to develop the musical properties of language to create new constellations of meaning. For Creeley, words' music also announces specifically poetic meaning. "Poems . . . are a structure of sounds and rhythms which cohere to inform the reader of their order. In this respect, I much agree with Zukofsky's note of his own poetics, which, as he says, comprise a function having as lower limit speech and upper limit music."[53] Creeley echoes Zukofsky's sounding of wood for violin-making as "sounding in the nature of the language those particulars of time and place."[54] As for Olson, the mind's response to place remains the impetus for poetry, but Creeley follows Zukofsky in interpreting this sounding not as bodily but as linguistic.

For Creeley and Duncan, sight and music enable Coleridgean dissolution of existing form. The independence of poetic language as a medium of the original imagination and a counterforce to colloquial idiom is, however, fragile. Although both poets initially imagined linguistic abstraction as the pure expression of the mind's forms, they became increasingly aware of language as an impersonal force influencing thought.[55] Whereas Creeley's *Words* (1967) and Duncan's *The Opening of the Field* (1960) hold creative personal vision and conventional public language in balance, the formal innovations of the later *Words* poems, Creeley's *Pieces* (1969), and Duncan's serial *Passages* (begun c. 1964) extend abstraction to dissolve personal voice and perception into linguistic structure as an impersonal agent in the poem. While they privileged this increasingly radical experimentation as a greater expression of artistic originality, Duncan and Creeley also came to perceive language as a force beyond the poet's control. What emerges in the free space of the poetic page is the shape and agency of language as institution structuring identity and communication.

2

If *For Love* explores language in its failure to embody natural order, Creeley's *Words* deliberately defamiliarizes language. The psychological focus of the earlier volumes begins to dissolve the tension between language as concrete reference and the strange nonreferentiality of seemingly transparent colloquial idiom. Rather than subordinating objects and words to personal emotion, Creeley experiments with allowing such dimensions of language as concrete reference and colloquial idiom to guide the poem's meaning. The effect is a disruption of conventional affect that begins to dissolve the poetic subject. The poem "Hello" reveals the absurdity of understanding language concretely by rendering the expression "catching one's eye" literal as "ripping" to hold attention "by / what flesh was left."[56] Such reduction of perception to physical terms may reflect the world's violent intrusion on Creeley's fragile self. However, the contrast between the ordinary greeting "Hello" and the melodramatic language of "ripping" and "shuddered" suggests irony and humor stemming from the limited analogy between linguistic and physical being. Artistic representation is stranger still. "The Chance" questions the motivation to create beauty in Frederick Sommer's photograph of an amputated leg on elegant black velvet. The still life's pretension to realism emerges as artificial distancing of its subject.

For whatever, it could
be done, simply
remove it, cut the

offending member. Once
in a photograph by
Frederick Sommer a leg

lay on what was apparently
black velvet cut
from its attachment

to the rest, the foot
showing the incised
wound whereof

the beauty
of all
reasons.[57]

Whereas medicine removes the diseased leg to save life, art reverses this motion, removing the imperfect world to isolate a single beautiful form. Creeley's comparison of the work of art to amputation mocks art's selective vision as a violence that distorts and wounds the continuum of real life.

Departing further from the illusion of reality that physical and psychological reference afford, Creeley attempts to articulate the life of language itself, not as structured by the subject or object but as possessing its own substance. "Waiting" seems to describe the typically Romantic epiphany straining the bounds of language from this perspective.

He pushes behind the words
which, awkward, catch
and turn him to a disturbed
and fumbling man.

What if it all stops.
Then silence
is as silence was
again.

What if the last time
he was moved to touch,

work out in his own mind,
such limits was the last—

and then a quiet, a dull
space of hanging actions, all
depending on some time
has come and gone.

God help him then
if such things can.
That risk
is all there is.[58]

In pushing the limits of language, the speaker renders not a shimmering vision of transcendence but a struggle with language, whose strange, independent character begins to emerge. Personified as independent agents, words become obstacle to rather than medium of vision. The tangible presence of words originates neither in the "silence" of thought nor in the actual experience of the moment. Nor can the god of "God help him," vacillating between literal presence and the cliché, ground language as logos. Although "depending" on the immediate moment and subjective presence in memory, words fit matter and thought only awkwardly. If "depending on" and "hanging from" allude to Williams's "so much depends," Creeley's words negate Williams's counterpoint of grammatical and physical reference. Colorless, unidentified actions, they "hang" in an uninspired empty space, negating the psychological meaning of "de-pendence" and sensual immediacy of Williams's poem. Further, the absence of grammatical connection in "depending on some time / has come and gone" indicates the inability of language to incorporate the past moment in subjective memory. As Heather McHugh writes of Creeley's poetry, "[t]he teeth of language tear as many holes as meaning mends."[59] Although the self may perceive its unity based on memory and anticipation, language cannot articulate that unity. Yet so powerful is language in rendering the self substantial that it forces the poet to "risk" such expression.

Awareness of language as artifice structured differently from both psychological and physical being makes location of the self in language increasingly difficult, rendering self both first-person and third-person constructs. "As soon as / I speak, I / speaks. It / wants to / be free but / impassive lies / in the direction / of its / words."[60] "The Invitation" seeks a basis for the self's coherence: "[T]hey / think in clusters / round the interminable / subject all but / lost to my mind. / Well, here I am , / they say, together. / Or here you are, / them, and it." Initially, parts of speech and syntactical units organize reality. As the poem progresses, however, words shift to physical reference, playfully destroying psychological and grammatical selves to construct a new self grounded in body. "Let's build a house of / human pieces, arms / and hair . . . the feet, face / facts as accumulations" to prove they can do "what flesh / can do."[61] The failure of the body to "house" self accentuates the discrepancy between physical and psychological identity.

As the final stanza drives the wedge further between psychological and physical reference and dissolves self, language replaces self as an independent agent: "home again / we'll say, / we'll fall down streets / rolling, / balls / of clear substance."[62] Creeley's play on a literary tradition of transparent spheres as figures of self, from Emerson's transcendent eyeball to Stevens's jar in Tennessee, accentuates not the transparent immediacy of perception but the autonomy and artificiality of this "clear substance." While the poem begins with words as a "they" who "think in clusters," the word patterns surround but never touch the subject or self. By the end of the poem, this "they" is the only speaking "we." Line breaks throw into relief the categories of thought communicated by different parts of speech, the gerund "rolling," the noun "balls" and the prepositional phrase "of clear substance." While all modify "we," the different texture of each shows words and the linguistic subject to be composites of radically different attributes and relations. Language's seemingly transparent objectification may be piecemeal and far from smooth or coherent.

Like *For Love*, *Words* reaches an impasse where both literal and colloquial valences retain lives of their own and impede the expression of private self in language. Love becomes hard to "locate" "some- / where in / teeth and / eyes. . . . Words / say everything / . . . I heard words / and words full / of holes."[63] The attempt to invest words with personal meaning and desire is increasingly difficult, as language disintegrates into physical reference and cliché. Only Creeley's virtuosic word play can invest the paradoxical presence and absence of language with desire, itself continually threatened with displacement as the language slides into other orbits of reference. *Words* turns from deforming colloquial language to the grammatical structure of language in itself as the most immediate expression of thought's forms. Creeley expresses his new conception of creativity in a letter to Olson.

Likewise I have been thinking of the so-called 'personal', involved with this in a sense—or reading in a book about language, that poets like they say would take syntax and what-not almost to the point of no return, or past, in an attempt to make the singular, etc. Viz, wouldn't this be what happens when you get an attempt to break clichés of association, on the most patently simple level, wherein the "name" has a presence completely dominated by customary contexts, etc.[64]

Words seeks new orders of syntax and naming to escape a rhetoric of personal emotion bound to "customary contexts."

As with Zukofsky's analogy of language to music in *"A,"* music emerges briefly as a self-referential system whose elaboration of theme, rhyme, and pun rearranges given meaning and history into new emotional patterns. Even this analogy is disrupted by words' difference from musical notes, however. Positioned on facing pages in Creeley's *Collected Poems*, "They" and "A Method" compare and contrast the nature of musical and linguistic sounds.

They

I wondered what had
happened to the chords.
There was a music,

they were following
a pattern. It was
an intention perhaps.

No field
but they walk
in it. No place

without them, any
discretion is useless.
They want a time, they

have a time, each
one in his place, an
endless arrival.

A Method

Patterns
of sounds, endless
discretions, whole
pauses of nouns,

clusters. This
and that, that
one, this
and that. Looking,

seeing, some
thing, being
some. A piece

of cake upon,
a face, a fact, that
description like
as if then.[65]

In "They," musical notes lack emotional significance without the context of other notes, acquiring meaning only in the greater "pattern" of chord or "intention" in melody's interplay of harmony and disharmony. Words' careful distinction—the "discretion" of discrete individuality—fails to reflect the fluidity of experience, for words introduce a direction or "endless arrival." Identity is thus both present and absent, articulated by the double meaning of "but" (although or except as) in the third stanza. Music does not exist fully in the single moment of a note or chord, yet it exists only through these moments. Identity is local and positional, emerging only through time, never fully realized in the implicit and changing structure and created anew in time by the responsive listener.

The sound patterns of language described in "A Method" act differently from those of music. Rather than disappearing into a flow toward "endless arrival," they "cluster" around "endless discretions," nouns or objects whose individual identities are either elaborated or modified by each word. Creeley's initial "this" and "that" sequences reflect the fissures or interstices produced in the system of language as it resolves into fixed "facts" in a place, as the face and cake form into a visualizable scene. As the poem moves toward a perception of language as a system more like that of music, however, the final stanza, "that / description like / as if then," undercuts visible scene and coherent phrasing. In the absence of coherent reference, words begin to behave like musical notes, their meaning changing with local context. "Like" and "as if" suggest units elaborating on description and "then" a different mode of discourse based on temporal or logical sequence. However, "description," "like . . . as," and "if . . . then" also represent three different logical patterns. By forcing the reader to group words in ways that do not follow conventional phrasing, the lineation accentuates the varied texture of parts of speech in themselves that emerges in the absence of their subordination to the physical world. Such groupings undercut all semblance of psychological expression. The emotional and metrical cadence of "endless arrival" in "They" indicates linguistic agency as radically at odds with the coherent subject and humanistic expression of affect.

In *Words*, grammar displaces self in determining the structures of thought in isolation from the rest of the world. Words diffuse and resynthesize the sensible world into an order radically different from that of things, whether subjective or objective. In *Pieces*, what begins as abstraction to articulate intimate emotion in language beyond the limits of colloquial convention dissolves into the impersonal structures and contingencies of language as system. Early *Pieces* poems disrupt conventional reference and syntax to reorient reading, away from personal meaning and toward examination of the internal structure of language. "WHERE WE are there must / be something to place us. / Look around. What do you see / that you can recognize."[66] Without concrete clues, "Where we are" is a purely verbal place defined by a shared linguistic consciousness multiple in its possibilities but no longer personal. Meaning is context-determined and thus multivalent or contradictory, generated by the relation between parts of speech and puns. Associations shift in the context of other words through rhyme, lineation, and sequence. The word *pieces* demonstrates such a process of creating meaning. "PIECES OF CAKE crumbling / in the hand trying to hold / them together to give each / of the seated guests a piece."[67] Simultaneously a disorderly fragment, a coherent part, and a deliberately constructed work of art, "piece" embodies a network of conceptual or linguistic meanings. Like the crumbling pieces of cake, Creeley's poems (pieces as works of art), though not complete in themselves, are parts of a system that is never fully present but revealed only as local orders that project possible contours of the system.

Some poems play with the reader's expectations of coherence, the effort to construct a visible scene from the poem, revealing the linguistic self's impulses toward form. "Willow, the house, an egg— / what do they make?"[68] Unable to compose a meaningful scene, the reader might identify this poem's "subject" as the character of nouns when introduced with or without different articles, nonmaterial linguistic categories of general versus specific. The poem "The" ends three of its six lines with "the," throwing into relief the unique character of this part of speech by separating it from the noun to which it is usually subordinate. "Again," and "THE WHICH it" seem to define these title words in the absence of reference, isolating structures of perception and logic into which language sorts experience.[69]

Toward the end of *Pieces*, Creeley abandons the extreme, impersonal abstraction generated by experiments with new word combinations as if to reconceive psychological experience from his new perspective. He no longer models self and language on the structure of things, but rather models things, including self, on the structure of language. Experience now resolves not into people and places but into the textures and changing contours of perception within a temporal continuum structured by the collective architecture of words. In "Numbers," portraits of numbers explore the ways personal experience shapes or distorts the individual's relation to this system. Perception is less passive reception of sensations than patterns accumulated over time. "Counting age as form / I feel the mark of one / who has been born and grown / to a little past return. / . . . Why the echo of / the old music / haunting all?"[70] Present experience has become inseparable from past, "haunted" by resonances of previously lived patterns. The dissolution and reformation of experience and the meaning constructed by the interaction between present experience and memory reveal the extent to which the meaning of individual facts resembles context-bound musical meaning.

If experience is ultimately structured like musical language, the self becomes a local order of moments whose coherence is grounded in a totality inaccessible to the subject. The boundaries and meaning of events and identity thus shift over time. The structure of *Pieces* reproduces this fluid, elusive system. Unlike Creeley's earlier volumes, in which one poem stands alone on each page, *Pieces* is a continuous flow of stanzas grouped or interrupted variously by bullet points, titles, and the capitalization of some first words or lines of stanzas. The reader cannot determine whether the book is a series of poems, some titled and some untitled, or a flow of stanzas within which discrete poems sometimes emerge. Creeley repeats the confusion of piece as part (fragment) and whole (work of art) on all levels, dissolving material world, self, poem, and language into systems whose structures remain implicit, overlapping and discontinuous, one ordering system displacing another. The shift from impersonal abstraction at the beginning of the volume to the more personal reflections at the end blurs the boundary between impersonal language and personal psychology as poles of a single continuum.

Rendering psychological structure indistinguishable from linguistic blurs the boundary between psychological and linguistic agency. While both agents have the potential for creative innovation, the poet as a distinct force using imagination to renovate language is no longer recognizable in the force field of the poem. Rather, the conventional lyric subject emerges sometimes as a force informing language, sometimes as mere affect clinging somewhat randomly to language structures. Creeley's poems track this disruption of self brilliantly to express its fragile dependence on language. While individual meditation may establish idiosyncratic patterns of force that seem to define self, these patterns are also subject to impersonal valences of language whose origin in an external world and a collective psyche remains an unpredictable yet integral element of self. Further, the vacillation of the speaker's relation to audience reveals a changing perception of language as communication. Either guests at a party or audience at a performance, Creeley's readers each receive a different "piece" of a whole that the artist struggles to hold together. The poem's communication is no longer modeled on communication between familiars but on language as an impersonal system that begins to interfere in interpersonal communication, its power as independent institution opening a breach between reader and writer.

3

Duncan's experiments in abstraction follow a course similar to Creeley's, from the personal redefinition of conventional idiom to exploration of the impersonal structures of cultural artifice. As in *Words*, dismemberment signals the violence language does to the body. Duncan undoes this violence through musical use of language. Like Creeley, Duncan seeks to understand the relation of language to the body, while also exploring the role of words in generating new meanings beyond such material reference. Whereas Creeley focuses on the contours of grammar and syntax, however, Duncan focuses on cultural and literary conventions, especially on literary and mythical figures as they personify aspects of the poetic and cultural imagination. *The Opening of the Field* uses linguistic music to transform the heterosexist cultural figures informing perceptions of homosexuality and traditional conceptions of poetic inspiration into figures that protect and inspire homosexual love poetry. While the lovers in *The Opening of the Field* create a private community in which to redefine the language of love, Duncan's 1964 *Roots and Branches* moves away from locating his poetry in this domestic haven to explore the poet's role in a larger production of tradition in which linguistic and literary figures become more powerful agents controlling meaning.

From his early writing, Duncan calls on art to provide constructive alternatives to the alienating, limiting norms for selfhood established by public consensus. His opposition to formal convention is inseparable from his desire to write as a homosexual in a predominantly hostile society and literary tradition. Duncan resists one explanation of the trend toward abstraction based on abstract expressionism in painting, what he sees as a "cult" of abnormality among fellow gay artists. His "The Homosexual in Society" (1944) condemns the view popular among artists and critics that modern abstract art is a homosexual phenomenon, its creativity emerging from a unique, exquisitely tormented sensibility of social alienation. He resisted what Maria Damon terms the "culture ghetto of an alienated superiority cult."[71] For Duncan, these artists attempted to "gain at the price if need be of any sort of prostitution, privilege for themselves, however ephemeral; [they] have been willing rather than to struggle toward self-recognition, to sell their product, to convert their deepest feelings into marketable oddities and sentimentalities."[72]

Duncan's early work is full of the pain of such self-ostracism. It describes sexual desire in the language of Christian morality, as lustful or demonic, a "magnet of a masst [*sic*] impurity." Love's "mirroring quest" is a "gleam of love as new perdition," mixed with rage and pain.[73] Redemption requires violent destruction of the body through Christianity's symbols of transcendence:

> But sun will overcome his beasts; see spring
> upon their racks his tigers, judges; afford a home
> for hawks; and answering self, see Tobit's
> toothless, clawless angel love make music
> not on harp or harpsichord but on
> the naked skin and lusty frame of crucifix. And if
> accept we then the loved deliberate bird,
> the beak and foot of death, the bone thereof
> is life, the brief burnd beast to rise
> upon his blackend wing.[74]

Animal nature and Christ alike are accusing judges against whose moral order the speaker struggles in the Manichean cosmos of Duncan's poetry. In these early poems, Duncan's primary image of spiritual growth is crucifixion, which achieves vision only through painful destruction of the body.

While Duncan cites Zukofsky's innocent eye and assertion that "[t]o see is to re-form all vision" as an important influence, it is primarily Gertrude

Stein's verbal revision through abstraction that enables Duncan to put Zukofsky's injunction into practice. Duncan writes in his Black Mountain College notebook of the value of Stein's "didactic nonsense" to free literature from the traditional burden of moral and metaphysical statement.[75] In a later interview, Duncan credited Stein with making "it possible for me to write about love when it was impossible to write any other way. . . . It was so painful to me, because I could see in every direction rejections of homosexual feelings."[76] Stein's attention to grammatical and sound patterns enabled him to break open conventional associations with symbol and affect, paving the way for a restructuring of self and emotion similar to that achieved by Creeley in *Words*.

Peter Quartermain demonstrates how Stein's sentence-level repetition and increment make the reader aware of the many ways that language constructs meaning and feeling.[77] Her displacement or omission of the conventional signs by which the reader judges or empathizes with characters reveals the extent to which emotional involvement and moral judgment depend on socially recognized cues. Two passages from Stein's *Three Lives*, the first of her works that Duncan read, exemplify this disruption of meaning and evaluation. "The Good Anna" parodies the narrative conventions, character, and diction of the Victorian novel in its protagonist Anna, a virtuous, hardworking servant who adopts stray dogs and attempts to "redeem" them by preventing them from mating.

Back would slink all the wicked-minded dogs at the sound of her hand upon the knob, and then they would sit desolate in their corners like a lot of disappointed children whose stolen sugar has been taken away from them.

Innocent blind old Baby was the only one who preserved the dignity becoming in a dog.

Anna found it hard to always know just why it was that things went wrong. Sometimes her glasses broke and then she knew that she had not done her duty by the church, just the way that she should do.[78]

Whereas Stein goes into great detail about the dogs' moral characters, she discusses the state of her protagonist's soul only briefly. The projection of moral feeling into the animals and the expectation that they remain "chaste" are comically inappropriate, yet where we would expect a moral psychology of Anna, Stein withholds it. Although Anna interprets broken glasses as a sign that she should go to church more often, Stein provides neither the circumstances nor the context to give moral standards and explanations of duty such as "just the way that she should do" meaning. Disruption of expectations concerning emotional and moral response allows the author to subvert conventional patterns of plot and character development.

Duncan's Stein imitations offer playful liberation from potentially oppressive meaning and new attention to the grammatical, phonetic, and colloquial units of language to channel the reader's thought. Such sound experiments as "loco-co moto mo mo / locomomo cotivecomo" and "turning into a man-naked memory / turning into a long avenue" disrupt the subordination of sound and grammatical structure to meaning. Elaboration of the phonetic and syntactical possibilities held in a single word breaks unilinear plot or argument to suggest multiple, branching meanings, placing violence in a new, transformative context: "The violence of a face cut open bleeding. / The violation of a form in a chin receding. / The violin of a figure disfigured for music. . . ."[79] Repetition and sound association shift the focus away from personal suffering to estheticize pain as a variation or formal disruption in nature, marring or creating beauty according to context. As early as these imitations, Duncan recognizes the potential of such abstraction for revising self-image. In *Derivations* he writes, "Poetry made up of sentences of words. Poetry in its regular irregular lines and divisions. Poetry in its steady revisions of the original vision, an accurate eye correcting its accuracies, an image of a man made in his own image inaccurately."[80] Sound play shades into revision of meaning in its gradual alteration of linguistic structures.

The Opening of the Field adapts Stein's technique to thematic revision of sexual convention, generating the transformative musical abstraction characteristic of Duncan's mature work. Duncan's decision to expand "The Homosexual in Society" for republication in 1959 signals his new poetic project.[81] In revising the essay, he notes that the artist's "alienation has not decreased but increased" to a general sense of the poet as a victim of society in the tortured "confessionalism" of Allen Ginsberg, Michael McClure, and Robert Lowell. For Duncan, these poets' internalization of social prejudice and power hierarchies as self-hatred reinforces the destructive belief that "the self is subject to society." His revision of the essay asserts a new purpose, to construct positive gay (and by extension any other marginalized) identity from negative conventional idiom.

Our sense of terms is built up from a constant renewed definition through shared information. . . . I have to push certain words from adverse meanings which as a social creature I share with the public to new meanings which might allow for an enlarged good. . . . I was trying to rid myself of one persona in order to give birth to another, and at the same time to communicate the process and relate it to what I called "society," a public responsibility.[82]

The Opening of the Field, in production at the same time for publication in 1960, records this process of self-transformation. Throughout the book, Duncan uses rhyme and pun, the materials of language, to transform heterosexist stereotypes from public opinion and literary tradition into a poetry and poetics of homosexual love.

   The Opening of the Field begins by invoking a female muse in "Often I am Permitted to Return to a Meadow" and ends with a poetic vision inspired by a male lover in "Food for Fire, Food for Thought." Structured on the ascent from Hell to Paradise in Dante's *Divine Comedy*, the volume moves from a poetry of a gay "Hell" of self-loathing to a recovery of paradise "purged / of whatever we thought we were to be."[83] While transforming Dante's ascent inspired by Beatrice, Duncan also transforms heterosexual figures of poetic and intellectual inspiration: the lady of courtly love as the male poet's muse, Cupid and Psyche, and Eros and Scientia. While feminine figures of inspiration continue to be significant throughout Duncan's oeuvre,[84] *The Opening of the Field* develops a poetics grounded in gay love and household. Like Creeley, Duncan works a Coleridgean diffusion and resynthesis of these topoi to render them habitable by figures of homosexual desire and imagination.

   Duncan's initiation of a new serial genre in *The Structure of Rime*, a series of prose poems articulating the relation of language, cosmology, social structure, and tradition in his new poetics, renders poetry an intervention in culture. Devin Johnston analyzes the influence of Blake and Shelley's mythopoetic writings and Whitehead's philosophy of organism on Duncan's interpretation of field composition at the time of *The Opening of the Field*. Conceiving the field as the full context of cosmic forces acting on the poet, Duncan perceives poetic form as embedded in cosmic structure. Poetry "dramatizes [the poet's] desire to participate in a meaningful universe"[85] and thus represents an occasion for transformation of that universe. As Duncan writes later in "The H. D. Book," "There is no physical reality that is not psychic or spiritual, for the universe appears real to us as the dreams of the body, soul and spirit become one dream; and what is most terrible about the world men have made is that it so embodies the dreams, the soul and spirit, of mean and vain imaginations."[86] *The Structure of Rhyme* constructs a cosmos in which "the Sentence" and "syntax," the laws of grammar, become the scientific and political laws that govern being. Inspired by Nietzsche's *Thus Spake Zarathustra*,[87] the series projects the transformation of inherited images of human nature to include homosexuality as natural, not aberrant. Nietzsche's Zarathustra challenges Enlightenment humanism by imagining humanity as one stage in the evolution of being from animal to Superhuman. Zarathustra looks to other forms of life as models of liberation—to the lion for the will to destroy in order to make room for change; to the snake for transgressive wisdom, especially of the body; and to the child for innocence.[88] Duncan's early *Structure of Rime* poems invoke Nietzsche's images of lion, snake, and child as allegories of revolutionary imagination. As the series progresses, however, "The Master of Rime" emerges as the primary agent of revolution.

Like Zukofsky, Duncan uses "rime" (a rhyme-like correspondence between terms based on any aspect of similarity, not only aural) to forge new connections between linguistic and literary figures. The poem that precedes *The Structure of Rime* I in *The Opening of the Field* presents "angelic Syntax" as a violent but transformative power with which the poet struggles.

> Look!   the Angel that made a man of Jacob
>   made Israel in His embrace
>
> was the Law,   was Syntax.
>
> Him I love is major mover.[89]

Like Jacob wrestling God, Duncan identifies syntax as antagonistic divine law. As for Zukofsky and Creeley, however, love is the source of change. The "embrace" of language personalizes the speaker's struggle into the aggressive and erotic encounter of Jacob wrestling the angel, opening the way to a conception of language as messenger and catalyst of change. The beloved will become a second creator, an alternate "major" mover invoking but pluralizing Aristotle's prime mover. Elsewhere, Duncan expresses the mutual definition of body and cosmos in the conflation of Dante's suicides as mutilated trees with the world tree Yggdrasil and in the allegorical Dr. Sea of "The Propositions," whose identity is as responsive to social opinion as the sea to the tides. Having "consume[d]" many books that reinforce belief in his deformity, Dr. Sea hardly recognizes his sick psyche as his own and dissects it with avid scientific curiosity. Careless of the pain he inflicts on himself, he "cuts the meat but sees / anatomies."[90] Both figures are so alienated from themselves that they damage their bodies in the name of science and law.

Andrew Mossin describes Duncan's "syncretic comprehension of the ways that the cultural markers of sexuality and difference can be usefully mined as sites of ontological transformation."[91] The "Master of Rime" uses the connection between natural and linguistic law to construct a Jacob's ladder to a new order of heavenly influences.

> O Outrider!
>   when you come to the threshold of the stars,
>   to the door beyond which moves celestial terror—
>
>   the kin at the hearth, the continual cauldron that feeds
>   forth the earth, the heart that comes into being through the blood,
>   the householder among his familiar animals, the beloved turning
>   to his beloved in the dark
>
>   create love as the leaves
>   create from the light   life
>   and return to the remote precincts where the courageous move
>   ramifications of the unknown that appear as trials.
>
>   The Master of Rime, time after time, came down the ar-
>   ranged ladders of vision or ascended the smoke and flame towers
>   of the opposite of vision, into or out of the language of daily life,
>   husband to one word, wife to the other, breath that leaps forward
>   upon the edge of dying.
>
>   Thus I said to the source of my happiness, I will return.
>   From the moment of your love eternity expands, and you are
>   mere man.
>
>   water   fire   earth   and air
>   all that simple elements were
>
>   guardians are.[92]

Located in the dark sky, the Master of Rime inhabits the realm of "celestial terror," the "unknown" world opposed to the natural world's familiar "light." If light represents the word of creation, darkness is the chaos beyond the known world defined by ordinary language. The Master of Rime, whose

orders of rhyme transgress conventional logic, inhabits this realm of uncre-
ated potential. Just as the near anagrams of hearth, earth, and heart suggest
the kinship and common home of earthly creatures, Duncan's alliteration of
"love," "leaves," "light," and "life" naturalizes human creation from the unknown through correspondences in the phonetic structure of language. As
the Master of Rime's logic prevails, the poem reverses the light-dark imagery
to render a celestial "ladder of vision" to a world in which sexual identity is
not fixed and lovers can change sex for each "partner."

The "ladder of vision" enables this new word's descent to transform
nature through creation of new verbal meaning. Whereas Stein removes
affective and evaluative language from her narrative, Duncan's allegorical
figures are almost pure affect, often to the exclusion of any physical characteristics. As such, they expose the subjective rather than objective foundation of language, heightening awareness of its malleability. The
incarnation of rime's new order in language destroys the old through
conflagration in the rising "smoke and flame towers," recalling the pillars
of cloud and flame that lead the Israelites through the desert to the
Promised Land in *Exodus*. Phonetic and thematic correspondences make
the basic physical and linguistic elements of the cosmos "guardians" of
the "source of happiness." The lovers' common "language of daily life"
and "mere man" thus become the creative center from which cosmic
order "expands," redefining a new natural order grounded in the lovers'
harmony.

The second section of "The Propositions" escapes Dr. Sea's entrapment and introduces eros as a "prime reality," an alternate gravitational
center capable of reshaping the cosmos. As the lovers' mutual care demands a healthier understanding of love, they establish this new center. In
Robert Duncan in San Francisco, Michael Rumaker argues that the domestic enclosure or "home," both as physical haven from anti-gay policing of
public spaces and as a place to create self in language, is crucial to Duncan's sexual liberation. Eric Keenaghan analyzes Duncan's "vulnerable
households" as spaces that violate Cold War attempts to establish barriers
between public and domestic, masculine and feminine, straight and gay to
create a more inclusive communal identity for the nation.[93] Duncan's
hearth in *The Opening of the Field* serves as the place for redefinition of the
"cosmos" defined by contemporary and literary convention. Love's private
speech community gives language new meaning.

When I summon intellect it is to the melody
    of this longing. Thy hand,
Beloved, restores
    the chords of this longing.
Here, in this thirst that defines Beauty,
    I have found kin.
Nerves tremble upon its reaches.
Sinews of the act have tone under its laws.[94]

Eros shapes a new cosmos, in which intellect serves shared desire and constructive love rather than painful dissection. Reciprocal desire renders the body beautiful, its "toned" sinews generating a new music of the spheres. Constituting a new "law," both scientific and political, the body's desire affirms homosexuality as part of the natural order. Elsewhere, language remains logos defining cosmic order. Born of the lovers' shared idiom, language articulates the law of nature in the body. Because language defines rather than reflects nature in a dialectically evolving cosmos, poetry plays a creative role in this evolution.

The musical overtones of language transform traditionally heterosexual figures of desire and imagination into figures of Duncan's poetic imagination. Like the young Paul Zukofsky of *"A,"* who confuses bloodshot and blood-shy, Duncan remembers his innocence of social value in the childhood mis-imagining of the hymn "Gladly, the cross I'd bear" as " 'Gladly, the cross-eyed bear.' " Punning, or "rime," generates a whimsical but revolutionary poetics of " 'double vision,' " an immediate, private rewriting of human nature grounded in Duncan's body and crossed eyes. "Across the pages of the completed man / tears of inward performance run."[95] The reader's collaborative performance discovers multiple private alternatives to what might seem to be a single authorial message. Not only may the seemingly "completed" meaning of "man" and page be torn open, but language itself generates new readings. While Duncan portrays reenactment initially as tearful sorrow at exclusion or condemnation, a second meaning of tears as semen gives them creative potential.[96] Palimpsestic accretion opens existing meaning to plural possibility.

Duncan's "rime" improvises on convention to achieve the ascent from hell to paradise. In "Nor is the Past Pure," punning literalization of Hades as the "underground," whose heavy physicality and decomposition are characteristic of Dante's Hell, becomes the mulch whose decay fertilizes new seed.[97] The final poem of *The Opening of the Field* restores life to Dante's suicides by interpreting the *Paradiso*'s heavenly rose as a symbol of community established by physical love between men. The broken world tree becomes the "good wood" from which passion "burst[s] forth," "all fiery youth," a projection of cosmic order that originates in the body and its desires. In Duncan's improvisation on tradition, Dante's infernal fire becomes passionate desire leading to heaven.

> This is what I wanted for the last poem,
> a loosening of conventions and return to open form.
>
> >Leonardo saw figures that were stains upon a wall.
> >Let the apparitions contain in the ground
> >   play as they will.
>
> You have carried a branch of tomorrow into the room.
> Its fragrance has awakend me — no,
> >   it was the sound of a fire on the hearth
>
> >leapd up where you bankd it, sparks of delight.
> >   Now I return the thought[98]

As with the page transformed by inward performance, conventions dissolve and reform, animated by the "play" of the imagination. Like Aeneas entering the underworld with the golden bough to awaken his lover from spiritual death, Duncan's lover revives not the world of shades but the intimate hearth, a place of communion that makes Dante's divine paradise real in the household. Duncan's puns fuse the secular love poetry of *La Vita Nuova* with the theological vision of *The Divine Comedy* to realize this epiphany in the body as divine order projected from lovers' sympathy. *La Vita Nuova*'s allegories of love as originating in the individual psyche driven by erotic desire merge with love as a gravitational attraction establishing a benevolent divine order in the creation. Images of male sexuality in the "green flame" and sparks of the lovers' sexual "branches" create a "hearth," a vital domestic space that becomes the center of a cosmos.

> >   . . . Did I stare
> >into the heart of desire burning
> >and see a radiant man? like those
> >fancy cities from fire into fire falling?

> We are close enough to childhood, so easily purged
> of whatever we thought we were to be,
>
>   flamey threads of firstness go out from your touch.[99]

Although embedded in the traditional Christian cosmology that produced the suffering of Duncan's early poems, this image shifts the origin of creation from divinity to the human lovers, who create domestic and cosmic home through the abstract, "riming" potential of language.

Although *The Opening of the Field* ends with a vision of personal fulfillment in domestic harmony, Duncan's experimentation soon shifted to explore a more impersonal potential of rime. Just as Creeley moved from personal deformation of colloquial idiom to exploration of the structure of language in itself in *Words* and *Pieces*, Duncan's writing shifted gradually from creation of personal meaning to discovery of impersonal structures present in the artifacts of culture. Body, hearth, and domestic community become less prominent forces in the evolving cosmos of *Roots and Branches* and *Bending the Bow*. Although Duncan differs from Creeley in linking poetic making to cosmic change, the *Passages* series begun in 1964 parallels Creeley's subordination of individual imagination to an encompassing cultural architecture. In a letter to Henry Rago, editor of *Poetry*, Duncan attributed the title *Passages* to Eliot's description of history's "many cunning passages, contrived corridors."[100] *Passages* explores the maze of culture that lures desire and self-realization among the artificial forces of a linguistic cosmos whose collective identity is created piecemeal and to some extent involuntarily by historical accretion.

Rather than portraying the music of the spheres as originating in the lovers' harmony, early *Passages* poems more often imagine the poet as lacking a panoramic view of connection and instead as tunneling in a solid ground or edifice of culture. Where personal desire no longer informs meaning, rime generates the arbitrary associations of language as a medium in itself. *Passages* 15, "Spelling," plays with sound and etymology much as Creeley does with grammar. Duncan plays out constellations of meaning suggested by Greek and Old English words containing the same letters or sounds to explore the role of alphabet and dictionary in shaping meaning.

> **Xaire**, rejoice **Xaos**, the yawning abyss. **Xarakter**,
>   the mark engraved, the *intaglio* of a man.
>   Xaris, Xaritas   grace, favor.

I want to see the sound of the names: **Kirke,   Kalypso**
(*kalypsis*, a curtain or veil)   **Kybele . . .** [Duncan's ellipsis]

Xalkis —there being **kopper** nearby,   **malaXite**
Xalkeos, of kopper, bronze, brazen   .[101]

The common letter *chi* suggests continuity between the Greek greeting *xaire* or "rejoice," chaos as the abyss of uncertain or inexhaustible emotion, and divine or human gifts of favor (charis/charitas) as structuring principles of the cosmos. These may "engrave" or delineate human nature, itself inscribed in the contours of language. The unaspirated [k] produces different associations with earth goddesses and witchcraft, associations that are visually separate from but aurally linked (in contemporary English though not in ancient Greek) to the *chi* (pronounced [ki] in English) of the previous stanza. Spelling reveals the permeability of any word to a variety of systems and its potential dissolution into patterns of sight or sound. Font and capitalization within sequences and words, whether pedagogical aids to emphasize historical affinity or the poet's manipulation of material, complicate understanding of the agency producing this poetic form. Like the bronze of the last stanza, an alloy of tin and copper, the meanings generated by blending *chi* and *k* may be deliberate, their production perhaps motivated by warfare, as was the production of bronze. That modern language no longer distinguishes between the aspirated and unaspirated [k] (Greek *chi* and English *k*) permits associations not available to the ancient Greeks, pointing to an open-ended evolution of language and its meanings.

In contrast to the lovers' re-creation of meaning in the local domestic community of *The Opening of the Field*, "Spelling" introduces the possibility that the individual may become lost in language. Duncan balances individual and collective agency, truth and falsehood in a more devious sense of linguistic and historical evolution. The explorer's point of view is limited and subject to error. "He did not come to the end of the corridor. / He could not see to the end of the corridor. / What came beyond he did not know."[102] Like Eliot's "cunning passages, false corridors" of history, language can mislead. Indeed, Duncan attributes the confusion of *k* and *chi* in English to Samuel Johnson, who changes Old English "ake" to "ache" because he is "ignorant of the history of the words and so erroneously derive[s] [ake] from the Greek *aXos*."[103] Recognition of such error changes the course of the poem from etymological and semantic correspondences to transpositions and misspellings based on pronunciation ("a naperon," "an ewt"[104]), perpetuating the distortion of meaning and form through misunderstanding. By the time he writes the 1968 preface to *Bending the Bow*, Duncan, "[w]orking in words,"[105] finds himself in a web where he can neither separate truth from falsehood nor control meaning.

4

Although I have not discussed Levertov in depth in this chapter, she too incorporates and transforms colloquial idiom in her poetry, making poetic revision a constructive force in field poetics. While her poems of the 1950s and early 1960s remain more firmly anchored in concrete description and setting than Creeley's and Duncan's, she uses alliteration and other forms of musicality to heighten the beauty of found world and language. The fragile personal control of meaning in Creeley's and Duncan's experiments reflects a change in their perception of language. While their initial experiments followed the late Zukofsky in emphasizing the role of love and private emotion in guiding language play, their experimentation developed toward an increasingly impersonal agency of language as medium in itself. As this medium became a more powerful agent in the force field of the poem, Creeley and Duncan relinquished some of the poet's power to craft the material of language. The role of the poet as individual shaping the meaning of common language dissolves into the agency of arbitrary, unexpected correspondences of language as mere artifact. While both poets continued to rearrange language to discover new constellations of meaning, their perception in the late 1950s of language as the place to secure private meaning gave way in *Pieces* and *Bending the Bow* to a perception of language as institution to whose agency the personal is subordinate.

The early Black Mountain experiments in abstraction are set in domestic contexts, implicitly locating renovation of colloquial idiom in communication between familiars. As with Zukofsky, the intimate sharing of meaning in family relationships represents the kind of speech community for which their poetry models the creation of new meanings. In their increasingly impersonal abstraction, Creeley and Duncan construct the relation between poet, language, and listener or reader differently. These poems abdicate personal negotiation of meaning to generate meaning from language itself. The more open forms of *Pieces* and *Passages* emerge in response to the poets' difficulty in achieving formal closure and control of meaning. As he began to work on *Passages*, Duncan wrote to Creeley that he was interested in a new poem sequence in which elements are "localities of an imagined structure that exists outside the frame of the writing."[106] Creeley responded enthusiastically that Duncan's idea led him (Creeley) to a new view of writing as "instances of poetry," inspiring him to break some of his longer poems into "parts,"[107] the result of which is *Pieces*. The poem is no longer the medium of private communication malleable to its users' meaning but increasingly a partial, local constellation in a larger cultural structure beyond their grasp.

This changing perception of language implies a shift in the conception of the public sphere poetry addresses. Creeley and Duncan's exchange over their emerging new poetics occurred in 1964, at a time when the New American poets and the larger counterculture of which they were a part had grown from a small local community to an increasingly established presence and force in the public sphere. The growth of poetic and political countercultures coincided with heightened awareness of the government's manipulation of language to conceal and then defend the war in Vietnam. While Creeley and Duncan do not state explicitly that they develop their poetics of formal abstraction as a response to a changing perception of the public forum for poetry, their innovations seemed to be closely linked to their changing perception of public language. Creeley's writing remained private and personal in focus, but Duncan and Levertov discussed the construction of public language and authority during the 1960s and wrote poetry that responded more explicitly to the public sphere. Although the writing discussed in this chapter holds personal and impersonal voice in balance, Duncan's and Levertov's increasingly public poetry of the late 1960s discussed in the next chapter registers different pressures on public language, pressures that profoundly destabilize the balance of poetic and public agency in field poetics.

Poetic Authority and Mass Audience
During the Vietnam War
in Duncan and Levertov

The Vietnam War strained the bonds of friendship between the Black Mountain poets and inspired some of their most troubled writing. Since the mid-1950s, they had adapted Olson's "composition by field" as a model of creative interaction between the forces of poetic imagination, language (colloquial and poetic), and things to make the ordinary new. Set in domestic contexts, the poetry of Creeley, Duncan, and Levertov grounds this renovation in communication between intimates and extends a similar familiarity to the reader. As Duncan writes to Creeley from the perspective of 1979, "we are also, you and I, more dedicated, or would be, to the practice of loving, the honor of those we love, the Romance of a Household."[1] While preserving the public vocation of the Modernist poet as giver of forms to his or her community, their poetry conforms to the "private world of the lyric" that Edward Brunner traces as characteristic of 1950s poetry.[2] Like the domestic poetry of Creeley and Duncan discussed in Chapter 3, Levertov's poetry of the same period discovers beauty in ordinary household objects and renders the business of everyday chores an epiphany enabling sacred communion with her family. All three poets generate alternatives to increasingly massified conventional idiom by presenting linguistic meaning as formed in the articulation of an intimate relation between individuals.

As they entered the public debate over the Vietnam War, Levertov and Duncan developed a sense of public communication as different from private that altered their poetics. They had conceived poetic imagination as a relatively autonomous "counterforce" rearranging everyday objects and colloquial language. Life at war blurred the boundaries between public and private, disrupting the integrity of the imagination and changing their conceptions of poetic control and agency.[3] Whereas their poetry of the late 1950s located renovation of colloquial language in domestic settings as communication between familiars, they began in the early 1960s to imagine the relation between reader and writer as more distant and to construct poetic voice in the image of authority in the mass public sphere. Although their different images of the public realm and the dynamics by which authority is created within it led to different theories of political poetry, the strained terms in which both attempted to legitimate the public authority of the poet reveal a widening gap between individual and collective voice.

1

As early as 1960, Duncan and Levertov became conscious of the destructive effects of public discourse on poetry brought eventually to crisis by the war. These early conceptions of mass community and their poetic response to it help to explain the changes in their Vietnam War poetry. Close friends and careful editors of each other's work from their initial correspondence in 1953, Duncan and Levertov grew closer in their shared resistance to what they perceived as a commercialization of poetry destructive to high art. The growing popularity of poetry in the 1950s made it possible for these poets to imagine poetry as a medium of communication to a mass audience. By the early 1960s, not only had the New American Poetry's counterculture begun to enjoy wider circulation through publication by established presses, but a growing trend of poetry readings brought these poets into direct contact with larger audiences. As charismatic figures like Olson and Ginsberg achieved near-guru status for many, Duncan and Levertov altered their poetics to oppose what they perceived as the dangers of a massified poetic persona.

For Duncan and Levertov, the demands of a mass audience were destructive to poetry. Writing for a mass audience narrows a poet's range, and the magnification of self in the media corrupted the poet's integrity.

In early 1960, Levertov complained to Duncan of the "Madison Avenue" "poison"[4] of many poetry magazines. Skeptical of a mass audience's ability to comprehend poetry, she felt that the desire to sell poetry caused writers to imitate genres produced for mass consumption. For her, Ginsberg's popularity reduced his writing to the sensationalism of "a newspaper report of victim's words at some catastrophe."[5] The "hero-worship" Olson won led him to cater to the crowd, distorting his idiosyncrasies and rendering him incapable of self-criticism.[6] Likewise, Duncan believed that popularity had corrupted the creative impetus of both Beat poetry and action painting. For him, Abstract Expressionism illustrated the "danger of securing the chic." Initially original and groundbreaking, Clyfford Still's abstract style now appeared to Duncan mass-produced, codified as an easily recognizable style appropriate to art's role as a status symbol for conspicuous consumption. While he continued to admire Still's work, Duncan condemned much of it as "grandiose, megalomaniac,"[7] an assertion of personality based on mass demand for spectacle rather than self-searching.

Levertov and Duncan attributed some of this corruption to the classifying of writers into "schools." While for Levertov some of the danger lay in producing coterie poetry, she felt that attention to audience expectation might override attention to form. "In all that school—or say, the interlocking schools—New York and Beat—there is a sense of the poets keeping their weather eye on the potential reader—not, as you say, 'living within the medium.' "[8] Although Duncan embraced coterie poetry as experimentation nourished by intimate community, he associated the idea of a publicly renowned school with commercial standardization.

Today, painting has all but become slave to the designs of market where Picassos DeKoonings or The New York School are analogous as conspicuous expenditure to Jaguars, and whatever fancy cars. Style must be like the signature on a check, unique but dependable recognizable=cash value. Now, while in the late forties and early fifties I had direct relation to what is rightly calld [*sic*] "action" painting, it was not then the commodity action painting, but a living movement.[9]

The mass market's demand for easily recognized style governed and corrupted creativity. Duncan's criticism came in the context of his experience of the homogenizing effect of large-scale publication. During the production of *The Opening of the Field* (1960), Duncan's Grove Press editor

Richard Seaver resisted Duncan's proposed cover design handmade by Jess (the design ultimately accepted for the first edition), preferring one closer to "the type of cover design of the *Evergreen* line."[10] Standardizing personal and artistic style to achieve popular fame or the easily consumable conventions of commercial styles replaces original self-creation with the inflated image of personality reflected in popular standards of celebrity. In this early exchange, Levertov and Duncan attribute corrupting power to both mass media and audience. They do not distinguish between mass popularity as a common denominator of taste and the media's power to shape audience reception but focus rather on the artist's image in the public eye and the threat this image poses to creativity.

Duncan and Levertov responded to the perceived massification of art by distancing artistic value and creative agency from audience demand and reception. Despite this distance, their constructions of poetic authority were shaped by images of power in the public sphere. Their decision to imagine a community of literary tradition opposing contemporary society signals their preference for the authority of the group over the individual to legitimate linguistic meaning. The group replaces the individual as the primary agent of linguistic meaning, and modes of collective communication alter the earlier model of communication between familiar individuals. Implicitly acknowledging the power of figures that live in the collective imagination, they ground inspiration in an alternate community of literary tradition rather than in political necessity or individual psyche. Individual agency dissolves in a legitimating poetic tradition whose collective identity and authority confront the power of mass stardom on its own terms.

Duncan's "The H. D. Book" traces a spiritual tradition within poetry that preserves a life of the imagination he believes absent in mass culture. Commissioned in 1960 by H. D.'s literary executor Norman Holmes Pearson in homage to H. D.,[11] "The H. D. Book" describes an ideal literary community of poetic precursors and contemporaries whose shared language counters the limited common meaning established by the mass media. Against the destruction of culture in his own time, Duncan imagines a city of "those who are devoted to Beauty," particularly "the beautiful English language," "an invisible city more real than the [historical] city in which they are," with its "squalid commercialism."[12] For Duncan, this ideal city preserves a richer range of expression than that tolerated by a modern "mass democratic State," which seeks to control popular consensus through mass communication as well as law and education,[13] to substitute "the mass-man" for "the individual."[14]

Duncan's image of poetic community thus both resists and adopts images of authority from mass culture to establish the public authority of poetry. His literary community is modeled on that of H. D.'s occult traditions,[15] whose mystical vision evolves within but apart from history. Invoking the sustaining creative spirit of a "company of the gods," H. D.'s *The Walls do not Fall* (1942) finds secret symbols which remain present for those who can read them in what seems to be the apocalyptic destruction of Western civilization during World War II.[16] For Duncan, H. D.'s collective " 'we' is used throughout [*The Walls do not Fall*] to refer to the community of a mystery within the larger society."[17] Like H. D., he seeks to legitimate poetic usage that departs from socially conditioned models of verse.[18] Poetic form thus originates not in the impulse of immediate environment but in an opposing literary field. However, Duncan's grounding of poetic authority in a collective consensus borrows public symbols of power with which to distinguish his literary heroes. Punning on the hero worship of movie stars, he creates his own "star cult" of fellow poets, both living and dead, as a projected universe of astral influences to elevate the poet to a similar stature.[19] Like the heroes of popular culture, these "star" poets seem to be natural forces shaping individual character.

In shifting his poetic roots from historical to ideal community, Duncan distances creative agency from the personal, locating it instead in the impersonal exigencies of art. Both "The H. D. Book" and the contemporaneous *Roots and Branches* (1964) replace the biological family with an artistic one. Poetry is "re-membering the Mother," "the Mother of those who have destroyed their mothers [and] . . . created their own mothers."[20] Duncan replaces his parents, who pressure him to follow a practical trade, with ideal progenitors of all poetry, "Father of roots and races, / Father of All, / Father who is King of the dream palace, . . . Father who is architect of the eternal city . . ." and "that other Great Mother / or metre, of the matter,"[21] rendering poetry the true measure and substance of reality. Although his "re-membering" implies both passive recall and active creation of his own heritage, this identification with an ideal community increasingly locates agency in a power and authority beyond the individual and the historical family. To Levertov, Duncan writes of the "schizophrenic aspects of the authority the art has over the artist."[22] "The H. D. Book" describes the world of poetry as an "autonomous play" or "melody of events" in which the artist is "cast,"[23] its plot replacing biological and social heritage. The title image of *Roots and Branches* refers to tradition as a world tree with "Authors . . . in eternity."[24] "And now the spring of an urgent life / pushes up from the trunk of the idea of me, / from a whole system of ramifications, / so many mortal entrances. . . ."[25] The individual is incorporated into this greater organism, the self's boundaries lost in the many branchings into other forms. Insufficient to establish meaning alone, the self becomes part of a larger communal being which shapes or confirms its vision.

Levertov's poetics undergo a similar transformation in the early 1960s, her dialogue with Duncan affirming and influencing changes in her work. She shares Duncan's admiration for H. D. and responds enthusiastically to his location of poetic authority in a living community of tradition. While maintaining a firm belief that poetry is grounded in the personal, Levertov admits increasingly the influence of forces beyond deliberate craft in poetic composition. She praises Duncan's formulation of H. D.'s gift as transcendence of the personal in "The H. D. Book," with its description of the poetry as "no longer *her* art but *The* Art."[26] Admiring H. D.'s power to evoke myth in the everyday world, "[t]he interpenetration of past and present, of mundane reality and intangible reality,"[27] Levertov distinguishes between historical and literary fields and affirms literary tradition as the ground of a spirit world beyond the mundane.

In the early 1960s, Levertov also distanced herself from colloquial language as the basis of poetic authenticity. Feeling the need to formulate her own poetics, she questions William Carlos Williams's "American Idiom" and Pound's injunction that "the natural object is always the adequate symbol," principles she had followed in training herself to become an "American" poet in the 1950s. In response to a negative comment from William Carlos Williams concerning her poem "The Jacob's Ladder," she writes that, while his "American Idiom" has been necessary to free some young poets from unsuitable literary language, she will not "put the idea of American Idiom *first*. For you it has always been a focus, almost a mission."[28] In 1964, she writes Duncan of her rediscovery of literary language in her personification of "Grief" in "A Lamentation" and of her return to the Romantic diction of her nineteenth-century British roots.[29] As with Duncan, literary tradition legitimates the development of her poetry and poetics.

Like Duncan, Levertov comes to imagine her poetic craft as part of a communal pursuit rather than as private or individual creation. "A Common Ground" articulates her new preference for literary over colloquial language. The poem distinguishes between different kinds of language, contrasting everyday speech, "gritty with pebbles," to literary "shining pebbles, / that soil where uncommon men / have labored in their virtue / and left a store / of seeds for planting!" Although the poem presents both kinds of language as seeds and later as grain capable of nourishing, it privileges poetic speech, "[n]ot 'common speech' / a dead level / but the uncommon speech of paradise."[30] Literary language invokes a reality more perfect than that of everyday speech. It is "necessary *for [artists] to keep in constant touch with masterpieces, so that the creative spirit may be maintained at its height* & prevented from backsliding."[31] Levertov's poetry of the 1960s uses the language of literature and tradition to frame epiphanic experience of the everyday, shifting inspiration from concrete objects to a community of kindred spirits. In contrast to her earlier use of alliteration to echo in words the harmony she perceives in spare concrete images,[32] "A Common Ground" articulates a more independent role of poetry in generating new images. The epigraph by Pasternak renders a voice from tradition rather than the concrete object the occasion of her image.

Allusion provides the basis for a widening visionary scope in Levertov's poems during the 1960s. By including various mythological figures such as Ishtar, elves, and angels as active presences in *The Jacob's Ladder* (1961) and *O Taste and See* (1964) and composing allegories of creative forces such as "the Spirit of Poetry," Levertov roots the imagination in a spirit world whose presence is maintained by poetic tradition. Beginning from an epigraph by Spinoza (as quoted by Pound) defining intellectual love, "A Vision" represents poetry as an elaboration of spiritual concepts transmitted through tradition. Levertov's vision of two angels provides concrete images of Spinoza's concept. In addition to more frequent literary epigraphs and personifications of spirit life, Levertov uses images and symbols from religious ritual to signal epiphany in the concrete. By structuring morning household routines around prayer, "Matins" fits daily activities into traditional ritual patterns for preparation to receive blessing. "The

Rainwalkers" transforms a rainy city street into a place of holiness by imagining it as a cathedral where "the avenue's / endless nave echoes notes of / liturgical red."[33] These symbols not only evoke the holy in the everyday but also reveal inherited structures of perception that inspire such epiphany. Levertov thus roots her imagination in a spirit world nourished by tradition.

Duncan and Levertov retain their belief in poetry as a more powerful mode of communication than the mass media through the mid-1960s. In the early stages of the Vietnam War, their poetry seems to stem from the belief that vivid poetic representation of war's brutality and injustice is sufficient to mobilize readers against the patriotic rhetoric and impersonal statistics of media reports. Levertov's early war poems such as "What Were They Like?" humanize the enemy by imagining Vietnamese culture and lamenting its destruction. "Life at War" challenges the language of military efficiency and prowess by contrasting the horror of planned killing with human beings' ability to enjoy and create beauty.[34] Levertov writes to Duncan of her effort in poetry "to grasp with the imagination what does happen in war—so that even if one hasn't been there, in the flesh, one doesn't let the horror of war just be an *empty* word—all our words have to be filled with, backed up by, imaginative experience."[35] Duncan concurs, praising the poignant humanity of the Vietnamese that Levertov evokes in "What Were They Like?" and expressing the similar purpose of his war poetry. "We labor to make the War *real*, to make it really happen so that it will speak to us."[36] Both poets affirm poetry's expressive, human voice as stronger than that of government rhetoric.

Increasing concern about the Vietnam War impels both poets to articulate the relation between literary and political communities more precisely. Although they begin to write poetry about the war with a common goal of making the war real to their readers, their conceptions of how to communicate this reality soon diverge. As the political demands of writing about the war challenge simple distinctions between poetic and political language, Duncan and Levertov develop new poetic forms to enable greater interplay between personal and public history not easily achieved in short lyric. Duncan's serial *Passages* imply sporadic interventions in history, imagined either as architectural connections in the edifice or birth canals in the organism of contemporary culture. Levertov subordinates poetic plot to history in her diary/documentary "Staying Alive." The debate in letters between Duncan and Levertov in which they attempt to justify their diverging poetics reveals the different character and relative authority each attributes to poetic and political voice.[37]

Duncan's *Bending the Bow* (1968) explores the relation between violence and creativity in literary tradition in order to create a mythical genealogy of the Vietnam conflict that would, in his words, "escape" its destructive anger.[38] Unable to sustain his belief in the transformative power of individual vision, Duncan gradually dissolves poetic voice into voices of public factions as monstrous agents driving history. For Levertov, in contrast, group voice is more powerful than individual, because it represents a community's democratic consensus. Levertov's *To Stay Alive* (1971) seeks to clarify the aims and ideals of war protesters in order to strengthen the presence of their opinions in the public realm. Like Duncan, however, she cannot sustain the authority of individual voice against public authority. The problems both Duncan and Levertov encounter in writing protest poetry reveal an increasing difficulty in resolving the tension between individual and collective voice as formed in the public arena of mass culture.

2

As the war intrudes on his imagination, Duncan shifts the ground of poetic creativity from an ideal literary community to history. The preface to *Bending the Bow* describes the displacement of private self into a national psyche through vicarious participation in the war as represented in the media.

We cannot rid ourselves of the form to which we now belong. And in this drama of our own desperation we are drawn into a foreign desperation. For our defense has invaded an area of our selves that troubled us. Cities laid waste, villages destroyd, men, women and children hunted down in their fields, forests poisond, herds of elephants screaming under our fire—it is all so distant from us we hear only what we imagine, making up what we surely are doing. When in moments of vision I see back of the photographt details and the daily body counts actual bodies in agony and hear—what I hear now is the desolate bellowing of some ox in a ditch—madness starts up in me. The pulse of this sentence beats before and beyond all proper bounds and we no longer inhabit what we thought properly our own.[39]

Historical form replaces artistic as the violent syntax of war overpowers the "proper bounds" of the ideally ordered world the poet would create. Punning on "proper" as both "decorous" and French for "one's own," Duncan renounces the poet's power for self-creation through art. The immediacy of news reporting awakens a fantasy internal to its culture rather than inspiring responsibility for a world outside the conscious self. At the same time, the mass media invade the home, forcing the private individual to recognize his or her participation in national identity. Duncan's "madness," insane rage at the war, attests to the power of the nation's deeds and its authority to shape individual thought. To escape this rage, the first thirty *Passages* poems, published in *Bending the Bow*, explore the role of violence in construction of identity and seek to transform heroic self-creation to eliminate its dependence on destruction of another.

The early *Passages* abandon the ideal "City" of artists defined in "The H. D. Book" to make the historical city or tribe the ground from which poetry springs. "Tribal Memories, *Passages* 1," describes this "City" as "scatterd thruout the countries and times of man." Poetry originates in memory, Mnemosyne, the mother of the Muses. Dozing at his work and entering a dream, the poet becomes the child born from the egg of memory. "I am beside myself with this / thought of the One in the World-Egg, / enclosed, in a shell of murmurings, / rimed round, / sound-chamberd child."[40] Leaving private self to be reborn from the world egg, the poet makes "rimes" that issue from its internal resonances. While the oneness of the world egg suggests an organic unity of all things, Duncan politicizes this interconnection to derive cosmic form from the relation between subject and object in history rather than in ideal rhymes that the poet can create. As Duncan engages the theme of war, he shifts from lyric to epic voice, public voice overpowering private to undercut his "escapist" poetics.

In "At the Loom, *Passages* 2," the war intrudes into the private, domestic world as the distant point on which the pet cat's eyes focus.

> The secret!   the secret!   It's hid
>   in its showing forth.
> The white cat kneads his paws
>   and sheathes his eyes in ecstasy against the light,
>   the light bounding from his fur as from a shield
>   held high in the midst of a battle.

What does the Worm work in His cocoon?

> There was such a want in the old ways
>   when craft came into our elements,
>   the art shall never be free of that forge,
>   that loom, that lyre—[41]

Like Homeric simile, Duncan's links domestic peace and public war as part of one culture, implicating his private domesticity in the larger conflict of the war. By introducing war from a domestic perspective and through the artifice of simile, Duncan preserves the capacity for distance and thus the potential for creative re-vision. Although entering the poem only in the comparison, the light displaces the ec-static cat and conceals its body behind flashing reflection. Interpreting his association as the immature larva in the cocoon, Duncan traces the intuitive association to a correspondence between the violent origin of poetry in Hermes' forge, Penelope's loom, and the lyre. The contrary motions of hammering, weaving, and plucking illustrate the poetic principle articulated in the "Preface" of "*how being at variance agrees with itself*."[42] The poem goes on to explore the etymologies of warp and shuttle that link violence and creation. Warp refers both to fertility ("*a laying of eggs*") and to the act of throwing. Shuttle refers to a ship, the bolt of a door and a "'*harpoon*'—a dart, an arrow."[43] These constellations of meaning link nest and home to the ships and weapons of Homeric warfare. By abandoning his impulse to forge order, Duncan allows the unresolved historical constellations of meaning to guide the poem and to expose the cultural fabric from which his associations spring.

From these constellations of meaning, Duncan recovers a vision of battle that interprets the "secret" of the cat's shining fur which, by the end of the poem, replaces the domestic scene, shifting focus to a public narrative of national identity that distorts the mutual reflection of heroes into that of patriotic hero and enemy-victim.

> withstanding,   each side
>
> facing its foe for the sake of
>   the alliance,
> allegiance, the legion, that the
>   vow that makes a nation
> one body not be broken.

Yet it is all, we know, a mêlée,
  a medley of mistaken themes
 grown dreadful and surmounting dread,

so that Achilles may have his wrath
   and throw down
  the heroic Hektor who raised
that reflection of the heroic

    in his shield. . . . [Duncan's ellipsis][44]

Like Homer, Duncan prevents easy nationalistic justification of war by humanizing both sides. However, by presenting the conflict first as that of generic "man" and "foe" bound by allegiance to a nation rather than that of individual heroes, Duncan separates actual battle from the images of national glory motivating war. The historical legacy of "mêlée" or mixing allows Duncan to recover the wrathful human against human violence concealed by the brilliance of heroic rhetoric. This divided reality explains the association of cat and war. Both cat and light are strangely displaced, known only indirectly through their shining. Just as the light is invisible except as the cat's fur reflects it, the cat's vision is ecstatic, "sheathed" or absent and thus protected from the light. The private individual disappears in the public sphere's hall of mirrors. In identifying with the national hero, private citizens bond in "the legion that the / vow that makes a nation / one body not be broken."[45]

  Duncan's literary understanding of war as a violent struggle between victim and aggressor challenges the government's one-sided image of a war for national glory. He seems to expose the violence inherent in current historical and poetic conceptions of democratic identity, both national and personal, so that human beings may learn to transcend them. Fighting in order that " 'free men everywhere' " " 'have the right / to shape their own destiny / in free elections' " supports American " 'free enterprise.' " American advertisements for " 'goods' " conflate ethical and economic value to perfume and deodorize the carnage of napalm-burned bodies in Vietnam, the victims of the American weapons industry. The terms of the television market represent not the true "odor of Man" but a falsely elegant "mannequin," "the Good Word and Work subverted by the Advertiser, / He-Who-Would-Avert-Our-Eyes-From-The-Truth."[46]

  The mass audience's hunger for political action is mediated by "the daily news," the power born of the seemingly greater reality of those in the political spotlight. "[E]nthralld by fear," private individuals are "caught in the *lascivia animi* of this vain sound."[47] "Vain" desire (both empty and proud) destroys television viewers, who are annihilated before media images. "Coercion, this is Ahriman. / In the endless Dark the T. V. screen , / the lying speech and pictures."[48] The inflated image of President Johnson, one of "the great simulacra of men," absorbs individual viewers into a national being, the president as "the swollen head of the nation" directing the rest of the body politic.[49] While images of light and reflection throughout *Bending the Bow* develop the displacements and projections of identity created by such mass identification with public figures, Duncan's counterpoint of carnage and physical mutilation registers the accompanying destruction of the private individual. As President Johnson, the "swollen head of the nation,"[50] replaces the democratic body politic of autonomous individuals with a hierarchical medieval one, private citizens disappear into "the endless Dark" surrounding the television screen, gaining substance only through consumption of its "goods," both economic and political.[51]

By providing a literary interpretation of history that challenges the current political terms of the conflict, Duncan invokes imaginative freedom as a tool to end war's violence. While incorporating violence into poetic making, he seeks to escape a legacy of historical violence that for him grounds American democracy and poetry. Discovering violence to be inherent in political and poetic tradition, he seeks to render violence productive. "Working in words I am an escapist; as if I could step out of my clothes and move naked as the wind in a world of words. But I want every part of the actual world involved in my escape. I bring the laws that bound me into an aerial structure in which they are unbound as outlines of a prison unfolding."[52]

"Escape" from violence through a reconstellation of current factions as well as Duncan's language of "form" as aerial structure and unbinding recall Shelley's *Prometheus Unbound*.[53] *Prometheus Unbound* (1820) represents the monstrous political factions of oppressor and oppressed as phantasms which, once recognized as such, may be reimagined to create a world in which self and other are in harmony rather than conflict. The drama of *Prometheus Unbound* evolves from a human condition determined by the myth of Jupiter's tyranny over Prometheus through a succession of intermediate mythic generations to an ethereal cosmos structured by harmony between humans and nature. Air is the element of reconstruction within which Shelley imagines the ideal. Such reimagination of conflict is possible for Shelley because he believes that the mind, although impressed and influenced by the objects of its environment, defines the relation between these objects in a single form.

> Every man's mind is, in this respect, modified by all the objects of nature and art; by every word and every suggestion which he ever admitted to act upon his consciousness; it is the mirror upon which all forms are reflected, and in which they compose one form. Poets, not otherwise than philosophers, painters, sculptors, and musicians, are, in one sense, the creators, and, in another, the creations, of their age. From this subjection the loftiest do not escape.[54]

While shaped by external objects, the mind shapes a cosmos that establishes the relation between them, expressing thereby the order or "form" of its age. Duncan's "Introduction" to *Bending the Bow* echoes Shelley's language in its emphasis on form as a moment in history of which the poet is a part. Although Shelley declines the possibility of escape, Duncan initially embraces it.[55] Having received the existing relation between "objects" of environment established by the age, the poet seeks to change them by creating new unities.

Bending the Bow searches literary tradition for examples of creative violence to enlarge contemporary discussion of the war and to render the great literary theme of war a positive element in soul making. In *Structure of Rime* XXIV, "the hideous city about us" contains "transitory hints of the eternal" and reinforces the power of the imagination for "rending the silence because what illusions? faeries? have awakend in the Real new impossibilities of harmonic conclusions? And we have made a station of the way to the hidden city in the rooms where we are."[56] Like musical discord, the poem may shift the ground of history from destructive conflict to progress toward a harmonious city now "hidden." Duncan also invokes mythological patterns of violence and resolution to render historical violence potentially productive. Several poems on the grail—"Shadows, *Passages* 11," "Sant Graal," and "Parsifal"—trace a traditional connection between wound or disease and the transcendence born of the spiritual knowledge that the chalice represents. "As in the Old Days, *Passages* 8" emphasizes the body's tearing and pain in giving birth. Later *Passages* explore the violence in Greek mythology as a conflict between parent and child working itself out through successive generations, as in *Prometheus Unbound*. Such recontextualizations remove the conflict from the mutually destructive factional conflict between nationalisms and exercise the mind to imagine positive solutions.

Although *Bending the Bow* seems initially to balance creative with deterministic production of poetic form, Duncan cannot sustain confidence in the individual's imagination to find ways of escape. Art's creative intervention in history becomes more tenuous as the book develops. "The Fire, *Passages* 13" suspends the relation between history, poetic dissolution, and the re-creation of form. The poem describes the power of Piero di Cosimo's painting of animals in a forest fire to create a new paradise "as if in Eden, in this panic / lion and lamb lie down."[57] Duncan traces a magic of poetry inherited from Orpheus as "chords and melodies of the spell that binds / the many in conflict in contrasts of one mind." Such music is lost "c. 1500" with Bosch's "opposing music" of conflict, however. Shifting abruptly to the present, the poem identifies the source of this loss in history as divisive nationalism. Although Duncan dates the beginnings of nationalism at 1500, he consistently links its destructive power to the representation of national authority in the media. The inflated images of national leaders absorb private individuals into their causes.[58] Both leaders and citizens are, as Duncan quotes Whitman, "aware of nothing further than the drip and spoil of politics—ignorant of principles. . . . [Duncan's ellipsis]." Politics, with its focus on the life of the nation, consumes the individual with its lust for power, the historical trajectory of the poem devouring the speaker's voice as well: "My name is Legion   and in every nation   I multiply / Over those who would be Great   Nations Great Evils."[59] This voice no longer opposes history but identifies with it.

As if to counter this trend, Duncan places grids of words unlinked by syntax or historical scene at the beginning and end of the poem. Containing words antithetical to the chaotic fire (e.g., cool, green, fish, leaf, purl), the grids appear to contain and dissolve destructive historical order into a syntactical chaos with liberating potential. In the context of the grid, "coin" and "bronze" suggest circles of light and the color of a stream rather than economic currency and warfare. The relation between the grids and the rest of the poem opens rich interpretive possibilities. Maria Damon reads this matrix as an isolation of words from their ordinary contexts to begin the process of redefining their meaning.[60] Mark Johnson traces the image of the matrix to the etymological "womb" and relates it to the generative power of language as the grand mother of images in *Passages* 22. Since the matrix in physics describes the characteristics of an object not as a field of matter composed of interchangeable atoms harnessed into patterns that can change, Johnson links the generative power of words to their liberation in field composition.[61] These interpretations describe well the liberating potential of field composition when it focuses on language in itself. However, what interests me here is the poem's separation of this linguistic field from the historical narrative, a separation that questions the relation of poetic composition to history. Lacking a direct syntactical link to the rest of the poem, these grids may either contain the fire or represent a static poetic world unable to intervene in history. While the grids force the reader to contemplate the relation between poetic and historical language, the disjunction suggests the failure of imaginative rearrangement to engage history.

As *Bending the Bow* progresses, Duncan renounces his earlier transforming poetic voice and assumes the role of epic poet who merges his voice with figures of public history. In "Orders, *Passages* 24," Duncan denies the power of the poet as "master / of enchanting words and magics" to "tell the beads, in the fearsome / street I see glimpses of."[62] Duncan does not stop shaping his poems; they are still crafted. However, he abandons personal voice to embody what he sees as the public forces generating the war. The creation of a mythological genealogy for political conflict like that of Shelley's *Prometheus Unbound* yields no resolution, only an unending cycle of violence.

"Stage Directions, *Passages* 30" exemplifies this violent reconfiguring of history. Although it is a story of hero and victim like that of Achilles and Hector in "At the Loom," "Stage Directions" denies the poet's interpretive freedom. It traces the mythological connection between poetry and violence in the simultaneous birth of Chrysaor, a mythological warrior, and Pegasus, emblem of poetry, from Medusa's decapitated body. Her beheading generates mythic creations as the main actors in history. Duncan's body imagery undercuts television's bloodless disembodied triangulation of identity, accentuating the construction of this new body politic from the dismemberment of private individual and local community.

He brings the camera in upon the gaping neck
    which now is an eye of bloody meat   glaring
    from the womb of whose pupil sight

springs to see,   two   children of adversity.

The Mother's baleful glance in romance's
                         head of writhing snakes haird

      freezes the ground.

                  Okeanos   roars,

wild oceanic father,   visage   compounded of fury and of wind

    (the whole poem becoming a storm   in which faces arise)

        Mouths yawn immensely   and hours,
                  as if they were mad brothers,
stare.
           From the body of the poem, all that words create

presses forth to be: [Chrysaor and Pegasus][63]

Against Classical heroic tradition, in which Perseus's shield protects him from Medusa's gaze and enables him to kill her, the poem focuses on Medusa. Duncan emphasizes the hero's creation from the victim, in context an unidentified decapitated body and possibly a war victim. Only under Perseus's sword does Medusa's gaze become threatening, that of the mortal individual challenging heroic violence. Replacing the head, site of reason and autonomy, the uncanny wound's "eye of bloody meat" is horrifically animate and inanimate. A new center of vision and agency radically unlike that of the embodied person, the wound becomes an eye only under the objectifying gaze of the camera, whose lack of compassion denies empathetic reciprocity. By destroying the individual's autonomous gaze, Perseus as mythic hero renders the wound a womb bearing a tautologically impersonal "sight" whose "seeing" produces a new family of monstrous agents: the "wild" Okeanos, the "mad brothers" of time, and ultimately Pegasus and Chrysaor, mythic animal and warrior linked for Duncan as figures of poetry. Just as the body representative of individual integrity fragments into discordant parts (eye, womb, pupil, head, face, mouth) each acquiring a life of its own, so the embodied person's vision is replaced by confusedly impersonal, disembodied viewers (camera and unidentified cameraman, wound, Medusa's severed head, staring mouths). Focus on the horrific wound and voraciously "yawning" mouths replaces the compassionate, familiar human gaze with dizzying abyss and appetite out of control.

Perseus emerges only at the end of the poem, "hounded" by his denial of the murder and bound in an unending tradition of violence and revenge. The drama unfolds in a series of violent mythological generations culminating in Geryon and Bellerophon, poets' guides leading respectively to infernal and divine inspiration and thus calling the value of this vision into doubt. Not only does Duncan extend this cycle of violence into recent history, but the poet's careful tracking of association in "At the Loom" gives way to the camera as agent, forcing the poet's eye to watch a drama beyond his control. Rhyme (sea and adversity, glance and romance) reinforces the viewer's harmonizing complicity while assonance of "o" and "ou" sounds draws individuals, time, and art into the gaping abyss of the maelstrom. If Duncan has in mind Zukofsky's Pegasus, a figure of poetry's flight beyond the earth,[64] he seems now to challenge poetry's power to transcend historical meaning, for the war hero Chrysaor and Pegasus are twins born of words inseparable from a body that is the victim of traumatic violence. The spectator stands by helpless as superhuman mythical figures, heirs of heroic violence, perpetuate themselves, taking center stage in human history and paralyzing the individual imagination.

This confusion resolves into the lineage of mythical creatures from Perseus and Medusa to Pegasus and Chrysaor, allying poetry and war. By the end of the poem, the poet's "dying body" merges with "the dying body of America."[65] Medusa's body preserves, however, the destruction of private integrity and the resultant inchoate welter of agency and affect exposed in the absence of conventional political agents. Although this chaos coalesces into the deceptively coherent national drama on an artificial "stage" whose action is focused by the camera's public eye, the passage's twisted syntax denaturalizes these mythic agents, revealing their roots in the violent destruction of the private body and resulting undefined loci of energy that propel history. Like the body of America, the "body" of language is not an organic unity but rather a "storm" of dismembered parts— heads, faces, mouths—freighted with the divisive violence of the public realm. Such language cannot create a coherent self. It has become an unstable being whose members acquire agency the poet cannot control.

Sublime

Forbidden intensities convert the personal,
      and from what *I* am
Masks of an old pageant, from my world and time
Portentous rimes, foreshadowings history become a plot demands.[66]

Duncan renders his own identity inseparable from the roles cast in history, placing the individual as the victim of a national drama.[67] Whereas Duncan emphasized the humanity of average soldiers in "At the Loom," the actors in "Stage Directions" are monstrous figures produced by heroism. The poet can no longer imagine alternatives but only speak through the masks of the greater factions that drive history.

    Duncan's abdication of individual control to monstrous agents is one of the most troubling aspects of his Vietnam poetry. It seems to justify, at times even revel in, war as an inevitable evolution rather than criticizing it because of human choice and responsibility. In the absence of imaginative alternatives, the historical rimes of cosmic unity generate brutality. The burning bodies of Albigensian and Caodaïste martyrs become elements of an evolving world order indifferent to human suffering. "[T]he name of the Roman Catholic Church with its heapt honors / stinks with the smell of their meat burning / enter as notes of a sublime sweetness, / the re-sounding chords of wrath and woe. Grandeur!"[68] Incapable of transcending history, the poet seems either to translate it into perverse artistic form or to wield abstract form with a violence equal to that of the persecutors.

    Nathaniel Mackey has characterized Duncan's war poems as born of a tension between "cosmologizing" and "humanist" stances, brutal theodicy and painful victimization.[69] Marjorie Perloff focuses on his poetics and treatment of the great theme of war independent of a specific political agenda.[70] These perspectives are certainly more fruitful for analysis of Duncan's Vietnam poetry than the search for an exhortation to a particular political action or opinion. The stances that Mackey identifies become more pronounced in Duncan's work as the war progresses, and he seems to embrace epic voice with increasing rage and irony. The multiple voices and playfully diverse poetic structures and themes at the beginning of *Bending the Bow* polarize into poems written from the perspective of either tyrant or victim. By tracing the evolution of this position, I would emphasize that Duncan's detachment from political advocacy emerges from the belief that neither private individuals nor poetry can be a force in public debate driven by radical new agents driving history. His poetry mirrors the process by which individual voice is subjected to the cultural cosmos created by representations of the war and its political controversy in the mass media, representations in which a radical discrepancy between public and private agency renders the individual the victim of the collective institution.

Duncan's theorizing in the late 1960s reflects his growing perception of language as instrument of power, a means to create and control political subjects rather than express self or domestic community. In his essay "Man's Fulfillment in Order or Strife" (1969), Duncan develops the effects of public language that exceed words' literal meaning. He presents the poet as both master and victim of language, the creative psyche formed by public structures of authority in the contemporary milieu. First, he compares the poet to the dictator able to mesmerize and control the crowd, recalling Hitler's presence in Leni Riefenstahl's *Triumph of the Will*. Duncan compares Hitler's power to his own childhood fascination at telling horror stories to work friends into hysteria with his "spellbinding" language.[71] For Duncan, the leader gains such power as a collective symbol with which individuals identify and in which they find security in times of cultural crisis. He suggests that images of powerful figures presented by the mass media exacerbate, if not induce, the individual's tendency to relinquish choice to the powerful public figure.

Identification with public power is one pole of a perpetually divided identity created by the mass media as described in "Man's Fulfillment." The other is the poet as the victim of figures of state power in the public arena. Writing of a new sense of himself as a prisoner of language that emerges while he composes *Bending the Bow*, Duncan compares language to a drug that carries him beyond himself by subjecting him to its "laws," "orders," and "prison,"[72] images that invade or restrict the integrity and freedom of the private body. If language transports, it has also become increasingly oppressive. Identification with its orders means grounding self in the same power imbalance that grounds the public identities of tyrant and crowd, while refusal of identification means silence.

Factional rage, which renders language weapon rather than message, ultimately erodes the integrity of poetic language and linguistic meaning. Duncan's "Santa Cruz Propositions" (c. 1968) open with despair at poetry's inability to transcend public faction. "Poetry! Would *Poetry* have sustain us? It's lovely / —and no more than a wave— to have rise / out of the debris, the stink and threat / —even to life— of daily speech."[73] The poem's second section, a collage of passages from a newspaper article and Plato's *Symposium*, embodies this corruption of poetry by reducing poetic voice to voices of public faction. The newspaper article describes the shooting of the wealthy Ohta family as part of a war on materialism by one Frazer, member of a countercultural utopian community that seeks "freedom" through "natural life."[74] Words have no power to inculcate their ideals. Rather, translation of idealistic words into material reality has an effect far different from the ideals words would articulate. The cause of this perversion may be the public arena, which distorts communication, for the newspaper focuses not on Frazer's meaning but on his unkempt appearance and marginal economic situation. Once Frazer's message is misrepresented and the dialogue that might lead to change of ideals denied, slogans like "materialism must die"[75] achieve a destructive literality in murder, subverting or multiplying meaning in disturbing ways.

The resonance between Frazer's story and Plato's *Symposium* reveals history's power to unsettle the figurative meaning of language and the ideals such figures would propose. Duncan's word play links Frazer to Plato's Eros, child of Resource and Penury, who mediates between the imperfect material world and the perfect world of the forms and draws the soul toward its perfection in the ideal. Like Eros, Frazer is poor, "evil and foul," "bold," and manipulative. "[A] ruthless hunter,"[76] he pursues his goal in a manner radically different from the ideal he seeks. Frazer's poverty and the Ohta family's wealth realize in social terms the spirit-matter division around which Plato's universe is structured. Just as Eros "spans the chasm which divides . . . the divine and the mortal," Frazer's ramshackle cabin is connected by a "flimsy swing bridge"[77] to his victims' wealthy neighborhood. Finally, Socrates learns of Eros through Diotima in a vision resembling Frazer's drug-induced vision of nonmaterialistic freedom. The translation of material and ideal into the "have" and "have not" of class skews the balance of power in public communication. Material possession gives the Ohta family more "substance" in society's eyes, driving Frazer to compensatory physical attack as the only way to achieve recognition and identity.

This unstable relation of the material and ideal dimensions of language disrupts Duncan's poetic control, leading him to focus on the uncontrollable materiality of language. Like Frazer's perverted translation of ideal into physical terms in the attempt to make his slogans reality, Duncan's imagination is invaded by alien meanings that the material form of language generates. The oceanic muse of the first section becomes a mockingly ruthless Mme. Defarge, who whispers new meanings into Plato's language. "'*Soccer Tease*,' she mutters / where he does not hear, / '*is my Saint, for he has drawn from the poisond deck / of youth's lure in his sight Alcibiades the Tyrant / . . . leers up from the fumes / of drunken Sleep with an assumed knowingness about his / gnawing Nothing . . .*'"[78] Whereas Plato's Socrates uses desire for the beautiful Alcibiades as a springboard to otherworldly beauty, this muse reduces Socrates' pose of knowledge to manipulative seduction. Conflating the boy Alcibiades whom Socrates woos in the *Symposium* with the tyrant Dionysius through whom Plato would realize his ideal state, Mme. Defarge converts love into pursuit of power, harmonious social relations into struggles for dominance. Socrates' claim to know nothing represents not wisdom and integrity but ravenous emptiness fed only by power over others. Language has no power to inculcate ideals. Rather, property and use of language determine the substance words confer on self, and the prior public possession of words determines their meaning for all.

In dissolving authoritative narrative voice into a collage of public dialogue, Duncan reveals the disintegration of individual or ideal vision into such dynamics of power. That public language has greater substance and therefore power than private renders language alien as well as familiar. While language remains the principal component of self, it resists individual meaning. During the war, Duncan portrays himself as victim rather than master of language—or if master, only through a sinister factionalism that derives identity by preying on others. His Vietnam War poetry enacts this violent opposition of oppressor and victim as the only voices available. The extreme crossings of form and content, ideal and material in his poetry expose the tremendous power cultural forms have to dissolve individual voice and the radically alien, chaotic forces released in the absence of the traditional subject. *Bending the Bow* traces the emergence of the alternating stances of cosmographer and victim, from the destruction of the individual through the power of inflated images in the public world and the corresponding destruction of poetic language and imagination as forces capable of resisting this public agency.

3

As for Duncan, the war disrupts Levertov's ability to create and maintain poetic vision. Whereas Duncan places the war in a mythological and literary context from which he constructs a drama of cause and attempts to imagine resolution of the conflict, Levertov anchors literary vision in concrete context, rendering poetry part of immediate public debate. Early war poems like "Advent 1966," which records the horrific incarnation of Southwell's vision of a burning Christ in the children burned in the war, present the war as a "monstrous insect" "blurring" her poetic sight[79] with an untransformable and poetically unredeemable reality.[80] Whereas Duncan believes poetic freedom is incompatible with public language, Levertov attempts to make poetic beauty an active force in history. In "Staying Alive," the long poem that comprises most of *To Stay Alive*, she focuses on the specific individual utterances by which public meaning is established to present public voice as the product of consensus, a direct representation of individuals' opinions in an open forum of debate. The poem establishes a continuum between individual and collective voice in the shifting, malleable communities whose usage defines collective meaning. *To Stay Alive* challenges the government's image of war, which predominates in the media, by solidifying and extending the voice of protesters in this debate as evidence of a widespread consensus opposing the government.

Like Duncan's "At the Loom," Levertov's "Staying Alive" presents war as an intrusion of public violence into the domestic world. "Staying Alive" opens with a conversation between two children who have internalized the duplicitous language of the government's rhetoric justifying war.

> Children in the laundromat
> waiting while their mothers fold sheets.
> A five-year-old boy addresses
> a four-year-old girl. "When I say,
> *Do you want some gum?* say *yes*."
> "Yes . . ." "Wait!—Now:
> Do you want some gum?"
> "Yes!" "Well, yes means no,
> so you can't have any."
> He chews. He pops a big, delicate bubble at her.

> O language, virtue
> of man, touchstone
> worn down by what
> gross friction . . .
>
>   And,
> " 'It became necessary
> to destroy the town to save it,'
> a United States major said today. [Levertov's ellipses][81]

Levertov's juxtaposition of the children's and the major's words links official with private usage, demonstrating the "erosion"[82] of social harmony at home by government rhetoric of war. Both Levertov and Duncan illustrate the influence of public language on private. Not only are domestic and public usage interrelated, but linguistic usage structures both individual identity and social relations. The structure of the passage expresses Levertov's awareness that private experience is fundamentally political. By placing her poetry within this political conversation, Levertov participates in the creation of her community's linguistic meaning. Everyday conversation is the occasion for her image of language as "touchstone" of morality, the direct quotations representing the ground of an established public usage from which her poetic language springs and to which it speaks.

While Duncan and Levertov recognize the war's intrusion and influence on domestic life, they represent the relation between domestic and public differently. Whereas Duncan introduces the interconnectedness of public and domestic in Homeric simile, Levertov juxtaposes the utterances of living people whose words she hears every day, sometimes nameless and typical individuals, sometimes well-known newsmakers. For her, the meanings language has accrued are not Duncan's researched and remembered intricacies of etymology, but those of current usage in a specific situation.

> O language, mother of thought,
> are you rejecting us as we reject you?
>
> Language, coral island
> accrued from human comprehensions,
> human dreams,
>
> you are eroded as war erodes us.[83]

The poetic image of language as a coral reef emerges from the concrete po-litical situation Levertov describes. Thus while she locates the impulse to poetry in history, she retains the poet's ability to infuse language with meaning against Duncan's abdication of authorial control to the historical evolution of etymology.

By rooting imagination in immediate social context, Levertov changes the conception of epiphany present in her earlier work, from a harmony in the world of things to social harmony. Whereas her earlier poems revealed beauty in the ordinary objects of everyday life, *To Stay Alive* describes the vivid suffering and violence of the war in Vietnam in order to make present the real but remote war that Americans would ignore, to create a "[s]mall stock of compassion / grown in us by the imagination."[84] In contrast to alle-gorical visions of a spirit world in her poems of the mid-1960s, Levertov's work now focuses on the communal context and function of theological concepts, reinterpreting them in social rather than theological or personal terms. The camera's image of life is "[c]onfirmation, / a sacrament," its "pulses" in "[r]adiant emanations of living tissue" a substantiation of the spirit's common "will to live" intuited in all living matter by the "mind's dream-eye."[85] "Communion" and "covenant" refer not to humans' relation to God but to the ideal of community sought by the supporters of revolu-tion protesting the war abroad and social injustice at home.[86] Epiphany be-comes a vision of the harmonious community toward which the protesters work and which their collaboration and celebration sometimes achieve.

Part I of "Staying Alive" exemplifies the emergence of individual identity and poetic voice from immediate community. Levertov reviews her life, particularly her personal past and Romantic identification with na-ture, in the light of recent political events through the collective idiom of revolutionary vocabulary. Structured around news reports of de Courcy Squire's hunger strike following imprisonment for civil disobedience as a draft protester, the section includes excerpts from news reports, Levertov's letters from and to friends, and diary entries as well as crafted poetry. Lev-ertov's childhood memories of the sea as a tranquil spirit in nature emerge not as experiences of eternal truths but as havens of peace antithetical to political events. Although current events change the significance of her previous identity, they also show memory to be a resource on which the private individual can draw to counter public authority. Levertov contin-ues this embedding of poetic composition in quotations and recent events throughout the poem, measuring her experience by the ideals and progress of the protest movement and linking her own development to its history. So completely does she fuse personal and public history that her personal development is simultaneously a historical record of the protest movement. Unlike Duncan, Levertov records this history as the interaction of specific historical voices and thus creates a place for poetry as one voice in a chorus shaping public meaning.

Because she believes linguistic meaning is established through specific instances of individual usage, Levertov sees authoritative public voice as emerging from a democratic consensus among individuals. Levertov fights the pervasive media rhetoric in favor of the war by representing public consensus against it. Group action is thus the vehicle of social change, for group voice represents democratic consensus in the public sphere. Levertov writes to lend her poetic voice to the group. She accepts the War Resisters' polar oppositions of "Revolution or death," adopting their image of the public realm as composed of two factions. In a letter to Duncan, she states her need to take part in the struggle convulsing the public realm, for silence would mean complicity with the pro-war authorities. "I don't see the sidelines, or Neutral Ground, as an alternative."[87] "*Which side are you on?* / Revolution, of course."[88] Levertov shares Duncan's sense that the public realm is composed of opposing factions, but for her individuals in these factions engage in open debate to determine the course of history.

If the first part of "Staying Alive" reviews Levertov's life through the ideals of the protest movement, the rest of the poem seeks to articulate the meaning of "Revolution or death" as a principle of personal life and social order shared by many protesters. In her "Preface" to *To Stay Alive*, Levertov establishes her authority not as a unique or privileged poet but as a typical citizen. She introduces the book as a political rather than poetic achievement, "a document of some historical value, a record of one person's inner/outer experience in America during the '60's and the beginning of the '70's, an experience which is shared by so many and transcends the peculiar details of each life, though it can only be expressed in and through such details."[89] Levertov not only seeks to establish the common sense of her ideas but also presents her poems as a conversation with the community of protesters. Her "Looking for the Devil Poems" emerge from a friend's exhortation, " 'Tell Denise to write about the devil.' "[90] "Judy's" " 'If you would write me a poem / I could live forever' "[91] inspires a meditation on her suicide. Levertov thus seeks to make "Staying Alive" a force in public debate that argues the revolutionaries' ideas in ethical terms to support widespread consensus that challenges the government's version of the war. The explicitly interpersonal source of her poetry reinforces its authority as expression of agreement within the group.

In contrast to Duncan's effort to preserve the authority of poetic tradition as escape from contemporary history and usage, Levertov seeks to demonstrate that the collective experience of the protest movement can realize its ideals in social practice. "Part I" of "Staying Alive" substantiates the group's ideals through instances of revolution and death drawn from protests, memories, and science. Subsequent sections record her effort to live in accord with these ideals and the rewarding emotional community achieved through political activism. She describes the "joy," "generosity and good humor" among members of a communal "collective" at a house party[92] and the immediate warmth and caring shared in an international community of political activists working for similar causes.[93]

Whereas Duncan understands the revolutionaries' energy etymologically as a turning back, a rage informed by vengeful confrontation with the current power structure, Levertov believes in the revolution's power to start over, embodied in this community, to be proof of a universal human goodness realized in social life. Drawing on a discussion of "revolution" in their letters, she writes, "Robert reminds me *revolution* / implies the circular: an exchange / of position, the high / brought low, the low / ascending, a revolving, / an endless rolling of the wheel. The wrong word." While she admits this is technically "the wrong word," she embraces group language: "But it's the only / word we have. . . ." [Levertov's ellipsis][94] Because the group can define meaning, it can transcend the etymological and historical legacy of language, as in the collective erasure of history implied in renaming 1969 as "The Year One."[95] Her example may inspire others to define linguistic meaning, to reshape cultural institutions in order to break with the past. In the same way, "Staying Alive" records the protesters' collective efforts to reclaim university land for a People's Park, to construct a harmonious community of individuals in nature.[96] Although the police destroyed the park, Levertov records the harmony between individual and group in the collaboration as testimony to the human ability to form a community that nourishes individual identity. The strength of her vision of peace gains confirmation as others share it.

This allegiance of poetry with the revolutionary aims of the group requires a rethinking of the politics of poetics. Levertov's protest poetry has often been criticized as a failure to represent political issues with the depth and subtlety of her earlier treatment of poetic subjects. Cary Nelson and Charles Altieri in particular argue that her poetics of epiphany in the concrete image is inadequate to represent war's violence and ethical dilemmas.[97] For Nelson, Levertov's earlier "fragile vision," "almost evanescent," has a limited range. It can express only the ironic failure of poetry to act in history or "vivid clichés of violent war."[98] Altieri criticizes Levertov's "aesthetics of presence" as representative of a postmodern poetic stance unaccommodating to political and ethical responsibility. For Altieri, contemporary "objectivist celebration of plenitude" is a secularized and self-conscious Romanticism that responds to visionary experience in the everyday not by construction of cosmology but by a more private "construction and reflection on stances and attitudes placing man in relation to experience."[99]

While I agree with these critics that *To Stay Alive* lacks the intensity of language play and imaginative integration of subject matter into an esthetic whole characteristic of Levertov's earlier poetics of "presence," I attribute this change to a different intent. Levertov herself criticizes her former poetics of presence in "Staying Alive," demanding political accountability for the value of its images. Repeatedly drawn into contemplation of natural beauty, she forces herself to return to the violent political arena: "(glistening crust of ice upon snow / in driftwaves, curves of stilled / wind-caress, bare to the moon / in silence of adoration). / If it were so for us! / But that's the moon's world."[100] Whereas Nelson and Altieri focus criticism on isolated images like those in Levertov's shorter poems, the position of these images in the context of the long poem is crucial to their significance. Subject to use by specific individuals and in specific events, they acquire unstable or shifting meaning as the poem progresses. The give-and-take between individual and collective shapes the narrative development, collective use determining the value of individual language and vision. Through this dialogue, "Staying Alive" experiments with different ways to understand the role of the community in determining artistic form and value.

Lorrie Smith describes the changes in Levertov's war poetry as born of the attempt to bridge the gap between individual and group. For Smith, the stronger presence of a collective "we" in Levertov's war poetry brings a greater "equilibrium" between inner and outer life than in her earlier poems. Her "montage" technique shows the painful split of personal and national that this expansion of vision involves.[101] Levertov's letters to Duncan during this period reinforce Smith's argument. They vacillate between "I" and "we" as she defends her activism to reflect the merging of private identity with that of the group. While Smith depicts well the troubled relation between private and public life in "Staying Alive," I will focus on the formal changes that emerge from Levertov's new effort to represent the relation between the two in the dramatic structure of the poem as another important development in her political poetry.

The narrative juxtapositions of "Staying Alive" enable Levertov to record the active social life of poetry as the measure of its value. Part II explores a new understanding of poetic meaning and epiphany not as cosmic or universal truth but as practical knowledge developed through the protest movement's reception of her poetry. Seeking an image for revolution, Levertov explores an image of drifted and moonlit snow. The glittering snowdrifts in the passage quoted above may present an ideal of the contemplative poet's ability to crystallize turbulence into an image of beauty. Having suggested this Romantic correspondence between nature and culture, Levertov rejects it, asserting a fundamental difference between natural and political process in her recognition that this is "the moon's world" and not necessarily the human one. Whereas Duncan politicizes the Romantic conception of form as a reflection of power relations between subject and object in the social realm, Levertov retains nature as a realm apart from history and an example of the harmony for which human beings strive. Although nature provides her with poetic images of harmony, she does not assert natural order as the foundation for human and therefore denies its power to govern the course of history.

Structured around swings from engagement in revolutionary struggle to withdrawal from it, "Staying Alive" develops the contradictory poetics of each situation, challenging Levertov's former emphasis on the life of appearances with a social engagement of the image. Traveling while on vacation, she feels nostalgia for the rootedness of a more conservative Europe and recovers joy in the epiphanic clarity of concrete detail learned from Williams. "[B]ut life is in me, a love for / what happens, for / the surfaces that are their own interior life . . . I bless / every stone I see, the / 'happy genius' not of my household perhaps / but of my solitude. . . ." [second ellipsis is Levertov's][102] As with the image of moon on snow, however, these clear images are difficult to integrate into a poetry of revolution.

Against solitary artistic creation, Levertov studies the relation of her images to history. As her poetry intervenes in history, it acquires meaning not as a reflection of eternal truths but in its use for the community. She records how protester Chuck Matthei reads her poem "A Man" (from *The Sorrow Dance* [1967]) at rallies around the country as a vehicle of protest, having "found in it / a message for all who resist war."[103] Not explicitly political, "A Man" describes the beauty of a face (Levertov's husband, Mitch) carved by time and culling its own wisdom and song from the years as indifferent "daughters of the Fates."[104] Matthei finds a social purpose in the poem's wisdom, rendering its general statement about fate relevant and active in a specific political situation. He distributes the poem on a mimeograph which contains other statements such as " 'THERE IS ONLY SO MUCH PEACE AS THERE ARE PEACEFUL PEOPLE' " and "*No one man can bring about a social change— / but each man's life is a whole and necessary part of his society, / a necessary step in any change, / and a powerful example of the possibility of life for others.*"[105] The poem becomes an empowering symbol for the origin of revolution in the individual engaging a historically specific time.

Although a powerful affirmation of her poem's value, such reception involves a construction of poetic meaning beyond Levertov's control, rendering the poem vulnerable as well as responsible to the rapid social change of attempted revolution. Echoing Marx, she writes that " '*things that seem to be solid are not.*' "[106] Not only are social and poetic values shaken by public opinion, but her positioning of this awareness reveals the emergence of increasingly tentative philosophical and poetic reflection as she experiences social change. Taken from a popular song by *The Doors* and drawing on *The Communist Manifesto*, these words describe the rapid change characteristic of Marx's bourgeois society, in which traditional values have been disrupted by an economy organized for efficiency:

All fixed, fast-frozen relations, with their train of ancient and venerable prejudices and opinions, are swept away, all new-formed ones become antiquated before they can ossify. All that is solid melts into air, all that is holy is profaned, and man is at last compelled to face with sober sense his real conditions of life and his relations with his kind.[107]

The rapidity of economic change bringing confrontation with "reality" that Marx describes complements Levertov's meaning. The awareness that what seems solid is not follows the description of People's Park and the destruction of this utopian space by the police. Levertov criticizes the state's opposition to the protesters' ideals as tyranny masked by democratic rhetoric. "The War / comes home to us."[108] This realization demands consideration of the uses of poetry and philosophy to intervene in historical process.

Again the positioning of images in the documentary context is important to poetic meaning. Between the passages on People's Park and the solidity passage, Levertov reproduces a flyer giving practical tips for demonstrators. An unpoetic but useful tool of revolution, the flyer relativizes poetry as merely one and not necessarily the most powerful element of social change. Although she goes on to represent the power of public opinion as threatening "floodwaters," Levertov embraces its potential for change. Her image of a tree torn from its roots and carried by the current transforms itself into a hand, leading her to see the water as "a sea full of swimmers." The energy of change emerges from a crowd of individuals like her, whose shared labor gives substance to the new. The feeling of solidarity renews confidence in change. "Maybe what seems / evanescent is solid. / Islands / step out of the waves on rock feet."[109] Although openness to social meaning threatens meaning's stability, it also enables the revolutionary community to change the meaning of language and to make new meanings real by living them.

Levertov recognizes her images as provisional and imperfect within this historical process by placing them in a fragmented relation to the poem's narrative. Although she wishes to represent history as a movement toward perfection of humanity, she cannot assure such progress and builds uncertain outcome into her projection of an ideal.

> Again to hold—'capture' they say—
> moments and their processions in palm
> of mind's hand.
>   Have you ever,
> in stream or sea,
>   felt the silver of fish
> pass through your hand-hold? not to stop it,
> block it from going onward, but feel it
> move in its wave-road?

> To make
> of song a chalice,
> of Time
> a communion wine.[110]

Departing from the current military meaning of capture, Levertov does not internalize its violence as Duncan might. Rather, she transforms its meaning with an image of nonviolent capture as a mode of participation in community. She stands in the stream of history seeking to record her experience without changing the collective momentum of the fish from which she gathers her moments. The basis for unity between individual and collective lies in the wave, which connects the progress of history with the sea's peace and healing from her childhood and a richness of poetic tradition in the modernized Anglo-Saxon "wave-road." Yet the imperfect correspondence between "feeling" and "silver" and the grammatical incongruity in the passage repeat the gap between the stream of history and crafted artistic form. Although the chalice is realized visually in the lineation, the description remains a sentence fragment, the infinitive "to make" an isolated crystallization of potential or wish. By placing such an image in her documentary poem, however, Levertov seems to convey the hope that the chalice will enter history actively to provide a model for social communion. Artistic order is incomplete in this political context but gains meaning and completion in the intersubjective process of history.

Consistent with Marx's conception of rapid change, the chalice becomes an inadequate image of community as the poem progresses. In the section entitled "The Year One," this traditional image is destroyed by history, "[t]he clamor / of unquenched desire's / radiant decibels shattering / the patient wineglasses / set out by private history's ignorant / quiet hands."[111] The traditional chalice cannot contain and shape the fluid energy of social change. Just as the "wineglasses" lack the spiritual power of the chalice for a community of believers, so the forms of peace drawn from personal history are inadequate to shape collective historical process. The gap between individual, nature, and society exposed in the snow passage pervades the overall structure of "Staying Alive" as well. Although images of water recur throughout the poem, they remain responses to specific situations and do not cohere or complement each other. Levertov's varied water imagery—the childhood images of the sea as an all-embracing tranquillity, water frozen into beautiful forms of snow and floodwaters perhaps yielding communion wine—suggest but do not realize a connection between fluid process and fixed meaning or between harmonious nature and turbulent history. The failure to resolve these images into coherent vision may be interpreted as typical of the failed intensity of craft for which many readers have criticized Levertov's Vietnam poetry. They may also reflect, however, the discontinuities of imagined cosmological or poetic order as they develop within history. Rather than resolving these images into a universal or unifying character of water, "Staying Alive" reveals the various local meanings as part of a world in the process of becoming, the discrepancies between individual and collective meanings revealing the inconsistent truths of historical process.

Like Duncan, Levertov finds it difficult to maintain individual voice in public debate. The authority of the group ultimately threatens her integrity and creative voice. Her love of the surface life of things and rituals is part of a personal identity incompatible with revolution. For Lorrie Smith, this incompatibility leads Levertov to identity crisis at the end of the poem. Increasingly exhausted and overextended, she fears loss of self to what she comes to perceive in the course of the diary poem as changing fads rather than emergent truths in the protest movement. Levertov distances herself from the unrelieved frenzy and anger of revolution during her return to Europe in later sections of "Staying Alive." She asserts her roots in tradition against change in the present, embracing traditional rituals of Christmas against the practical compulsion to learn "karate, / soybean cookery, / or how to shoot."[112]

Although the collage notebook form of "Staying Alive" implies Levertov's belief in a liberal democratic public form, the development of the poem's narrative and imagery expresses her growing difficulty in embracing such a conception of the public sphere. In setting her own memories, letters, and poetry in dialogue with those of other specifically named protesters and politicians, Levertov represents political advocacy as a debate among autonomous individuals on the model of face-to-face community. Even as the poem records her increasing exhaustion and despair in dedication to long-term activism, it continues to assert the distinction between private and public spheres, "daily life" and "history," and to project their ideal "meshing" in "song."[113] By the end of the poem, however, the private realm has shrunk from expansive, sustaining havens of childhood memory and vacation landscapes to a barely accessible "well" in the "grim middle of the tunnel."[114] Threats to the private realm disrupt Levertov's dialogue of individual voices as the principal political agents.

Against the imagery of solid ground and territorial boundaries that distinguish private from public in "Staying Alive," Levertov portrays the private individual as increasingly overwhelmed by history's turbulent floodwaters, which threaten to erode the distinction between public and private. Although Levertov's earlier water imagery also links public and private, it does so in more constructive ways: the reviving force of the sea in childhood memory,[115] a flood that becomes a crowd of swimmers capable of creating solid land in their solidarity,[116] and social energy that in the right form may become "communion wine."[117] By the end of the poem, however, water has become an unfathomable "roaring silence." Its formless, inhuman power mesmerizes but destroys, as in the suicides of two revolutionaries, Judy and Grandin, whom Levertov views as casualties of history. "Judy ignored the world outside herself, / Grandin was flooded by it. / There is no suicide in our time unrelated to history."[118] Grandin's death by "flooding" signals directly the invasion of the private individual by public history. Although less directly public, Judy's solipsism also represents intolerable alienation from self in activism.

Levertov's lament of these deaths focuses on the loss of nurturing community that might have saved the revolutionaries. Letters and conversation give way to eulogy and address to the dead. In attempting to remember these individuals, "to gather up the fragments of it, fragments of her [Judy],"[119] Levertov attempts to recompose the integrity of the private individual "smashed" in political struggle. The vacillation between "it" and "her" indicates the fragility of the individual person possessed or transformed into an impersonal historical event. Levertov has trouble focusing her memory. Her imagination gravitates instead to the reason for the suicides, reflecting her preoccupation with broken community. "Further away than 17th-century China / nearer than my hand, you smashed / the world in the image of yourself, smashed the horror of a world lonely Judy, / silently plunging forever / into her own eyes' icy green."[120] Judy's "mirror" refers most immediately to the pool whose depths she sought as a child to fathom, but Levertov's water imagery links the pool to the inhospitable waters of history to suggest Judy's isolation and self-absorption in the commitment to activism, her entrapment in the foreign self history reflects back to her. Like the vacillation between "you" and "her," Levertov's contradictory feeling of unity with Judy yet inability to reach her reveals the alienating displacements of identity in the revolutionary community. Judy simultaneously looms powerfully as an actor in the political struggle to which Levertov has dedicated herself and remains unreachable, cut off from the personal communication of letters or conversation by her status as a public figure.

4

For both Duncan and Levertov, the tension between public and private identity during the war strains poetic voice. The formal changes in their war poetry emerge from efforts to render poetry an active force in the public arena. Their long poems develop the interplay between personal and public history but do not resolve the two easily in a single framework. While Duncan's serial *Passages* and Levertov's diary/documentary "Staying Alive" allow exploration of contradictory public and private stances, the very different forms of their long poems reflect their different conceptions of public voice and its relation to poetic agency. The debate in letters between Duncan and Levertov in which they attempt to justify their diverging poetics articulates the conceptions of the public arena and the poet's relation to it which motivate these different formal innovations in their war poetry. Although they began to write poetry about the war with a common goal of making the war real to their readers, Levertov and Duncan developed conflicting conceptions of the real war to be represented and thus different theories of how to write political poetry. Duncan roots the truth of the war in a literary field whose free imaginative expression grasps a fuller human significance of violence than that afforded by the narrow terms of contemporary political debate. For Duncan, Levertov's allegiance to the War Resistance Movement narrows her writing about war, compromising her poetic integrity. Commenting on Levertov's appearance at a women's peace rally televised in a PBS Report on the Rankin Brigade in March 1968, Duncan interprets Levertov's frenzied appearance as embodying the collective energy of the enraged crowd, "the demotic urgency, the arousal of the group against an enemy." "The person that the *demos*, the *citoyen*-mass of an aroused party, awakes is so different from the individual person . . . the *soul* is sacrificed to the demotic persona that fires itself from spirit."[121] Although he may agree with Levertov's political views, Duncan resists group advocacy as a means of activism, believing that it binds the participating individual to the group and thus prevents free thought.

And hardest of all, just here where we might be thought to be in agreement, to drive thru to the doubts I have in the area of agreement, the resistance to Resistance [the activist organization RESIST urged opposition to the draft and protested the war]. And driving thru I find I go with a free morality, I do not assent to whatever social covenant nor do I assent to the inner command as *authority*; but seek a complex obedience to "What is Happening."[122]

Duncan finds both allegiance to political faction and "inner" opinion inadequate. As he seeks to define this "complex obedience to 'What is Happening,'" his criticism and Levertov's response develop into a debate on "Staying Alive," particularly the poem's engagement of group activism and the language of political advocacy to which Levertov lends her voice. Duncan criticizes *To Stay Alive* for its engagement of group activism and the language of political advocacy to which Levertov lends and attempts to mold her voice. Marjorie Perloff has discussed the esthetic terms of the early debate over poetic language.[123] I focus here on the later debate surrounding the publication of *To Stay Alive* in 1971. For Duncan, both this polarized public debate between government and protesters and the war itself represent the "loss of relation between the individual organism and its ecological field." Both groups assume identities modeled on a destructively competitive ideology of nationalism. Nation is no longer one force among many shaping a universal "humanity," but an end in itself, its energy dividing rather than unifying the international totality of "Man."[124] Throughout their discussion, Duncan insists that the poet must resist the "commanding conscience" of embattled contemporary perspectives[125] to "imagine" or reinterpret the war in the context of an evolving cosmic drama.

Duncan's view of the radical discrepancy between literary and public voice, here that of political faction, in the representation of political debate motivates his attack on Levertov's style in *To Stay Alive*. Duncan resists Levertov's effort to merge her poetry with the protest movement's language as loss of poetic freedom in deadlocked political faction. For him, its members articulate no new order of peace but merely confrontation with the government. The slogan "Revolution or death" expresses the same destructive doublespeak of the U.S. Major whom Levertov quoted as destroying a town to save it. Doubting the ability of the embattled group to effect social change, Duncan also rejects Levertov's view of People's Park as an idyllic community. For him, the protesters work not to create political utopia but rather to release rage and revenge against the state's tyranny. Too angry to engage in constructive creation, the protesters mouth "empty and vain slogans" and moralize "war waged under the banner of peace."[126]

Duncan's understanding of the relation between the literary field and history changes during the war. Although his liberating vision gives way to a representation of the monstrous, polarized character of public voices behind their patriotic rhetoric during the war, he maintains the radical separation of literary from colloquial language as essential to poetic truth. The multiplicity of perspectives in the early *Passages* poems preserves the poet's role as enricher of humanity beyond conventional public rhetoric and involvement in factional debate. Poets must "get the words *right*," "keep alive in the language definitions as well as forces, to create crises in meaning, yes—but this is to create meanings in which we are more aware of the crisis involved, of what is at issue."[127] "[T]hat is the urgency that demands the poet to reveal what is back of the political slogans and persuasions."[128] Redefining "revolution" as a new start betrays the complexity that its etymology of return implies.

Brecht's "*Alles oder Nichts*" is, like your "*Revolution or Death*" and the American general's "*It became necessary to destroy the town to save it*" are [sic] poetically exemplary as embodying with great concentration the very principle of the world view they belong to. Ideologically, they are totalitarian and do not dissemble, sentimentalize, or delude us. But I would refuse such an ideology myself. I am and remain a pluralist.[129]

Duncan criticizes Levertov's poetry for what he perceives as an embrace of the narrow views created by public faction like that of her husband Mitch's resistance to the draft. "Your confrontation, Mitch, is not *against* the War but within it; bringing into the ground of What is Happening a war within the war, a multiplicity of potentialities."[130] Such action for Duncan may criticize contemporary specifics of the war but does not achieve the distance necessary to criticize the underlying reasons for the war or the idea of war itself.

The idea of the multiphasic character of *language* and of the poem as a vehicle of the multiplicity of phases is more and more central to my thought. The most important rimes are the resonances in which we sound these phases in their variety of depths . . . —the resonances that depend upon our acknowledgement in our work of what we know of the range of meanings in the language.[131]

If the early *Passages* adopt the stance of the individual antithetical to group faction, the later ones assume the monstrous voice of public power to expose the true nature of political faction. Such power destroys the poetic effort to forge ideals that would guide history. History driven by such force becomes "evolution—which as far as we know is the way in which life actually meets its test and creates its self." Consequently, Duncan writes, "I feel that revolution, politics, making history, is one of the great falsehoods."[132] Poetry's separation from history alters the function of poetry as creation of ideals. "The poet's role is not to oppose evil, but to imagine it."[133] During this period of crisis, Duncan thus abandons representation of an ideal order to identify with the existing conflict and expose the forces of evolution driving history beneath the conscious terms and intent of the public debate.

Levertov resists the view of the crowd as possessing energy radically different from that of the individual. Her involvement in and representation of the protest movement seek to maintain the power of the individual to shape public meaning.[134] Viewing the public arena as a vehicle for direct communication rather than distortion of individual voice, she defends her appearance at the rally not as an incitement to collective violence but as a message of peace. Her letter to Duncan cites her actual words ("Mothers, don't let your sons learn to kill and be killed. / Teachers, don't let your students learn to kill and be killed. / Wives and sweethearts, don't let your lovers learn to kill and be killed. / Aid, abet, and counsel young men to resist the draft!")[135] [I have supplied repeated words that Levertov indicates with ditto marks] to emphasize her speech rather than appearance on the screen as the essence of her message. Describing her role at the rally as that of private citizen rather than poet, she grounds her authority in a representative rather than special understanding of the war and prefers colloquial dialogue and public debate to literary language as the most appropriate medium of communication.

Levertov's letter condemns Duncan's resistance as "DISGUSTINGLY ELITIST." For her, verbatim conversation, correspondence among members of the movement, and the group's political slogans constitute appropriate, authentic poetic language to record this struggle.

> In the whole poem ["An Interim"] I attempted to range in language from the tra-
> ditional literate that is my heritage to the flippest colloquial that is also part of me
> and that I use just as much. A long diary kind of poem gave me the opportunity
> to swing between extremes in diction (just as in my life at that point I was swing-
> ing between extremes of gloom and cheerfulness etc etc [*sic*]) which short lyrics
> don't give.[136]

While leveling the hierarchy (although not abolishing the distinction) between poetic and colloquial diction, Levertov admits both as essential elements of her expression. Part of a continuum of individual utterances that
establish public meaning, poetry can engage colloquial idiom directly and
transform it. The revolutionaries' activism thus constitutes not rebellious
revenge, but the effort to realize the community sketched in their rhetoric.
For Levertov, the intent of People's Park is inviolable. Her perception that
the collaborators *"stayed together and wd not be driven away by intimidation,
and we did experience love and community"* affirms ideals that can build social harmony. Because collective inspiration radicalizes many to devote
themselves to such goals, revolutionary slogans, although imprecise and
changing, represent important progress. "This is a movement that can only
learn by doing. (And by and large it does.)"[137] The common language
of slogan articulates this emerging community backed by the power of its
shared experiences. Levertov's identification with group language represents not loss of freedom but positive, mutual transformation of self and
community.

Levertov comes to measure the worth of self and poetry by their
contribution to the protest movement. Her poetic language is rooted in
and responsive to the colloquial rather than the literary world. The community of protesters replaces tradition as the standard of poetic worth. "I
feel again that I have spoken and been audible, and that is much, very
much, to me; one does not want to have lived in vain."[138] By presenting
society as a combination of smaller dialogues, Levertov reveals the process
by which the individual influences public meaning and presents her poetry
as part of a broad continuum of communication. Although her poetry is
vulnerable to public reception and the group consensus with which she
identifies herself, she does not encounter Duncan's problems of authority

in resisting what he views as superhuman distortions of personality in the public realm.

Despite their efforts to render poetry an active force in history, both Duncan and Levertov find intense openness to the public world unsustainable. The third section of Duncan's "Santa Cruz Propositions" quotes a letter from Levertov lamenting their gradual estrangement. Duncan portrays their friendship as issuing in a rage born of her participation in public politics. Like the debased Socrates of the poem's second section, whose love is need, Levertov desires love to fill the lack born of rage at others' power: "she cries / from the center of terror / that is the still eye of the storm in her: / '*There comes a time when only Anger is Love.*' "[139] Here too, rage converts Levertov's language into a power-seeking doublespeak equivalent to the military language she criticizes in "Staying Alive." Just as Levertov lives the protesters' words, so Duncan comes to live hers, her equation of anger and love concluding his poem to reveal the contagious spread of violence through all social relations.

For both poets, modeling poetic authority on public does violence to individual voice. Just as Levertov finds her political poetry inadequate to both revolution and self and expresses exhaustion at the effort to blend the two at the end of "Staying Alive," Duncan's focus on the public world ultimately undermines his conception of what is real and of his own poetic power. "Bring It Up From The Dark" describes the extreme disorientation produced by the discrepancy between public and private reality. "It will be news from behind the horizon. / Refugees, nameless people. Who are they? / What is happening? I do not know. / Out there. Where we can see nothing. / Where we can do nothing. Men of our own country / send deadly messengers we would not send." The effort to visualize and incorporate world history in one's own becoming overextends and consumes the individual. Duncan concludes by assuming the role of pliant survivor. "I too am Ishmael."[140]

Recent theories of the public sphere enable us to trace Duncan's and Levertov's conflicting poetics to different conceptions of the public sphere and of political subjectivity and agency within it. Whereas Levertov's presentation of the poet as representative citizen and of group language as the product of democratic consensus projects a Habermasian bourgeois public sphere of private individuals engaging in rational debate, Duncan's assertion that the "demotic" persona of the crowd possesses and overpowers individual agency resembles in some aspects Habermas's massified public sphere, in which the individual achieves identity by bonding with the crowd through anonymous collective consumption of a common object, whether commodity or celebrity.[141] While Levertov and Duncan clash in their letters over the nature of poetic and political agency, their Vietnam poetry shares location at the crisis-ridden threshold between different images of the public sphere. Both find that public forms of authority subvert imagination in powerfully troubling ways. Their war poetry ends in disorientation and awareness of the painfully intolerable stances into which their commitments have led them. Both poets find themselves in what Wendy Brown calls "politics out of history," the radical confusion concerning identity and historical process that follows loss of faith in such foundational concepts of liberal democracy as "personhood," "right," "free will," and "progress."[142] Reading their poetry in the context of this historical crisis illuminates alternate forms of political subjectivity and public culture that their extreme poetry struggles to articulate.

Although Levertov and Duncan imagine political agency differently, their political engagement produces intense rage. For both, Judy Collins's "There comes a time when only anger is love" becomes a touchstone for the erosion of utopian domestic community in the public sphere.[143] This rage seems to come from their awareness of an imbalance of power and the unjust terms of their struggle. The public sphere polarizes into victim and aggressor, a phenomenon Brown traces as emerging when liberalism's "egalitarian ideal is shattered." For Brown, conceiving one's status as unprivileged victim or dissenter rather than equal citizen produces an "identity rooted in injury" that requires repeated victimization or imaginative identification with other victims to affirm one's identity as different.[144] The marked individual who despairs of inclusion in the universal remains bound to the dominant political order through this need for definition. "But restaging the trauma of suffering reassures us that what we need or love—the social order that originally hurt or failed us but to which we were and remain terribly attached—is still there."[145]

For Brown, imagining oneself as victim produces political paralysis like that fueling Duncan's and Levertov's doubts concerning activism. Levertov focuses increasingly on the martyrdom of political activists through police aggression. Nancy Sisko argues that Levertov's desire to make poetry purely a form of political action produces vacillation between self-hatred and hagiography of political activists in "Staying Alive."[146] Likewise, Duncan's agency polarizes around victim and hero aggressor. That Duncan theorizes his poetic voice during the war alternately as that of the fascist dictator[147] and as a prisoner of the law and order of language[148] reflects the interconnection of these subject positions in a post-liberal public sphere.

The difficulties of relating poetic and public generation of meaning in both Duncan's and Levertov's Vietnam poetry reveal the pressures of public opinion communicated by mass culture to which the poetry of the 1970s will respond. Both poets doubt the integrity and agency of the individual and question whether collective or public voice controls individuals. For both, the agency of collective forces has the power to render poetic meaning unreal due to the destabilizing discrepancy between poetic and public voice. Although both poets recover a separate space for poetry in the early 1970s, the stylistic differences between Levertov's and Duncan's war poetry emerge from diverging conceptions of agency based on collective and individual voice. The rupture in their friendship coincides with the end of the close contact among the Black Mountain poets as a group. Although some correspondence continues, their poetic concerns no longer overlap as significantly as they did from the late 1950s to the mid-1960s.

The crisis that political engagement produces in Duncan's and Levertov's poetry and their attempts to theorize this crisis as they justify their poetics reveal the powerful influence of the public sphere of national politics. Characterizing this public sphere as a threshold between either bourgeois and mass culture (Habermas) or liberal and post-liberal political culture (Brown) helps to explain not only the extravagances of their Vietnam War poetry but also the fate of field poetics. Duncan's and Levertov's opposed positions, privileging mass and individual agency, respectively, reflect the imbalance of power in the public sphere that strains the force field's model of productive interplay and foreshadows the next generation's need to develop new poetic strategies.

5

The Problem of Political Poetry
and the Polarization of the Field
in Levertov and Dorn

The striking difference between the late poetry of Levertov and Dorn illustrates the breakdown of field poetics as a model of political poetry. Until the late 1960s, field poetics provided the Black Mountain poets I have been discussing with a structure for representing the relation between individual and collective agency in a widening public sphere. Concerned from the late 1950s onward with the renovation rather than representation of colloquial speech, these poets asserted the individual's imaginative power to transform collective institutions. The Vietnam War shook Duncan's and Levertov's faith in the individual's power to influence political debate in the public arena of mass culture. Political factions as represented in the media threatened individual voice and undermined poetic authority through their seeming ubiquity and larger-than-life stature. Because Levertov and Dorn wrote a large body of explicitly political poetry during and after the war, their work articulates most clearly the social forces influencing field poetry from the late 1960s onward. Their understanding of the public arena and of historical process reveals the experience of collective institutions such as language to which Creeley and Duncan respond as well. In their divergent approaches to writing political poetry, Levertov and Dorn exemplify the polarization of the field created by this increasing distance between individual and collective voice.

Levertov and Dorn met in the late 1950s, when Dorn submitted poems to the issue of *Origin* guest edited by Levertov. Levertov's relation to Dorn was that of a mentor, she helping him to find publication opportunities and he posing somewhat uneasily as the younger writer grateful for help. He admires Levertov's craft and expresses insecurity about the prosaic quality of his writing.[1] Although Levertov and Dorn ceased to correspond in the mid-1960s, their subsequent political poetry diverges in directions significant for the development of a Black Mountain conception of the force field as a model of social agency. Initially, both poets used the force field of the poem as a place in which individual and collective agency interact productively, a place where the individual could criticize and transform common language and thereby the public arena of communication. In the early 1970s, however, both came to perceive individual voice and agency as radically different from collective and to reconfigure the poem to represent and address the different public spheres they perceived.

Unable to represent individual and group or institution as agents in a single political process, Levertov and Dorn gravitated toward viewing history from the perspective of one or the other. Levertov increasingly employed individual voice and Dorn that of institution. As Levertov's attempt to open poetic value to group determination ended in exhaustion and impasse at the end of *To Stay Alive*, she sought to establish a healthier relation between individual and group and to render the private imagination an agent of social change. During the mid-1970s she developed a theory of political poetry and activism as grounded in personal voice. *Candles in Babylon* (1982) attempts to create the conditions within which personal voice may survive in mass culture and to use this voice in constructing a public space in which the individual imagination may flourish. Although Dorn's idea of political poetry also changed, he rejected the group activism within which Levertov immersed herself. When asked in a 1992 interview his opinion of the connections between domestic and political life that Levertov makes in her political poetry, Dorn expressed confusion that shows how completely he separates the life of the body politic from that of the family or the domestic sphere.

If the mind makes a kind of a metaphorical leap from the household to transnational events or characteristics, I suppose that's possible, but I think it stretches the possibility so thin that I'm not interested in it. . . . [I]t seems to me that domestic preoccupations in art are just an excuse to not actually take mental responsibility for something larger. . . . [W]hen the television comes into your house, I don't consider that domestic property. Anything you see on television is not

I don't think one can accurately measure the historical effectiveness of a poem; but one does know, of course, that books influence individuals; and individuals, although they are part of large economic and social processes, influence history. Every mass is after all made up of millions of individuals.[9]

Imagining poetry as a force that influences the course of history, Levertov reduces the mass to thinking individuals capable of reimagining their world and thus transforming society.

The effort to write of personal experience as relevant to public seems to shape Levertov's subsequent work. In the introductory note to *Life in the Forest*, she writes of her desire to "avoid overuse of the autobiographical, the dominant first-person singular" prevalent in contemporary poetry and "to find a new way to explore more expansive means." Although she mentions having achieved this expansion earlier "by resort to a diarylike form, a poem long enough to include prose passages and discrete lyrics— to vary a habitual lyric mode,"[10] presumably in "Staying Alive," she rejects documentary style and her former emphasis on the representative quality of her experience as a typical citizen. Instead, she cites the influence of Cesare Pavese's *Hard Labor* (1943), with its invented genres of "poem-story" and "landscape." Pavese's note to the volume describes his desire to go beyond the merely personal, "to avoid the usual abstract introspection expressed in that bookish and allusive language which, with so little warrant passes for essential."[11] Against lyric as a distillation of pure emotion freed of the contingencies of time and place, Pavese develops the "poem-story" and "landscape" as vehicles through which to represent emotion emerging from concrete setting. For Pavese, these genres establish "an *imaginative relationship* or *link*" between person and place, rooting poetic figure in place and expressing a shared experience of place that constitutes the villagers' local culture.[12] Imprisoned by the fascist government and then living in hiding in the Piedmont countryside, Pavese resists Italy's national culture through his portrait of a regional culture whose beauty and integrity exist independently. Personal experience reflects a cultural imagination of time and place that nurtures individual vitality and wisdom.[13]

Levertov seems to graft Pavese's conception of local culture as a collective experience of place onto her view of the individual as active creator of culture. In doing so, she develops an ideal of culture as the shared meaning with which individuals invest their environment through careful use and communication. "Metamorphic Journal," the poem sequence concluding *Life in the Forest*, presents the origin of the imagination and its social extension into culture as the product of empathetic reflection between individuals. In contrast to the political journal "Staying Alive," "Metamorphic Journal" imagines a private love relationship. Seeking to articulate the origin of her love, the speaker compares her feeling for her lover to her childhood delight in embracing different elements of her natural environment, trees to feel their solidity and a river so that her "mind would sink like a stone / and shine underwater / dry dull brown / turned to an amber glow" in order "to know / the river's riveriness with my self."[14] Imagined identification with other beings helps her to self-understanding.

Continuing this refraction of self through environment, the speaker goes on to interpret her love as the desire alternately for something stable (treelike) to cling to, for a river's flow toward dissolution in the sea, and for a flickering flame akin to watery fluidity. The poem weaves the four elements—earth, water, fire, air—into a cosmos that symbolizes selves defined through love. The search for correlatives for desire and the self formed through it sparks imaginative growth and action:

> When you love me well
>   it is when
>   Imagination has flicked
>   its fire-tongue over you,
>   you are freed
>   by that act of the mind
>   to act.[15]

Love and "Imagination" thus exist in reciprocal relation, love awakening the imagination through which the self creates its own meaning. Ideally, such empathy fosters the growth of both individuals, for the cosmos that each creates enriches and confirms the other's experience as expressed through symbolic understanding of their shared environment.

Pig Dreams (1981), a poem cycle portraying a pet pig Sylvia's life on a Vermont farm, extends "Metamorphic Journal's" conception of individual and collective imagination as formed in mutual reflection into an ideal society. A whimsical version of Wordsworth's *Prelude* as it might have been written by a pig, *Pig Dreams* traces the spiritual development of the pet pig

Sylvia from birth to religious enlightenment and a vision of paradise. Like the speaker of "Metamorphic Journal," Sylvia comes to understand herself through her relation to others. Levertov's playful poetic forms express the varied perspectives into which she enters through her friends. Taken from her mother to become a house pet, Sylvia learns gregariousness from her "dogbrothers," contemplation from the solitary cat, and mortality from the seasons. The slow, stepwise form of "Her Sister" embodies the ruminant contemplation the cow communicates to her.

> Kaya, my gentle
> > Jersey cowfriend,
> > > you are no pig,
> you are slow to think,
> > your moods
> > > are like rounded clouds
> drifting over the pasture,
> > casting
> > > pleasant shadows.[16]

Thinking her way into Kaya's mind, Sylvia discovers its peace to be harmonious existence between earth and sky. This harmony is imagined in terms of the local environment, the pasture, which the animals share. Beginning from an articulation of difference which lured empathetic identity, Sylvia discovers a deeper kinship with Kaya in their worship of the same goddess (Isis), in the human love domesticated animals enjoy, and in appreciation of nature.[17]

While Kaya arrives at these beliefs and feelings through rumination, Sylvia's discovery is "porcine." Imagining touch as the primary sense through which a pig would perceive and enjoy its world, Levertov presents the "pigpatterns" Sylvia makes trotting in the mud after the rain as shining and reflecting the sky with the same light as Kaya's eyes. The many compound words Levertov coins in *Pig Dreams* ("cowfriend," "pigpatterns," "dogbrothers," "She-human," "pigwisdom," to name a few) represent this hybrid quality of the imagination formed through contact with others.[18] Despite different modes of perception, the animals' pleasure in their environment converges in their common perception of harmony among its elements. Sylvia's imaginative agility enables her to understand each animal's unique appreciation of this shared environment and thus deepens her understanding of the interplay of similarity and difference among the farm animals that creates such harmony in diversity.

Sylvia's feeling of kinship with other animals inspires a vision of cosmic unity. In the absence of her pig mother, she learns to drink milk from a bowl by watching her adoptive human father.

> At last
>> in the full moon's sacred light
>> in the human room where I'd run
>> in circles till my tapping trotters
>> almost gave way,
> the He-human
>>> naked and white as my
>>> lost mother,
> bent on all-fours over my untouched bowl,
> his beard a veil before me,
> and with musical loud sounds of guzzling
> showed me *eating*. Gave me
> the joy of survival.[19]

Beyond its charming pig's eye view of a person from the beard up, the passage establishes a familial relation of nurture between pig and human through their shared need for physical nourishment. Dependence on physical environment establishes affective associations with physical objects that resonate through Sylvia's life to form a cosmology. The emotional bond formed from shared physical appetite creates a Wordsworthian sense of a common being that rolls through all, echoed whimsically in the whiteness of pig, human, and milk. Sylvia's childhood joy in drinking milk returns in a sublime experience of union with nature during a sledding party in which white moon, snow, and pig are united as the "most snow-and-moon-and-midnight-bewitched / pig in the world!"[20] Interaction with one's environment to maintain physical existence thus grounds the imaginative transformation of environment that forms culture.

Each animal's potential for culture is based on the particular way it perceives its world. Ethical taboos originate in physical danger, water being "forbidden" by "the Law" because pigs cannot swim. The constellation of the "Great Boar," "invisible save to me [Sylvia],"[21] projects a heavenly counterpart of her earthly mate, "My Lord Boar."[22] As befits her hybrid being as domesticated pig, Sylvia's religion is Egyptian, involving worship of deities who combine animal and human characteristics and a cosmology deeply informed by geographical setting, perhaps most importantly creation from mud. For her piglets, Sylvia founds "civilization" based on touch, treasuring "an inheritance of shapes, / textures, mysterious substances—/ Rubber! Velvet! Aluminum! Paper!" Her appreciation of human culture also focuses on touch in her love of humans' dexterity in practical crafts of comfort—rugs, hearth, bowls, refrigeration.[23] By grounding imaginative life in physical life, Levertov presents culture not as a uniquely human creation but as each animal's particular means of survival and pleasure.

Pig Dreams' imaginative identification with an animal extends Levertov's portrayal of culture as formed in mutual reflection beyond humans to animals and ultimately all elements of one's environment. Her ideal social order is one in which all beings grow through such mutual reflection, preserving the ecologically balanced interaction that maintains this environment through respect for and pleasure in other modes of being. For Levertov, empathy is essential to cultural richness and physical survival, since sensitivity to each being's particular relation to environment deepens one's own appreciation of it.[24] Beliefs that prevent mutual reflection destroy the interdependent lives in a community. "Her Judgment" condemns humans' "swinish" view of pigs as mere bacon to feed human appetite.

> . . . Us they fatten,
> us they exchange for this [money];
>
> and they breed us not that our life
> may be whole, pig-life
> thriving alongside dog-life, bird-life,
> grass-life, all
> the lives of earth-creatures,
>
> but that we may be devoured.[25]

By viewing other animals only as the source of wealth and food, humans restrict animals' lives, denying them the capacity to enjoy their world that Levertov imagines in Sylvia. This self-centeredly utilitarian view limits not only pig life but also human life by preventing the empathetic extension through which imagination grows. It denies the physically and spiritually nourishing vitality of environment on which each individual's life depends. By viewing human culture through pig consciousness, Levertov offers a fresh, playful understanding of human culture as essentially animal and of animals as part of a common "life" deserving equal respect. Levertov's poetry attempts to foster such imaginative empathy as both ethical imperative and esthetic pleasure through chameleonlike translation into other perspectives.

The ideal of mutual empathy constitutes Levertov's test of cultural institutions in her subsequent poetry. She praises institutions that foster mutual vitality and condemns those that deny it. Republished as one section of *Candles in Babylon*, *Pig Dreams* represents an ideal of selective, local community through which to evaluate our larger and more complicated contemporary culture. In this broader context, empathetic reflection becomes more dangerous, rendering poetic voice vulnerable to the destructive institutions that deny imaginative life. *Candles in Babylon* begins from a position of exile and orphanhood that represents alienation from a hostile environment. The opening and title poem of *Candles in Babylon* presents the public world as antithetical to nourishing reflection.

> Through the midnight streets of Babylon
> between the steel towers of their arsenals,
> between the torture castles with no windows,
> we race by barefoot, holding tight
> our candles, trying to shield
> the shivering flames, crying
> "Sleepers Awake!"[26]

While fragile individual vision survives, armor and aggression thwart imaginative interaction, rendering the public world inhospitable and lonely. Those opposing the rigid institutions that form public space are powerless to create communion. The ideal persists only in an art increasingly remote from experience, in their "hoping / the rhyme's promise was true."[27] By presenting the repressive forces as "sleepers," however, Levertov renders imprisonment a state of mind. Beginning from the imagination's exile from the public world, *Candles in Babylon* seeks handholds by which the imagination may establish its place in history.

Levertov's distancing of poetic vision from Romantic identification with nature may emerge in part from the inappropriateness of innocent identification with nature in the face of contemporary history. "The Soothsayer" presents the poet as a weaver whose art establishes private rather than public identity. Unlike Homer's Penelope, who weaves the heroic public history of the Trojan War by day and unravels it by night, the soothsayer weaves "fictions, tapestries / from which she pulls / only a single thread each day, pursuing / the theme at night." Her private imagination creates a cocoon only partially undone by public day. While she allies herself with mortal nature, her "daughters" or poetic creations possess a vital but nonorganic beauty, the "[d]elicate bloom / of polished stone. Their hair / ripples and shines like water, and mine / is dry and crisp as moss in fall." Although art possesses vitality like that of nature, its relation to nature remains unclear. "My daughters / have yet to bear / their fruit, / they have not imagined / the weight of it."[28] Early poems in *Candles in Babylon* present poetic vision as an illusory beauty nourishing to the self but uprooted from the world, like theatricality and fairy tale as imagined in the theater's red and gold pomp suspended in the "chill" of ennui[29] and the magical view afforded by seven-league boots, "fertile dreams, / acts of passage, hovering / journeys over the fathomless waters."[30] The poems reestablish the integrity of private imagination shaken in *To Stay Alive* but remain unsure of the significance of its role in the public world.

As *Candles in Babylon* progresses, it anchors the imagination in people and things outside the conventional structures of perception that mediate their subjects' relation to the world. "The Art of the Octopus: Variations on a Found Theme" explores selective imaginative reflection as a "solitary dance" through which the self may choose which elements of the world to inhabit.

> *The octopus is a solitary creature, and for it,*
> *any shelter it can find is home*
>
> . . .
>
> *When it gave up its protective shell it developed*
> *many skills and virtues.*
>
> It can, for example, curl itself small
> to live in attics where daybreak
> is an alertness of red rooftiles that a moment ago
> were a vague brown at the western window,
> or it can untwine, stretching out starbeams into voluptuous
> unexplored chains of high-vaulted thronerooms
> beyond the scan of hurried, bone-aching throngs
> below in the long streets.[31]

Since individuals are vulnerable to environment, they need a "home," a structure that places them in nurturing, familial relation with the world.[32] Only out-of-the-way places provide shelter from the rushed, painfully invasive crowd and wearyingly "long streets" defining conventional commonplaces. Flexibility enables unique views within the confines of existing cultural edifices, however cramped, and expansion into an imagined royal house beyond the already built-up earth. That Levertov's octopus is not soft by nature, but vulnerable from having given up its shell, suggests the fluidity of the individual created through interaction with environment. The need for a protective home comes from an aggressively invasive environment.

Much of *Candles in Babylon* provides examples of homes created by inhabiting one's own environment and thus rendering it familiar. "Two Artists" opens with sculptor Rosemarie Gascoigne's creation of a household from found objects, old nails arranged like flowers in a pot, feathers woven into one side of a picket fence to suggest enclosure, tiny turret shells placed in a bowl like millet, and a coat of arms made from carpenter's scraps. By bringing cast-off and unusual objects home, Gascoigne creates kitchen and hearth from an alien world, encouraging intimacy with the foreign by incorporating it into her everyday household. Such intimacy allows imaginative exploration of these objects in the interplay of similarity and difference between their qualities and those of the household objects for which they stand. The shells produce a "music of jostled brittleness"[33] different from the millet to which they are compared, awakening a delight in textures that embellishes physical utility. Simultaneously, domesticating the foreign expands the mind's range of interaction with its environment and thus overcomes isolation. Another artist, Memphis Wood, creates a similar interplay between artwork and raw material by combining brightly colored hanks of cloth in a pattern "never / disowning its origins."[34] Both artists enact the imagination's development from anchors outside it to reveal the importance of creating a cosmos of objects that encourages empathetic identification and pleasure.

In contrast to such nurturing imaginary homes as a tool for social reform, contemporary culture produces an environment debilitating to the imagination. The final section of *Candles in Babylon*, "Age of Terror," criticizes the cultural organization of space currently mediating relations between individuals. Echoing the shivering flames of the title poem, "Talk in the Dark" shows isolated voices lamenting their condition as "flies on the hide of Leviathan," waiting to see "where my own road's going" but feeling powerless against an impersonal "history."[35] The threat of mass death in nuclear war is overwhelming. "Each day's terror [is] almost / a form of boredom—madmen / at the wheel and / stepping on the gas and / the brakes no good."[36] Because vital contact with such horror is unsustainable, empathy becomes apathy. Levertov's most developed image of the cultural space that produces this apathy is the movie theater, where the audience loses itself in the superhuman illusions on the screen. "A Speech: For Antidraft Rally, D. C., March 22, 1980" exposes the media's power to isolate individuals from empathetic selection and creation of community and thus render them pawns of ready-made ideology. Listening to students' speculations about what they'll do " '[i]f there's a war,' " the speaker laments their ignorance of history and the real violence of war. Filtered through the dualistic Cold War framework dominant in the news and the unreal violence of cartoons, war seems a clean and noble struggle between abstract good and evil, between "Commies" and "the *Free World*." Violence has become a familiar yet unfelt aspect of everyday life.

> No violence they've seen
> on the flickering living-room screen familiar since infancy
> or the movies of adolescent dates, the dark
> so much fuller of themselves, of each other's presence than of
> history (and the history anyway
> twisted—not that they have a way to know that)—
>> the dark
>> vibrant with themselves, with warm breath,
>> half suppressed mirth, the wonder
>> of being alive, terrified, entranced
>> by sexual fragrance each gives off
>> among popcorn. . . .[37]

Television's domestic familiarity and film's associations of heroism and adolescent romance suffuse violence with heady glamour, while sheltering viewers from the physical and personal effects of violence. The cultural spaces within which one views film and television not only control the emotions associated with information but also provide the concepts through which individuals interpret their world. The media serve the concerns of a society turned in on itself. Rather than generating culture in face-to-face interaction, individuals channel desire into existing public spaces:

> . . . They think
> they would die for something they call America,
> vague, as true dreams are not; something they call
> *freedom*, the *Free World*, without ever knowing
> what *freedom* means, what *torture* means, what *relative*
>   means.
> They are free to spray walls with crude
> assertions—numbers, pathetic names; free
> to disco, to disagree—if they're in school—
> with the professor.[38]

Not only the ideals through which the students shape themselves but also their sense of their power to change these ideals conform to the space social institutions allow them—the wall, the disco, the classroom. Freedom means rebellion within controlled structures, articulation of the conventionally scandalous on a blank wall rather than destruction of the wall. For Levertov, this freedom leaves the imagination "criminally neglected"[39] in its refusal to foster the empathetic identification that would allow individuals to generate culture from intimate communication.

"A Speech" attempts to break through such ideology by presenting its real effects on human subjects. The poem contrasts the neatly compartmentalized science of modern warfare—bureaucratic politicians who know nothing of the effects of the bombs and lasers they deploy or of the lives of the young they send to war, scientific designers of weapons who know their effects but may not control their use, and young draftees inspired by heroic fantasies—with the violent interaction of real war, "the way war always meant / not only dying but killing, / not only killing but seeing / not only your buddy dying but / your buddy in the act of killing."[40] Levertov's syntax resists the distancing power of modern technology. She reveals the cruelty and messy irresolution of war as it forces rupture of emotional bonds and denial of another's humanity. The poem's verbal repetition articulates war's mutual entanglement of death, violence, and friendship, of killer and victim.

Subsequent poems seek to move beyond the isolating darkness. "Writing in the Dark" hopes for "minds that are big enough / to imagine love, imagine peace, imagine community,"[41] to find "words that may have the power / to make the sun rise again."[42] Meditating on the theater's power to defuse emotional response to a movie on lynching, "In Memory of Muriel Rukeyser" attempts to reimagine public space:

> You cross
> the darkness
>
> still shaking, enter
> the house you've been given,
>
> turn up the desk light,
> sit down to plan
>
> the next day. How else
> to show your respect?
>
> 'No one
> to drive the car.' *Well,*
> *let's walk then,* she says,
> when you imagine her.
>
> Now. Stop shaking. Imagine her.
>
> She was a cathedral.[43]

Moving through the alien darkness of the socially constructed space around her, Levertov feels helpless and confined. Her house is not her own. Whereas "No one to drive the car," quoted from William Carlos Williams's "For Elsie," expresses Williams's sense of seemingly rootless contingency as the essence of American culture, Rukeyser's "*let's walk*" replaces Williams's passive submission to a driverless machine with self-directed immediacy. Unlike the movie theater, the cathedral is a communally created social place for worship of a shared divinity.

Christianity provides the metaphysical foundation for the link between Levertov's ideal of selective community and the dominant culture she criticizes. At the end of *Candles in Babylon*, "A Mass for the Day of St. Thomas Didymus" expresses the vital relation between the two that emerges in Levertov's poetry at the time of her conversion to Christianity. Grounded in the belief that the world is the creation of a wise and good creator, the "Mass" presents empathy as the natural response to the harmony and unity of all beings. The "Mass" creates a script for Rukeyser's cathedral, a construction of social space as a place for discovery, worship, and protection of common life beyond the self. Beginning from the "cacophony of malevolence"[44] that renders history an impersonal "destructive vortex," "downspin of time,"[45] "freefalling / forever . . . [toward] the violent closure of all,"[46] the poem seeks to combat the doubt and apathy bred by such a hostile environment. Initially, the individual knows its divine source only as an inner "deep unknown, guttering candle" as evidence of shared being with others. "Praise / the invisible sun burning beyond / the white cold sky, giving us / light and the chimney's shadow."[47] Knowledge of this source is acquired only indirectly, through the objects illuminated by remote divinity and the shadows or absence of light that the limited individual hearth produces. The "Mass" progresses from individual recognition of this divine core to the communal responsibility such recognition entails. Metaphysical unity affects history insofar as it remains part of the collective imagination, for names for the gods are "all that Imagination / has wrought . . . naming, forming—to give / to the Vast Loneliness / a hearth, a locus."[48]

Just as the candle represents both individual vision and divine light, so also "Imagination" and "the word" refer throughout the "Mass" to human and divine qualities, representing deity as both superhuman creator and human creature, who defines this creation through exploration of and interchange with other forms of being. As in *Pig Dreams*, Levertov grounds the common nature of divinity in the physical need that renders individuals interdependent. The "Benedictus" finds "[t]he name of the spirit . . . written / in woodgrain, windripple, crystal, / in crystals of snow."[49] Levertov's compound words and sensual and verbal alliteration express the mutual reflection through which all knowledge emerges. "[W]indripple" makes wind akin to water. The repetition of "w" in "woodgrain" and "windripple" establishes a correspondence between patterns of wood, wind, and water. The contrasting sharpness of "crystal" embodies the difference of texture between water and ice, the diversity within unity brought full circle in the final "w" of snow.

Faith in a common conception of deity is essential to overcoming the isolation and alienation that characterize the "Age of Terror." In "Agnus Dei," divinity is an ideal common essence in the relation between natural and human being and Biblical word. By deriving the essence of the "Lamb of God" from the concrete attributes of earthly lambs, Levertov unites spiritual language with the concrete referents in a mutual enfolding of deity and physical nature. Representing the lamb as "afraid and foolish," "vigorous / to nuzzle at milky dugs,"[50] the poem affirms divinity as vulnerable innocence that must be protected. "God then, / encompassing all things, is / defenseless?" "[B]orn in bloody snowdrifts, / licked by forbearing / dogs more intelligent than its entire flock," the lamb is part of nature, protected less by divine power than by the collaboration of an extended family of other animals. Recognition that all beings are as vulnerable as oneself renders the self a nurturing mother as well as an orphan seeking a home. Isolated individuals thus merge into a collective voice. "[W]e / must protect this perversely weak / animal, whose muzzle's nudgings / suppose there is milk to be found in us? / Must hold to our icy hearts / a shivering God?"[51] While both human and lamb are cold, each seeks nourishment in the other. The concluding "Let's try"[52] dissolves the ideological and technological structures that compartmentalize individuals whose fragile beauty demands the responsibility of mutual protection. The "Mass" thus recovers the firm purpose for the imagination shaken and uprooted at the beginning of *Candles in Babylon*. The imagination becomes the agent of compassion through which the isolated "shivering" candles may form a nurturing community, Levertov's Christian conception of deity providing a metaphysical basis for the common essence discovered in empathetic reflection.

Within a Christian context, Levertov's ideal of local community resonates with importance beyond the fulfillment it offers its members. Albert Gelpi has described Levertov's Christianity as "the transcendent third term that bridges the rupture between individual epiphany and public calamity."[53] For Levertov, a Christian understanding of suffering and its power to inspire compassion seems to render the public sphere not a numbing debilitating darkness but rather a ground within which selective local community may retain productive potential for its members and for the rest of society. In the "Mass," the fragile lamb inspires the compassion from which nurturing community may form.

2

While both Levertov and Dorn believed any political poetry must engage the public institutions that inform the individual imagination, Levertov's poetry seeks to reinforce private havens for the imagination, while Dorn's focuses on representing the cultural mechanisms that seem to him to govern public life. Unlike Levertov, Dorn had little faith in the force of individual imagination over social institutions. The different stances Levertov and Dorn adopted toward the little magazines and literary community of New American poets in the early 1960s foreshadow their future poetic representations of the relation between individual and group. In their correspondence, Levertov admonished Dorn not to submit work to *Evergreen* and *Yugen*, because she believed these journals had uneven literary standards. Dorn responded that he knew little about either journal but that literary infighting was inevitable in journals that follow a particular poetic program.[54] Levertov's careful choice of her community and her effort to shape its beliefs reveal her conviction of the reciprocal relation between public and private identity. Dorn in contrast felt himself an outsider to the institutions that define community, viewing them as shaped by the inherent character of the institution rather than by individuals' efforts to control their meaning. Having lived in poverty for much of his life, his childhood and early adulthood unsettled by his family's nomadic search for factory or farm work, Dorn often viewed culture from the outside. His novel *The Rites of Passage* (1965) records how economic, social, and educational institutions which mediate basic physical and emotional needs seem relatively transparent to those with money but mysterious and opaque to those without it.

Dorn's early writing concentrates on the material workings of local culture, much on the model of Olson's poetic treatment of Gloucester in the *Maximus Poems*. His social protest laments the destruction of Romantic innocence and sentimental caring by the harsh natural and economic realities of his life in the northwestern United States. Unlike Levertov, Dorn portrays individual sentiment as fragile, if not powerless, in this struggle and turns to satire rather than visionary ideal to articulate his criticism. Whereas Levertov's political poetry criticizes and seeks to reform public institutions through assertion of an alternative vision of community, Dorn attempts to represent the independent life of public institutions as it renders them resistant to individual control.

In contrast to Levertov's assertion of individual agency, Dorn focuses on the material aspects of culture, whose independent evolution belies individual attempts to infuse them with meaning. Ideas are incapable of governing the meaning that material presence establishes. In a 1963 essay on a racist incident in his town, Pocatello, Idaho, Dorn begins to articulate the failure of language and ideas to govern the meaning of things. He comments that whites treat blacks unequally even though they understand the language of "rights of man" and Civil Rights. "Talk *is* cheap. Talk about 'human rights' is particularly cheap. Rights have nothing to do with general colors, shapes of eyes or forms of noses. . . . Race *is* an exotic recognition, mostly visual, and always a momentary interest."[55] The physical presence of a different skin color perceived as "exotic" was more powerful than the idea of equality, the material reality rendering words ineffective. For Dorn, this material aspect of culture hinders human efforts to control its course. Its agency lies in the material forms it assumes, forms that develop a life different from the intent with which individuals created them. Elsewhere, Dorn quotes from Fox and Frobenius. "Culture is an independent organism. Man is not its subject but rather its object or bearer. Man does not produce culture. Culture permeates man."[56] Dorn's primary interest is in identifying the mechanisms that produce this independent dynamic of culture.

In his early poetry, Dorn undercuts the Romantic empathy with spiritualized nature and humanistic value on which Levertov grounds her ideal of social harmony by representing the unexpected or arbitrary material forms culture takes. His poem "On the Debt My Mother Owed to Sears Roebuck" begins with a powerful evocation of the drought and locusts that destroyed farms in the early 1940s, sending the speaker's parents into debt in 1943. While the debt paid for the child's clothes, the family's struggle for subsistence, fraught with worry and guilt, renders absurd the nation's heroic war rhetoric, which made farmers, frequently women, the "*stay at home army.*" The speaker's mother gains no spiritual freedom or insight from her life on the prairie.

> [A]nd my mother brooded
> in the rooms of the house, the kitchen, waiting
> for the men she knew, her husband, her son
> from work, from school, from the air of locusts
> and dust masking the hedges of fields she knew
> in her eye as a vague land where she lived,
> boundaries, whose tractors chugged pulling harrows
> pulling discs, pulling great yields from the earth
> pulse for the armies in two hemispheres, 1943

and she was part of that *stay at home army* to keep
things going, owing that debt.[57]

The mother's confrontation with nature is immediate and powerful, but it possesses neither the grandeur nor the enlightening purification of the classic pioneer experience. Dust and locusts create physical and economic barriers to her mind's expansive identification with nature. The noise and shape of farm machinery rather than national ideology or poetic sense of place anchor her imagination. Technology mediates a vague, haphazard vision of the land which contrasts sharply with the ordered, purposeful economic and moral order projected in the war propaganda. The driving force of culture and its relation to nature remain unclear. The "pulse" that drives the "stay at home army" renders agency diffuse. The long chain of causes that defines the pulse links machines, machine parts, natural resources, and political causes without establishing either clear beginning or causal relation between the elements. Rhetoric not only fails to conform to reality but also bears little relation to the material structures to which people cling.

Dorn rejects political poetry that advances ideological argument or prescriptive vision. In a 1958 letter to Levertov, he criticizes Bly's magazine *The Fifties* for its "strange naifness of social comment, apparently to revive [Pound and the Imagists], but as if things hadn't progressed even a little toward the impossibility of the poem as a social coercive."[58] Dorn's resistance to the poet as social visionary deepened through his friendship with LeRoi Jones, a friendship made and broken through their mutual interest in political poetry. Robert Von Hallberg analyzes a disagreement carried on in the correspondence between Dorn and Jones over Dorn's poem on the sentencing of Olga Herrera Marcos, purportedly the first woman sentenced to death in the Cuban Revolution. Dorn focuses on Herrera Marcos's terror as shown in a newspaper photo rather than on the political issues surrounding her arrest. Jones criticizes Dorn's poem as counterrevolutionary for its failure to address ideology and finds Dorn's response that he wished only to express Herrera Marcos's public shame unacceptably relativistic. Von Hallberg argues that Dorn uses the guise of "sentiment" or occasional writing to lift image and fact out of ideological embroilment, "challeng[ing] ideological certainties by pitting contingent events against the categories commonly used to hold political history in order."[59] Von

Hallberg thus places Dorn squarely in the Black Mountain tradition of refreshing conventional opinion and language, rendering the difference between Dorn's ironist and Olson's explainer one of degree rather than essence.

I would argue that *Gunslinger* mirrors rather than disrupts the material process by which culture develops through collective use. Dorn interprets other Black Mountain poetry not as a renovation of language but as a revelation of its social subtext. He interprets Creeley's *Pieces* not as the liberating construction of new linguistic meaning through disruption of conventional syntax but as the use of poetic language to reveal the social conventions woven into the reading process. In a review of *Pieces*, Dorn writes of each poem as "a precise social property," each poem representing "a model of a social universe" ordered by a strict ear "or by the fanatically balanced structures of cultural memory."[60] Dorn reads Creeley's constructions as warpings of the social fabric that expose its usually transparent norms rather than as autonomous art objects whose meaning transcends and expands conventional usage. For Dorn, language cannot escape this social fabric. Creeley's poems make explicit the expectations of word order and connotation inescapable in individual comprehension of language, revealing how much even creative writing draws upon socially established conventions of meaning.

While nature is a powerful force in Dorn's pre–Vietnam War poems of the American West, his writing turns in the late 1960s to examine the mechanics of culture in itself, particularly those of mass culture. Culture has the capacity for radical distance from nature. "It is one of the lovely qualities of Western Man that he is abstract. What I mean by abstract is, as far purely away from nature as he can get."[61] Dorn sees institutions as inflexible to individual expression, as possessing a life of their own that shapes the individuals who claim to run them. Describing his experience as editor of the mock newspaper *Bean News*, Dorn mentioned the staff's awareness of the constraints that newspaper form imposes. "[H]ow different can you make a newspaper? What is there left that would be distinctive?"[62] The conventional structure of the newspaper limits both the material it can include and the way people read it, this format rather than the actual content of the paper establishing the meaning people derive from the newspaper. For Dorn, the same has happened with the self: "[I] . . . is a habit that really has seen its day. It's not that it doesn't persist, but it turns out that everybody's everybody else. All our stories are so interchangeable. If they're significant they seem to be more interchangeable."[63]

Gunslinger illustrates the active role the media play in structuring individual life by creating a world in which fictional images from the media rather than specific humans are the main actors. This mock epic of the Wild West satirizes the unrealistic dimensions of the world of the heroic cowboy as represented in a television serial. The main characters are not individuals but cultural fictions, larger-than-life elements of popular culture that shape a public conception of reality remote from physical limitations. The characters are stock types from the movies, such as the sharpshooter Slinger and the stereotypical Western madam Lil, a generic artist "the Poet" and popular expressions such as "Kool Everything" brought to life. So pervasive are such genres, phrases, and images when magnified by the media that the narrative's landscape and plot change suddenly to conform to the dimensions of the fictional world associated with each character.[64]

Cultural fictions introduce conceptions of being that no longer conform to the laws of objective, local time, and space. The opening encounter between Slinger and the narrator exemplifies the supernatural power of cultural fictions.

> I met in Mesilla
> The Cautious Gunslinger
> of impeccable personal smoothness
> and slender leather encased hands
> folded casually
> to make his knock.
> He would show you his map.
> There is your domain.
> Is it the domicile it looks to be
> or simply a retinal block
> of seats in,
> he will flip the phrase
> the theater of impatience.[65]

Nature and culture, psychological and physical qualities blend to produce a landscape of cultural illusion like that of the television Western. Slinger is the stereotypical cowboy, an extension of his fictional genre. His body is cased in leather rather than skin, and he can draw his pistol faster than the speed of light. We learn that he is no mere mortal but a "semidiós" who has traveled from ancient Smyrna to the American West. A resilient cultural type of the hero, he is reborn in new forms throughout history. A product of popular imagination, he slows down "at noon / from the inertia of National Lunch."[66] As a mythical hero larger than life, Slinger has the power to translate time and space into his own idiom. He possesses the map of the world and defines the narrator's place in it. Although Slinger describes the narrator's space as a "domicile" or "domain," implying privacy and autonomy, the narrator remains a passive viewer in Slinger's "theater of impatience," the world of suspense and adventure of the cowboy movie. His gun, loaded with bullets of "pure information,"[67] shoots not to kill but to "Describe" people, forcing them to live and perceive within the dimensions of his world.

Power rests in the ability to control people's conception of reality by replacing objective time and space with the illusory reality of a television genre. The main characters travel in Slinger's "stage," a coach that transposes them into the idealized landscape and plot of the Wild West. Slinger's shootout with "a Stockholder" results in the Stockholder's "description" as "a plain, unassorted white citizen" without proper name. Investing their economic and imaginative resources in film heroes, ordinary individuals become mere "extras,"[68] background for the stars' lives on the movie set. Individuals are superseded by the fictions they have produced.

The early sections of *Gunslinger* develop the narrator's bewilderment and the inadequacy of conventional conceptions of identity in this world of mass cultural fictions. His confusion arises from the assumption that he can identify stable beings and events ordered in terms of objective time and space. Asking "who," "what," "where," "when," and "why," he strives without success to interpret cause and effect and the meaning of events and images. Such a "mortal" conception of being pales beside the manic action of the demigods of the television Western. The narrator's conception of reality proves old-fashioned, unable to adapt to a world that no longer conforms to the conventional distinctions between past, present, and future, life and death, and being and nonbeing.

Why do these conventional ideas of being no longer hold? Michael Davidson argues that, for Dorn, global capitalism destroys the local by manipulating our image of reality through its mass distribution of signs.[69] Such distribution destroys the local individual by reducing it to something that can be produced over and over. With such reproduction, particular details become signs of an original that is no longer familiar to most of the audience, as in the idealized character of the cowboy of film, who resembles few real life cowboys. Even art and philosophy become prey to this mechanism. In an interview, Dorn states that the arguments of the particular philosophers mentioned in *Gunslinger*—Zeno, Parmenides, Descartes, Heidegger, Lévi-Strauss—are "not important to the poem at all. I want these characters to have the possibility of such names: they are widely evocable intellectual signs. . . . The intellectual community is a mass community as much as the cotton picker's or the trucker's."[70] The apparent originality of philosophical thought is destroyed by its mass distribution and reception. Even self is not free from such massification. Somewhere in the course of Book I the reader realizes that even the first person narrator is not a specific person recounting his unique experience but a third person character I, whose being conforms solely to the Cartesian sense of self as rationally thinking being. The apparent authenticity of first person narration loses specificity, becoming a cultural fiction whose categories of subject and object define the traditional self. I's encounter with other characters reveals his outdated notion of identity in this landscape inhabited by figures of the collective imagination.

The death of I signals the impossibility of maintaining a discrete identity within this world of cultural signs. That I's decomposing body threatens to create a stench in the small space of the stagecoach suggests an unpleasant dissolution of the world organized around I's conception of identity as discrete beings inhabiting the same objective dimensions of time and space. When the Poet suggests preserving I's body as the container for Kool Everything's "batch" of pure acid, the hallucinatory vision of the crowd, I is integrated into the powerful collective imagination of mass culture. Rather than creating boundaries to bolster individual integrity from invasion by mass media as Levertov does, Dorn shifts from private lyric voice to a representation of this collective imagination in a pop epic.

The Poet's voice is as much a culturally structured system as Slinger's. The Poet translates the landscape through which the characters travel into his own terms. A parody of Romantic poets, particularly Keats and Whitman, the Poet transforms Slinger's stagecoach into a tree house, an organically structured home. "So this raga disperses / as the shimmering of its sense goes out, / Into the dry brilliance of the desert morning / . . . Into the upper reaches of the Yggdrasillic yoga / Over inner structure of the Human Thing / like Unto the formation of the pinnate ash / in which our tree house sways."[71] Mocking Whitman's invocation of natural origin in the opening phrases of "Out of the Cradle, Endlessly Rocking" the song expands into nature, its structure conforming to that of the world tree and an objectified, naturalized human being in harmony with this mythical order. Although the Poet presents his song as a loss of self in nature, it is his "shimmering" song that creates this illusion of inspiration. Against the fantasy world of the other characters, the Poet's mimetic incantation of natural process, "Make the sun hes [*sic*] comin up / Make the bird shes gonna sing,"[72] seems limited and redundant.

The Poet's Romantic vision does not exist free of the modern technological world of the other characters. Not only is this vision associated with a hallucinogen, as are the other major characters', but his language mingles with that of the rock star, the modern equivalent of the bard. "Light the mornin light the light / Thats the natchral thats all right / Oh baby, light the morning like the light."[73] Dorn translates Romantic vision into modern rock diction. The past cannot maintain its independent being and is thus configured to contemporary modes of expression and being. Likewise, while his portrait of Lil follows the metaphysical poets' figure of the lover's face as a book, the Poet incorporates elements of the modern world as part of the metaphysical context of contemporary love poetry. "And in the Yellow Rose of Dawn / Miss Lil reads her encyclopaedia / in a slender handled mirror / . . . that ancient argument of amaranthine flesh / the quick aniline of flawless brow. . . ."[74] Mingled with the traditional topoi of book and blazon, "aniline," a poison used in manufacturing rubber, dye, and varnish, expands conventional metaphors for beauty into the realm of industrial production, finding the latest chemical equivalents for Lil's supple, shining skin. The world of the Romantic poet is one system interpenetrating others in mass culture.

Although we learn in Book II that I has died, his death is no Romantic death of consciousness into nature. Slinger affirms that I, like the other characters, is not dead but merely undergoing a reincarnation.

But wheres he at
If I aint dead?

    Life and Death
are attributes of the Soul
not of things. The Ego
is costumed as the road manager
of the soul, every time
the soul plays a date in another town
I goes ahead to set up
the bleechers, or book the hall
as they now have it,
the phenomenon is reported by the phrase
I got there ahead of myself
I got there ahead of my I
is the fact[75]

Again, Dorn translates Whitman into the theater of the modern rock concert, parodying the complex relation between me, myself, and I of "Song
of Myself." We learn the ego is a thing, part of the material presence of culture, which is consistent with *Gunslinger's* scrambled interaction of matter
and spirit. Although costumed and thus part of the artificial drama of culture, the Ego sets the stage for the soul's drama, creating the setting within
which emotional tensions and life struggle to achieve meaning. Having internalized the theater of the rock concert, I plays out his drama on the
stage of mass stardom, inseparable from the self magnified in the eyes of a
mass audience. That this image of self emerges from the literalization of
the colloquial expression "I got there ahead of myself" reveals the power
of popular idiom in shaping psychology.

    The Poet's striving toward a transcendent, timeless perfection in
lyric,[76] what Slinger calls his "abso-lute,"[77] is inappropriate in such a radically changing world. Public voice overtaking private, Book II modulates
from the Poet's Whitmanic lyric to public epic in the saga "The Cycle of
Robart's Wallet" performed by Slinger. Introducing Howard Hughes, alias
Robart, as the hero of Universe City, The Cycle presents the type of the
entrepreneur as ancestral hero, "the Valfather of his race," in an epic not
of war but of "the Cycle of [monetary] Acquisition."[78] A hero because he
best manipulates advertising to hold the crowd's attention, Robart illustrates the power of money to alter the character of being.

Like Slinger, Hughes embodies his genre, the world of commercial advertising that he has manipulated successfully to become rich. He has no human body but is composed entirely of brand names and commercial products. Adorned with Kleenex, he rides "industrial brooms." Like his reclusive historical counterpart, he arouses but never satisfies the public's appetite, appearing only as a succession of electronic images that change rapidly to hold public attention. In the course of two pages, he mutates from the "cheeze in a burger" to a "Save the Cheese" campaign,[79] taking advantage of the popular trends of fast food and ecological consciousness to sell his products. Such change enables him to manipulate the latest fashion to his own ends and prevents others from consuming him for theirs. He adapts the heroic war epic in the same way, incorporating "the muse / Singing Used War for Sale" into his "system"[80] in a sideswipe at the economic motivations for U.S. intervention in the Vietnam War and its propaganda.

Robart's manipulation of cultural fictions to maintain his life in the popular imagination reveals the shift of identity from discrete essence to sign system. Conventional distinctions of identity are labeled the ancient "Beenville paradoxes." Like Zeno's paradoxical divisions of time and space, the "Beenville paradoxes" separate artificially what is continuous in the new world of mass communication. Developing unexpected ways in which material culture shapes reality, the paradoxes play on the power of language to create as well as describe reality. For example, the statement that "Nature abhors a vacuum / but for nature, A VACUUM'S / GOT NOTHING AT ALL" presents a vacuum as absence yet also as a qualitative concept opposing being. Although the vacuum literally has no content, the colloquial phrase "got nothing at all for" adds a meaning beyond the literal, half personifying the vacuum as having no emotion for nature. Feeling nothing describes a psychological state rather than the absence of being. Literal and colloquial psychological meanings cross to produce an odd hybrid of physical and psychological nothingness. In the same way, words for times other than the present refer not to an objective past but to concrete things in the present distinguished by the aspect of pastness. "To Be in Beenville Was / IS / To be in Beanville still."[81] Being in the past endures ("IS") in the present as a physical sediment, the participle "Been" shifting inaudibly to the concrete "Bean." So complete is absorption in the immediate act that it obliterates any objective conception of the past by translating history into the frame of the present. The "pseudoparadoxes" articulate a similarly arbitrary translation of matter into idea. Just as "Nothing" and pastness may acquire concrete status as things, so also the concrete may be as illusory as a hallucination: "the mass of me you have in your coach / can never be longer than yesterday's roach."[82] The equivalence of image to the roach that produced it conflates material being and perceived illusion while emphasizing the incongruous, hallucinatory relation between material culture and the worldview that it produces. This scrambling of physical and linguistic being, reinforced by the awkwardly rhyme-driven line, characterizes the unpredictable way cultural forms generate meaning and reality.

This breakdown in an objective concept of being renders identity fluid. Meaning shifts through the many possibilities for association with contingent cultural systems.

> Time is more fundamental than space.
> It is, indeed, the most pervasive
> of all the categories
> in other words
> theres plenty of it.
> And it stretches things themselves
> until they blend into one,
> so if youve [*sic*] seen one thing
> youve seen them all.[83]

Time replaces objective space as the principal structuring identity and the relation between things. Formerly identified by position in space, beings have become systems that maintain their existence by undergoing radical change, as in the rebirth of cultural fictions in different ages. Money enables this fluidity and potential unity of all things in mass culture. Structured around Parmenides' preface to his philosophical vision of the unity of all Being beyond appearance, Book III renders the truth of Parmenides' vision for mass culture. "Sllab," "balls" spelled backward, parodies the conception of Parmenides' (and Heidegger's) "Being" as the progenitor of reality. Since access to the original truth of the past is impossible, the "giant bronze bean" is "sllab's messenger / that memory's now obsolete."[84] Money governs Sllab's meaning in the present. Transformed into a tourist attraction that plays a recorded message for a nickel, Sllab's *Logos* is based not on eternal truth but on "a random sample" from consumers, "Western Man" and the Sublime advertised as cinematic spectacles.[85] Describing the United States as a nation produced by "reason / & corn," Sllab laments its transformation "by the seething masses" into "commentary," the loss of distinct mind and matter to performative exclamations "TREMENDOUS! FANTISTACK!"[86] The distinction between appearance and essence thus gives way to the succession of media illusions which now constitutes reality.

History progresses not by the deeds of individuals but by the manic and unusual action of signs manipulated by economic interest. Whereas individuals have some inherent identity, signs assume a different meaning depending on context, that is, on the system of which they are a part. The color red, for example, may signify love if shaped like a heart but stop if shaped like an octagon. For Dorn, the self was once the center of such a system, defining other beings as discrete and autonomous like itself, but it has become weak and outdated in contemporary mass capitalism. I's development throughout the book reveals the more powerful cultural systems to which the self is subject. After his philosophical confusion in Book I, I returns, having adapted to the rigorous conditions of mass culture. The place of I's reappearance, Café Sahagún, reflects his change from thinker to consumer. No longer an absolute, human knowledge is seen as a "psychognosis," a hybrid of the specifically human mind and knowledge. Twirled like a cheerleader's baton for show and competitive spirit, it presents no serious description of reality[87] but remains subordinate to vested interest. The main actors in the scene at Café Sahagún are Lil and "Kool Everything," a personification of popular opinion represented appropriately by a slang phrase so pervasive in colloquial language that it is a part of everyone's mentality.

> Hello Everything, thought you'd
> Never get here
> HI there Lil, did you all
> keep me in minde, oh Looke
> I wish I had some of Those Things
> Everything's eating
>
> *That's a dish of Etzalqualiztli!*
> Lil said, extending her hand
> *Corn & beans*
>
> Fascinating, I said, taking it

Everything you got Produce
all Over your lapel, say
whats that other bowl of matter
stationed before you
like a Hollywood award.[88]

I's former faculties, observation and thought, exist now only in archaic form, in the spelling of "looke" and "minde." Formerly a passive questioner, I is now the perfect consumer. He no longer observes, but desires. As a good consumer, he wants whatever the character Everything has. To him, Everything's nondescript "bowl of matter" resembles a "Hollywood award," the sign of stardom and thus of collective desire. Whereas the specific items consumed are vague at best, the commercial category "Produce" becomes something substantial enough to have on one's lapel. Likewise, Lil, former keeper of a brothel, mediates the exchange by marketing these "things" to make them attractive to the consumer. She renames simple "Corn & beans" as exotic "Etzalqualiztli," the Aztec word for the sixth month of the year, referring etymologically to the eating of corn mush at a religious festival during that month. Lil thus appropriates the sacredness of religious tradition to lend the commercial product mystery and increase its appeal. Lil's erotic power further enhances this image, for the passage leaves open whether I takes her hand or the corn and beans and which of the two he pronounces fascinating. Desire, seduction, and consumption thus replace the pose of objective inquiry that formerly structured I's vision. The object of consumption has no inherent value but arouses desire only through association with another system of values.

The radically changing and discontinuous narrative world of *Gunslinger* reflects history driven by systems rather than by individuals. Dorn calls this historical development "mutation," the radical change in the dimensions of character or reality produced by these interacting sign systems. The characters' interaction reveals systems as dynamic and permeable, capable of living and growing by absorbing others and transforming themselves to infiltrate and appropriate other systems. They either supplant other systems' meaning with their own or adapt their own meaning to coexist with the fluctuation of neighboring systems. Slinger not only "describes" mere mortals in terms of his "theater of impatience," but also expands into other systems by transforming himself into their terms. When the Poet transforms the "stage" into a tree house, Slinger appears as Yggdrasil, the world tree that structures the universe by becoming a tree, preserving his earlier dominance in this organic version of his earlier mapping power.

Human nature changes through participation in the system of economic circulation. When Everything receives the check in Café Sahagún, the manager sticks his finger in Everything's ear, making Everything's head a slot machine in which his eyes roll and turn up two "plumbs."[89] Plugged into the economic system through consumption (or rather, this system plugged into him, his energy contributing to its existence while it dominates him), Everything becomes subject to its lottery, the random relation between price and value. Unable to get the finger out, he is advised either to get another finger for the other ear or to get a ring to show they are married.[90] Acceptance of his new hybrid identity reveals the adaptation to the new configurations produced among systems. The character of cultural fictions is not consistent but changes radically as they attempt to secure or maintain a place in the collective imagination. For Dorn, their power to determine the categories of individual perception shapes the course of history with a power far greater than that of the individual.

As *Gunslinger* develops, one realizes that I is a relatively minor character in a battle between two dominant cultural fictions, Slinger, the romantic cowboy of the American West, and the capitalist entrepreneur represented by the millionaire Howard Hughes. Despite their qualitative differences, both characters act like systems, fighting to survive and expand in the cultural landscape created by mass communication. The struggle between Slinger and Hughes occurs on the battleground of public opinion, where both seek to win viewers and expand their lives in the popular imagination. Their combat reveals the forces of desire and consumption that pervade the cowboy myth as represented in mass culture as well as the business world. Aided by Taco Desoxin, a master of "environmental modification,"[91] Slinger challenges Hughes's "cheezeburgers" with the southwestern mystique of tacos, meeting Hughes on the common ground of fast food emblematic of the process of marketing and consumption through which they woo their audience. Hughes defends himself with the Mogollones, transforming these natural rock formations of Monument Valley into octane-powered automata through the power of commercial advertising.

The final confrontation is appropriately anticlimactic. Both Slinger and Hughes avoid the potential destruction of a dramatic shootout. Each adopts useful qualities of the other to continue his expansion. Hughes heads toward "Chile" to exploit the exotic appeal of Hispanic culture Slinger had introduced. Slinger adapts Hughes's ability to defer conclusion and thus to hold his audience's attention in his parting words, "Hasta la Vista [until next time]," true to television serial form.[92] Since it was Slinger who introduced Hughes as his adversary in the epic "Cycle," one wonders whether Slinger presents Hughes as a decoy to cover the traces of the economic production in which Slinger himself is involved. Their mutual accommodation reveals the interaction and coexistence of systems that shape the cultural landscape of mass commercial capitalism.

The process of mutation by which systems adapt to each other is unpredictable and capable of changing reality in unexpected ways. Introduced by pseudobiologist Dr. Jean Flamboyant, author of the Beanville Paradoxes, mutation describes the garbled transmission of digital information. Transmitted as electronic signals to Universe City to meet the other characters, Dr. Flamboyant arrives one body part at a time, his body itself a spectacular but radically discontinuous fluctuation of codes for electronic representation.[93] Although the main plot is structured around the contest between Slinger and Hughes, the surface of this story is crazed with other systems that the characters have absorbed into their own plots. Just as the Poet's appropriation of rock lyrics transforms his subjectivity, so Lil's use of foreignly named Etzalqualiztli for corn and beans continues an appropriation of foreign names for food, as in Hughes's transformation of his car into "chile relleño [*sic*]" to escape an angry crowd.[94] Gradually, the elements of Hispanic culture appropriated through Taco Desoxin as weapons of mystique in Slinger's fight against Hughes become an independent language. Following Lil's sale of Etzalqualiztli, the use of Spanish proliferates to disrupt the story with I's seeming non sequitur, "Los cajeros llena menguante nueva,"[95] "the bank tellers, full, waning, new." Whether this line is simply nonsense (the noun does not agree with the adjectives) or naturalizes cash flow in terms of the phases of the moon is unclear. However, this eruption of Spanish takes over I's voice, rendering it incomprehensible and dissolving him into yet another system. Elements of Hispanic culture become a stronger presence, not only in Slinger's and Hughes's dependence on Hispanic characters to fight for them, but also in the spelling of English words as if pronounced with a Spanish accent, particularly in the speech of "Portland Beel [Bill]." Infiltrating the voice of non-Hispanic characters and even the voice of the omniscient narrator, this accent indicates the power of an appropriated system to engulf the culture that appropriated it.

Thomas Foster argues that *Gunslinger*'s "reproduction of racial stereotypes" demonstrates "the limits of the postmodern [understood as pastiche] critique of subjectivity as the basis for a multicultural public sphere." While the ascendency of "the Hispanic" toward the end of the poem does translate it into representation in terms of the capitalist commercialism the poem protests, Foster assumes a space outside the system, a position of countercultural critique,[96] that Dorn's poem denies. All media are subject to similar subversion. Styles, phonetic and spelling distortions, and typographical techniques like italics and capitalization spread unexpectedly and without apparent logic. Initially employed in the conventional way, to lend emphasis, these writerly elements gradually acquire a life of their own independent of the meaning of those who use them. Crooning like a rock singer, the poet translates the *hodos* or "way" of Olson's careful met-hodology as the means of separating human from natural categories "intointoo . . . the hoodoos / lying around the foot of our future."[97] Contemporary pronunciation creates new meanings through the material resemblance between elements of culture, here reducing philosophical truth to a magic that produces our image of the future. Although italics sometimes distinguish Lil's voice from others, Dorn does not use them consistently. In some cases, emphasis appears arbitrary and suggests different possible meanings within a single sentence, as in "*I ain't dead.* [Slinger] / *I* know *that, Slinger* [Lil]."[98] Dorn's text thus enacts the way in which any aspect of material culture can generate a new system, producing a reality of shifting signs and centers of agency which change along unpredictable lines of force. The world of mass media is volatile, and its material forms are capable of mutating beyond their use in a specific situation to produce a world transformed beyond recognition.

3

The discrepancy between individual and collective agency is so great for Levertov and Dorn that it produces incompatible visions of social process. To affirm the individual as the center of agency, Levertov must deny the specific influence of institutions and ideology, relegating them to dark spaces or vague, inert machines. To represent the mechanisms by which cultural institutions evolve, Dorn reduces self to a similar institution or an intersection of cultural frameworks. His attention to cultural fictions emphasizes a pervasiveness of mass media that eliminates a private realm of the individual. Neither Levertov nor Dorn can synthesize the two perspectives, and each presents one to the exclusion of the other. So great is the interference of mass culture as a medium of social communication that it prevents purposeful interaction between individual and institution. While acknowledging the presence of these mass institutions, each poet responds with a different conception of creativity. For Levertov, poetry constitutes a private, individual use of language separate from and transcending social convention in its ability to create new meanings. Art remains a realm apart from but capable of influencing social conventions. Institutions are conventional structures established by a community of familiars and therefore malleable to individual use and expression. For Dorn, in contrast, language and self are part of the material process of history and subject to the contingent processes of institutions, processes beyond the control of individual intention. Dorn's portrait of popular culture disperses individual voice to represent it as a product of the more powerful fictions of the mass media. Satire replaces the Romantic poet's power to construct an alternative, personal vision with which to counter these mass fictions. While moving toward opposing extremes on a spectrum of possible constructions of agency in political poetry, Levertov and Dorn also exemplify the difficulty of bringing these extremes into fruitful interplay in contemporary mass culture.

Conclusion

Gunslinger received a cool initial reception from Creeley, Duncan, and Levertov. Their responses reveal the extent to which Dorn's poem challenged beliefs about poetry that these poets shared through the 1960s. Dorn's adaptation of field poetics in *Gunslinger* is ironic, undercutting the personal authenticity crucial to the other poets' representations of self as a force in this force field. Dorn portrays such authenticity as impossible because mass culture has become the dominant force shaping language and identity, overpowering others and preventing the creative interaction of individual imagination and language that made the force field such a valuable model for poetics a decade earlier. While Dorn's writing shares some characteristics both of Black Mountain field poetics and of a younger generation of Language poets, his ability to alienate both groups signals his position as a transitional figure. The tensions in his work and in its reception help to explain the problematic position of field poetics in the changing poetic landscape of the 1970s and 1980s.

The Black Mountain poets were uncomfortable with Dorn's satire, his rejection of the poet's role as serious renovator, whether representative or privileged, of communal language. From the hindsight of 1978, Creeley attributed the ambivalent Black Mountain reception of *Gunslinger* to "fear of the 'ironic.'"[1] Creeley, like other 1960s poets, rejected the New Critics' affinity for dramatic and structural irony and advocated a personal expression and authenticity essential to poetry as self-creation and communication. In a 1971 interview, Duncan reflected on Creeley's initial response to *Gun-slinger*, identifying the importance of poetic imagination as a creative force in field poetics.

Creeley says that *Gun Slinger* [*sic*] doesn't have the emotion. You see, at Black Mountain, poetry was . . . [complement unstated]. This stems from *Pisan Cantoes* [*sic*] and from *Paterson*. Poetry was a private . . . personal mystery in a different way, it did engage one at the conscience . . . the coexistence of consciousness and conscience in that [. . .] And in *Gun Slinger* it's an entertainment. It begins to be able to use all situations and convert them to it and entertain them. And it's cool in its style, something Creeley may prepare for but never is. Gone from *Gun Slinger* is Creeley's absolute, immediate, existential crisis, which is there no matter where you are in a Creeley thing. And I think that absence of crisis, Creeley reads as . . . well, *cool* means "where is the emotion." As long as the emotion's not there, you're cool. That was not ever part of the Black Mountain scene. That was very much what was going on. For Charles, better to be sick, as Wieners is frequently, and be in the truth of yourself, than be wise to the whole thing. His criticism of me [in "Of Wisdom As Such"] was that I tended to be wise to every situation and not actually to come to the crisis. . . . This is a crisis School. [ellipses in brackets indicate my omission; the rest indicate pauses in the interview][2]

For Duncan, a Black Mountain poem's emotion is personal, the poem's precise tracking of individual or cultural consciousness a moral commitment. For Olson and Creeley, the poem's adherence to a train of thought constitutes the only authentic record of self in the fluid force field and thus the only access to identity. Although Creeley's and Duncan's more impersonal writing refracts the self through forms of cultural or linguistic artifice, both the pervasive presence of the poet's voice and their emphasis on the warping or shattering of self when subordinate to such institutional structures reveal the consistent presence of individual perspective as one significant agent among others in the force field. Because the individual remains a crucial force shaping community, the poet's responsibility extends beyond the personal to the social. Poetic imagination must remain a constructive counterforce to the other influences in its environment. To depart from such assertion and integrity of the poetic self is to betray the poet's personal and social responsibility, as Duncan's use of "entertainment," both exploration of possibility and leisured pastime, suggests.

To this way of thinking, Dorn's masquerade of different perspectives implied frivolity, a disregard for the ethical commitment involved in placing self and using the shared medium of language. For Creeley and Duncan, *Gunslinger*'s playfulness and satire of Olson marked the passing of an era. For Duncan, speaking a year after Olson's death,

the age of Olson is over [. . .] a whole new world of poetry was disengaging itself from, I guess. . . . A part of it I think is that it was too grievous of an engagement with. . . . [object unstated] Well, but there have been disengagements from . . . formal disengagements. When Pop Art goes back to the grand chic of the twenties, it's disengaged itself from the almost grievous levels of engagement that there were in abstract expressionism.[3] [ellipsis in brackets mine; the rest indicate pauses in the interview]

Duncan understands Pop Art's parody as a reaction against the "too grievous" personal involvement that makes poetry the articulation of increasingly isolated personal meaning. (He may have been thinking of the intensely personal use of color and form in Pollock's crisis-ridden drip paintings or of the similar use of local detail and myth in Olson's late *Maximus Poems*.) In contrast, Pop Art—whether painterly or literary—avoids the personal through parody of public material, rendering poetic self a mere reflection of collective institution. Although Duncan finds it hard to name what poetry disengages from, he goes on to suggest a middle way between these esthetic extremes that preserves the poet as a source of imaginative freedom. "And part of what's happened now I think is when you politicize the engagement, you have actually removed yourself from the one field you are responsible to . . . The imagination. [my ellipsis]"[4] Duncan identifies a creative space in which personal and public may interact and a role of the poet as shaper of forms for popular culture. If Duncan's hesitation indicates the difficulty of theorizing his position, he nevertheless maintains imagination as a constructive locus in his poetic practice, something Creeley and Levertov also maintain or reestablish in their work of the 1970s and 1980s.

While Duncan's "too grievously engaged" probably refers to the personal emotion of Abstract Expressionism he mentions earlier in the interview, it may also indicate his ambivalence about the extent to which personal crisis and emotion were social or political, delicate issues for Duncan as he emerged from his painful, enraged poetry of the Vietnam War. To insulate the poem from such collective voice, Duncan locates an independent source of poetry in a realm (whether psychological, spiritual, or other) outside the force field of contemporary history and politics. Duncan articulates his common ground with Creeley, Levertov, and Olson as follows: "it is certainly in this that I see you [Creeley], me, Denise, Charles strongly united that the ground of the poem is a circuit in which experience and language are united in a process of ongoing creation of our situation."[5] Poetry emerges from—or is grounded in and by—a place defined as the flow of energy between experience and language. Duncan's wording preserves a fundamental connection between individual and social, implying their mutual influence in the creation of collective culture, "our situation." If the relation between poem and circuit remains ambiguous, "the ground of the poem" suggesting both the poem itself as ground and an anterior origin outside the poem, Duncan's imagery preserves fluidity. The flow of energy between individual and collective in the medium of language maintains the power of imaginative freedom as a social force. The desire for creative interaction of individual and social, experiential, and linguistic forces makes the force field a productive model of poetic structure.

Dorn's work after *Gunslinger* loses faith in the relative autonomy of multiple agents and their fluid interaction in the field. It intensifies the erosion of the personal in a massified public sphere and the impasse this erosion represents for field poetics. Dorn retains the intense Black Mountain engagement with colloquial idiom and custom, representing himself as the gadfly of his local Denver community and other discursive communities, such as those of the academy or of political liberalism. His portrayal of the impersonal interests of institutions invading the local and overpowering the individual's construction of meaning leaves little room, however, for the creative interaction of person, language, and institution that had been characteristic of Black Mountain field poetics. Grant Jenkins characterizes Dorn's stance as thoroughgoing rejection of idealism and utopian solutions. In an interview with John Wright, he states, "I don't really have any politics"[6] and emphasizes the difficulty of escaping complicity with the media and institutions. Against Olson, Dorn characterizes his work as "anti-polis,"[7] resisting any conception of a public sphere as the place for political or literary intervention. Consistent with this vision of self and community, Dorn's narrative personae satirize, the only option for a voice that rages against but cannot escape the powerful, arbitrary action of these institutions.

While *Gunslinger* uses playful mock epic humor to satirize the massification of such cultural fields as television Western, structuralist philosophy, and Romantic poetry, many of Dorn's later poems focus on local and
personal or private subjects where loss of autonomy is more painful
and controversial, as well as politically charged issues like identity politics
and minority solidarity. His 1990 *Abhorrences* attack such liberal causes as
AIDS awareness, politically correct language, and Native American rights.
Dorn's satire insists relentlessly that local and personal refuges of idealistic
thinking are illusory. For him, such refuges are shaped as much by institutional interest and power as are the more explicitly massified cultural institutions of *Gunslinger*. In both subject matter and style, Dorn finds class
complicity and hypocrisy not only in establishment interests but also in
liberal idealism and personal sentiment. His criticisms of politically correct
slang and jargon are especially sharp, revealing the failure of language and
liberal sentiment to transcend self-interest. One "Abhorrence," "Something we can all agree on," mocks liberalism's bureaucratic and rhetorical
strategies for responding to poverty.

> Suppose there were a new
> acronym for an old disease—
> very awful and very incurable.
> Let's call it HELPS for
>   Heritable Endemic Longrange
>   Poverty Syndrome
>
> Now here's the question:
> do you think there would be
> much tea & sympathy for this plague?
> Neither do I.[8]

Dorn criticizes the power of the catchy acronym to attract public attention
for its cause. Recalling AIDS, HELPS suggests that new acronyms capitalize
on the emotional power of others. But beyond calling poverty a "plague" acquired like AIDS from social contact rather than a product solely of individual responsibility, the poem makes no gesture to escape the social channels
for liberal dismissal of the problem without guilt. Once the acronym transforms the problem into a bureaucratic issue or a media event, it removes the
problem of poverty from concern for those who suffer. The questioner's
"neither do I" implies and sanctions the reader's apathy, indicating facile

preference for the popular opinion whose authority he or she mimics rather than challenges. Such institutionally framed consensus relieves the speaker of responsibility and allows sentimental contemplation and dismissal of prepackaged controversies, which are diffused by the dynamics of the opinion poll or news report rather than by solution of the problem.

If HELPS mocks institutional and public naming to allow self-righteous evasion of social problems, other "abhorrences" attack the individual's idealistic power to change consciousness by changing language. For Dorn, poetic and intellectual language use cannot transcend the power dynamics of contemporary culture to work change. "Every Man for Herself"[9] mocks the attempt to reform sexist language by propping women's power on phallic "Man's" authority. Dorn's late work erodes the last vestiges of personal and imaginative idealism by revealing their complicity with existing power structures. When he departs from such satire, as in some of the more private love poems of *Love Songs*, he adopts unconventional and oblique structures of language that resemble Creeley or some of the Language poets, as if to shield private emotion from the too-pervasive truisms of popular convention.

1

Whereas Dorn responded to the crisis of poetry's openness to political process in the late 1960s and early 1970s with the satirical distance of *Gunslinger*, Levertov, Duncan, and Creeley rework their poetics, emerging from periods of intense, if uneven, experimentation to establish greater equilibrium. Their subsequent work restores the poet's ability to mold impersonal form and institution, at least to some extent. Although the wounds to their friendship never healed completely, Duncan and Levertov recovered a space for greater imaginative freedom in the early 1970s, and their grounding of this space in poetic tradition as the source of topoi from which the poet can respond to contemporary culture reveals their deep affinity. Creeley moved away from the grammatical abstraction of linguistic structure in *Pieces* to integrate language into different contexts of communication and nonverbal experience. These poets made their choices in the context of new poetic communities shaped at least to some extent by the diverging conceptions of agency I have discussed in Levertov's and

Dorn's poetry, communities that abandon or transform field poetry's fluid interaction between individual and collective agency to favor one form of agency or the other and develop different formal concerns.

The choices Creeley, Duncan, Levertov, and Dorn made led to palpable differences of form and subject matter in their work. Perhaps most dramatically, Dorn's focus on a local popular audience and public voice and Levertov's political activism and poetry of Christian belief lead them to develop different themes than Duncan and Creeley, with their greater emphasis on formal experimentation with language. If Dorn's sense of his vulnerability to public voice marks him as typical of a younger generation, Creeley, Duncan, and Levertov remain strongly linked by common personal and poetic concerns, despite their significant differences. Poems like Duncan's "The Torn Cloth" and Levertov's "For Robert Duncan" and Creeley's last prose tributes to Levertov[10] express mutual devotion and a strong sense of common purpose, not less because they struggle to comprehend the serious issues that created breaches where friendship and shared understanding of poetry were so strong. The late work of these three poets, while influenced by the different communities in which they come to participate, reveals the continuing influence of field poetics as the basis of this affinity.

I have discussed how Levertov's late poetry balances individual voice with group consensus as a source of social change. Local community established through empathetic reflection remained central to Levertov's political writing after *Candles in Babylon*. The major political poems of her next two volumes, "The Showings: Lady Julian of Norwich, 1342–1416" and "El Salvador: Requiem and Invocation" (published in *Breathing the Water* [1987] and *A Door in the Hive* [1989], respectively), explore the possibilities and tensions that arise from this stance. Julian's childhood home and precolonial Mayan culture are models of vital interaction between individual and environment, in which daily work is worship of one's materials, deity a nurturing parent. Levertov's meditations on nature in *Evening Train* (1992) and *Sands of the Well* (1996), written as she made a new home in the Pacific Northwest, reveal the beauty and wisdom gained from imaginative communion with neighboring mountain, heron, forest, and sea. Protest poems expose the technological and linguistic structures by which culture destroys such communion. "Those Who Want Out," for example, depicts the thoroughly artificial environment and language of researchers who devote their lives to leaving the earth to found a colony in outer space.[11] "News Report, September 1991" is a collage of the military rhetoric used to desensitize soldiers to brutal killing during the Gulf War.[12]

The greatest challenge to Levertov's poetics of empathetic reflection is representing how her vision of harmony becomes a force for political change, and some of her poems explore this problem. "Where is the Angel?" expresses frustration at the peaceful beauty of a "mild September" through which "History / mouths, the volume turned off."[13] *Evening Train's* section "Witnessing from Afar" provides one solution to this problem by tracing the small yet significant effects at home of apparently remote violence to reveal the vital interconnection of life on earth. Levertov's most frequent strategy seems, however, to be to reveal the discrepancy between harmony and violence through juxtaposition of the two in poems whose tone ranges from pathos to irony, outrage, and occasional bitterness.

Levertov's renewed interest in Christianity frequently grounds the dynamic relation between local harmony and world history. As Levertov began to explore the Christian visionary tradition after *Candles in Babylon*, she was drawn to the writings of Julian of Norwich for her faith in love and mercy during the horrors of war and plague. Although Julian "lived in dark times, as we do," she was able to laugh at the devil and "[cling] to joy though tears and sweat / rolled down her face."[14] A Christian tradition of compassionate response to suffering enabled Levertov to remain hopeful and active in a hostile environment. "El Salvador" finds examples of this faith in four martyrs to the nation's struggle for peace. Although the poem portrays the knowledge and harmony of ancient Mayan culture and nature as an ideal, it considers them "lost,"[15] ineffectual in the current struggle. The Christian martyrs' belief and example that "all of us *are* / our brother's keepers , / members one of another , / responsible, culpable, and— / *able to change*" render their lives "seeds" of knowledge and power.[16] Faith in a Christian cosmology to give meaning to suffering and compassion gives Levertov a fuller, unifying context in which to relate the local communities of which she writes as forces of change in history.

Although the Christian conception of compassion grounds long political poems that approach the scope of "Staying Alive," in "The Showings" and "El Salvador," Levertov does not develop an exclusively Christian perspective in her last books. Ecopoetic respect and compassion for environment also permit the communion of beings that her Christian belief supports. While *Evening Train* and *Sands of the Well* continue to reflect her concern with the relation among private imagination, empathetic reflection, and community, individual poems address the problem from different perspectives. A poem imagining polluted earth as a leper deserving charity[17] may be followed by one in which the speaker ponders the significance of the moon's distant serenity against the face of "earth's cries of anguish."[18] Returning to the spare juxtapositions of facts or events used in her shorter political lyrics, Levertov resists adherence to a single philosophical, ideological, or religious framework.[19] "Dom Helder Camara at the Nuclear Test Site"[20] provides a microcosm of such shifts of perspective. The poem describes protesters for peace celebrating Mass, confronting marshals at the site, and then joining in a circle dance that fuses individuals "in the unity that brought us here, / instinct pulls us into the ancient / rotation," presumably the earth's turning.

Dom Helder, the focus of the poem but not explicitly named the catalyst of this communion, leads the Mass and "dances at the turning core" of the circle. The poem demonstrates the birth of harmonious community through an act of political resistance where shared imagination becomes a cohesive force. Levertov does not, however, provide a formula for activism. She suggests that both religion and nature, leader and various individuals may be forces in the creation of this harmony, for the poem gives preference to neither cause and leaves the tension between them unresolved. The impression is rather of a unique and spontaneous, if willed, coalescence. Levertov's diversity of perspective seems to come from her fidelity to the concrete particular, from the priority her poetry gives to expression of vivid sensuous and spiritual experience. The diversity of her work grows not just from representing these particulars but from exploring the meaning of the relation between them.

Like Levertov, Duncan develops a poetics that distances voice and form from those of political faction. After fifteen years of self-imposed silence, Duncan published *Ground Work: Before the War* (1984). The volume records a significant rethinking of his poetics to distance himself from the epic voice and possession by national history with which *Bending the Bow* ended. While *Passages* 33, "Transmissions" characterizes the field as both destructive and creative, "vortex" and "compost," it also reasserts "the creative" as one of "many energies [that] shape the field."[21] The book's progression from the opening "Achilles' Song," with its specific date and allusions to Homer's (and H. D.'s) war poetry, to the closing undated and cyclical (whether biological or esthetic) "Circulations of the Song" locates Duncan's poetry in a universe larger than history.

Duncan recovers distance from epic rage by reconceiving public history as one among many different orders and agents in interrelated but autonomous local communities rather than as subjects in a hierarchy of power. Stephen Collis argues that Duncan's construction of architectural space in his poetry of the 1960s enabled the interpenetration of public and private to make the domestic sphere a public space and thus a force for political change.[22] *Ground Work: Before the War* continues to develop this connection but also uses architecture to establish boundaries. "Structure of Rime XXVIII, IN MEMORIAM WALLACE STEVENS" praises the imagination's power to erect "a Gate" "beyond the boundaries of all government. . . ."[23] "The Museum" represents such architecture. Its sheltering solidity preserves ways of seeing and thinking from other eras. A "treasure room" of memory, the building's "carving out of thought" and "route of seeing carved in stone" provide perspectives outside natural and historical destruction.

The museum's order is incomplete and provisional, however. Although the museum represents a source of inspiration outside history, the poet sees not the totality of the edifice, "the radiant space in building" into which the muses "gaze," but the earthly negative he inhabits and thus perceives only from the inside. Duncan characterizes this space as "a shadowd space, a shell in time, a silent alcove in thunder, in which the stony everlasting gaze looses itself in my coming into its plan. It is an horizon coming from what we cannot see."[24] Although the museum provides shelter and silence against an implicitly turbulent, threatening environment, the shadowed interior is only the "horizon" or interface with another world, not full vision of it. The animating, inspirational effect seems to come from the physical structure itself, whose "stony everlasting gaze" recalls Medusa's. Duncan represents art and tradition as valuable but warns of taking art's vision as absolute. The rest of the poem renders the museum's chambers indistinguishable from those of the heart and demands that its rigid architecture give way to the natural force of earthquakes. Although the museum houses a tradition that recovers the autonomy of artistic vision apart from history, Duncan voices anxiety about this autonomy as both fragile and deadly to the natural vitality of which it is an integral part.

The poem sequences that follow "The Museum" ("Poems from the Margins of Thom Gunn's *Moly*, "A Seventeenth Century Suite in Homage to the Metaphysical Genius in English Poetry," and "Dante Études") move beyond "The Museum's" tentative assertion of art's autonomy to preserve imaginative freedom but integrate art more fully into life. The "Dante Études" conceive of art as one among many interlocking and mutually influencing symbolic orders and language communities. Duncan draws on Dante's understanding of language as richly polysemous, its meaning and character defined in multiple social contexts and branches of knowledge, to affirm the integrity of local community and place it in fruitful contact with the larger political communities of state and empire. In contrast to the local meanings of "daily speech" corrupted by the bloodthirsty voice of the nation in the "Santa Cruz Propositions," the vernacular in the "Dante Études" is learned in the intimacy of the infant's contact with its parents and grows with the child's gradually expanding community. Knowledge of language expands outward from the family as primary center to include the "language" of pets and natural environment, as well as first articulations of self-consciousness and identity. These meanings are firmly established before the individual comes into contact with public and political discourse in the city state and empire or their modern equivalents. As part of this early development, the study of "grammar" at school nurtures awareness of the abstract, "reflective" power of language. Linguistic "constructions" or "floor-plans" form "a felt architectonics . . . of the numinous"[25] that open the way for creative intervention in the architecture of the cosmos.

By establishing multiple symbolic orders, Duncan frees language from the public authority that would make it a tool of political domination and secures the creative role of the imagination in shaping the human cosmos. The "Dante Études" recover and extend the multiplicity of perspective of the early *Passages* in the autonomy but interdependence of familial, natural, political, literary, and divine orders, "[t]he individual man / having his nature and truth / outlined / in relation to groups / appropriate to his household."[26] In making the "household" central to the definition of truth, Duncan subordinates "the meaning of 'nation'" to "the speculative intellect / whose devotions [are] / to the general the good / of the total design thereof." Because this speculation "extends into the actual / as the practical intellect," "speculation" is not only static mirroring but practical action in the world. Active synthetic imagination overcomes rigid architectural conceptions of form to intervene in and contribute to the fuller evolution of life in "the Process of Man."[27]

Attention to the unique formal integrity of local experience as participation in a cosmos that includes many orders of being from cell to empire inspires the continually evolving cosmic vision of the rest of Duncan's poetry. Embracing the intensely temporal, ephemeral character of existence presents the fullest possibility of understanding cosmic "design," for it renders poetic form responsive to the full trajectory of the individual's physical, historical, and spiritual life. Just as Duncan's earlier work developed shifting foci of sexuality, love, family, art, and citizenship crucial to his personal growth, *Ground Work II: In the Dark* (1987) tracks the withdrawal of self into "my first and final place"[28] in illness and aging to construct new visions of cosmos afforded by mortality. Norman Finkelstein describes the volume as turning away from eros and the body to face death, particularly the void or absence of embodied being and the impending chaos of physical "decreation."[29] Poetically, this shift is no small change for, as I argued in my analysis of *The Opening of the Field*, the lover and domestic household constituted by erotic desire generate the gravitational force that shapes Duncan's cosmos. Leaving eros behind alters this cosmos fundamentally, displacing its "center of gravity" from the beloved to unknown death. No longer anchored by his relation to his lover, Duncan feels dispossessed, "not my own / yet forever now in this playing a part of me."[30] Eternity displaces him from his body's time, subverting his former sense of self by involving it in a plot foreign to him, that of "forever" in death.

Form and imagery in *Ground Work II* explore the evolution of spirit accompanying this dissolution of the body. The shape of the poems alternately narrows to reflect the diminishing self and, as Michael Davidson argues of the late *Passages* poems, expands into the margins of the page to depict the body's vulnerability to and invasion by disease.[31] Duncan weaves this new perspective of the cosmos through a revision of tropes from his oeuvre. The "ladder" to heaven of the erect phallus (as in *The Opening of the Field*) gives way to downward "well" and sphincter,[32] which tap the body's sources in the river Styx and regulate the boundary between vital organism and abject matter. Images of relationship to the beloved as the life-giving "heart of a solar mirror" that causes "the whole to shine" cede to images of self reflected in a dark crystal or mirror and in black water, the unknown beyond the body's life. That Duncan writes his death into the book's final line "—an eternal arrest"[33]—makes the body's mortality the ultimate source of poetic form. While recognizing the gaps, inconsistencies, and partial correspondences of imperfect understanding, his commitment to the changing form of embodied temporal experience affords the fullest range of perspectives through which to fulfill the speculative imagination's potential.

Although Creeley's response to the social turmoil of the late 1960s is less explicitly political than Duncan's and Levertov's, his concern with language as impersonal institution reflects similar concerns about the individual's ability to control language as a medium of communication and expression. In the decade after *Pieces*, Creeley continued to explore language as a depersonalizing artistic medium. In *A Day Book* (1972), the private self of diary dissolves into formlessness through translation into language. *Presences* (1976), composed in collaboration with sculptor Marisol Escobar, explores the ways in which formal media, whether sociopolitical or esthetic, distort human form. A collage of artwork and prose in which one of each pair of facing pages is Creeley's text and the other (not always the same side) a photograph of a Marisol sculpture, *Presences* continually shifts perspective, its radically different formal foci creating a sequence of discontinuous forms. Marisol's sculptures subject the human figure to nonbiological forms in a variety of ways: embedding body in geometrical blocks of wood, distorting body parts into geometric regularity or stamping them with stylized patterns, allowing the medium (e.g., woodgrain) to disrupt facial features, labeling people with numbers. From these forms, distinctly individual faces stare out with a range of expressions, from terror to worry, tooth-gritting preservation of appearances, and haunting melancholy. Sequencing the photographs from close-ups of parts of the sculptures framed as autonomous compositions to more distanced shots of the whole sculpture further decomposes the object into disorienting, radically discontinuous perspectives.

Creeley's text shows similar distortion. Composed of prose passages of varying length separated by a double space, it fills the page completely (there are no margins). Creeley's prose ranges from what might be loose ekphrasis or personal association inspired by the visual images to narrative.

Some of the concerns in the prose parallel Marisol's distortion of human form. Section titles are permutations of the numbers 1, 2, and 3, and character names shift between proper nouns and letters of the alphabet. Some passages explore the relation between social forms of behavior (from professions to family roles) and identity. Early passages meditate on the uniform as the form of the person who wears it and express paranoia about the intrusive presence of the police. Verbal form interferes with this political focus, however, generating odd conjunctions of thought, such as "*Fire delights in its form.* Firemen delight in their form? Inform us, policemen. . . . Firemen and snowmen share other fates, the one burning, the one melting."[34] While the word "form" drives the meditation, it raises questions about the relation between form and essence, information and influence, political and esthetic form, and grammatical structure and meaning. The text destroys "presence" as the illusion of continuous reality, dissolving the individual into profoundly decontextualized, discontinuous forms whose origins are unclear. Near but not full collage, *Presences* gestures at personal agency and artistic control, sometimes providing images of complete sculptures and nodes of narrative coherence. Because the idea of governing intention remains implicit, the absence of a visible agent controlling form becomes all the more sinister.

Presences does not sustain this radical dislocation, however. A short way into the last section (2.3.1 Five), with the phrase "The stories keep coming back," the prose coalesces into personal narrative or the meditation of a single voice. While the visual art remains disruptive in its abstraction, the narrative establishes a background or context for the images, creating a coherent semantic field that limits the images' range of meanings. This reemergence of personal voice forecasts Creeley's return to more personal voice and social orientation that anchors experimentation with language in his subsequent work. As the titles of his books from the 1980s and 1990s indicate (*Mirrors* [1983], *Memory Gardens* [1986], *Windows* [1987], *Echoes* [1993]), he no longer views poems as things or objects (as in *Words* and *Pieces*) but as traces, reflections, frames and pastoral arrangements of a world outside language. The epigraph to *Echoes*, taken from Coleridge's "Frost at Midnight," expresses this return to measuring self by an external world beyond linguistic form in the "idling Spirit / . . . every where / Echo or mirror seeking of itself."[35] Creeley's work of the last two decades explores personal identity as reflected back to him in multiple contexts, reestablishing language as a crucial element of self-definition in a circuit of social and natural experiences.

The transitional *Later* (1979) develops a range of ways that language gives form to experience and self in Creeley's subsequent writing. Poems set at shorelines, beaches, dawn, and dusk portray consciousness as an interface or frontier rather than an isolated structure. Recurrent images of decaying or abandoned edifices suggest the permeability of language to a world beyond it and the poem's emergence from entrapment in the formal structure of language. "The House," for example, opens the edifice of the poem to nature. The ruin's "crumbling stucco" and "debris" allow "spring / [to] come in at the windows" to "make / this song."[36] No longer a self-contained medium determining reality, architecture merely frames and channels natural process, which inspires the poet. In the same way, language becomes open and responsive to nature, conceived as one force in a field of experiences. Due in part to renewed connection to his body in love and aging, Creeley's return to the relation between physical experience and language leads him to portray both the body and language at times as potentially entrapping structures. These shifts of perspective reveal, however, the multiple points of view that relativize linguistic order and open new directions in his late poetry.

Poems about poetics in *Later* explore the relation between words and physical being anew. A three-poem sequence exemplifies Creeley's attention to the different roles of language in its experiential contexts. "For Pen," a love poem to Creeley's wife Penelope, roots the meaning and purpose of language in interpersonal relationships, the poem inspired by the desire to "sing this / weather"[37] that their life together creates. While in this poem language records interpersonal place or mood beyond the physical, the next poem shifts from social to sensual experience. Whereas *Pieces* accentuated the absurdity of analogy between words and objects, "Love" reintegrates language into sensual experience, savoring "words voluptuous / as flesh."[38] The third poem, "Erotica," undercuts this analogy but comically plays out the tension and desire that the discrepancies engender to construct human desire as both physical and linguistic. Describing the speaker's reaction to a scene in which torn pages of pornographic magazines litter a landscape that includes a dump and two mounds of dirt, the poem traces the way the desire that the pictures arouse leads the speaker to construct the landscape erotically. After contemplating frenzied embrace of the breast-like piles, Creeley leaves the poem suspended between the inadequate but titillating "paper shreds / . . . dirty pictures"[39] and the quite different "mystery" of the real body that the pictures cannot present. The pictures awaken a desire different from the desire for nature, indicated by the ambivalence of "dirty" as socially transgressive and smudged with unerotic literal dirt. Like the crumbling edifices elsewhere in *Later*, the torn pages dispel the illusion of art's completeness and invoke other forms of presence that words cannot capture. The interplay of multiple desires and the confusion that the speaker expresses suggest that the full range of art's meaning and pleasure is accessible only through the dynamic interaction of sensual, verbal, and social experience.

Formally eclectic, *Later* explores the wide variety of ways that language gives experience enduring form and defines the social context within which such forms are possible. The poems alternately track moment-by-moment perception in concrete images (such as the movement of sunlight on a wall), construct abstract word patterns to convey original feeling, and delight in storytelling, slang, and other forms of oral expression that realize self in community. Creeley's order and juxtaposition of the poems in *Later* accentuate the richly textured contrasts of these possibilities. As the poems return to "presence" as a continuum of experience, however, they define this context as intensely personal and individual, resisting the pressure to ground authenticity in new imperatives of political correctness and identity politics. Creeley preserves the fluid interaction of elements in the field by exploring the life of language in intimate community. Much like the Dorn of "abhorrences," Creeley mocks the authority of public language as unreal and empty. "News of the World" reduces the indignant catalogues of atrocity in the news to numbing unreality.[40] Poems like "Eddie" relish reproducing personal voice that includes ethnic or class markers but do not reduce individual style to socially representative identities.[41] Creeley's late poetry thus registers but resists formal entrapment in language as impersonal institution by recovering its uses in local communication and expression. Authenticity depends on the originality of a personal present against ready-made public expression.

The differences in the late work of Creeley, Dorn, Duncan, and Levertov are palpable, born of the political and social contexts they choose to address as well as the intensely personal experience of language for each. These differences have led poets and critics to question the common ground of their early association and identification as "Black Mountain" poets. The public debates Levertov and Dorn engage in the 1980s and 1990s compel them to attribute greater authority to forms of public discourse than do Creeley and Duncan. Levertov's Christian metaphysics and belief in the political importance of community consensus motivate her to establish greater coherence in her poetic forms, while her adherence to the sensual particular also sets her apart. If poetic tradition is a valuable source of inspiration and alternate community for Creeley, Duncan, and Levertov, it is especially important as an alternate community of meaning and inspiration for Duncan and Levertov. Creeley and Duncan experiment most fully with language as artifice, yet the significance of this artifice is different for each. Duncan's experience of language as an articulation of cosmic order gives poetic form a symbolic and spatial dimension as part of a metaphysical totality. In contrast, Creeley's constant awareness of time and of the ephemeral nature of experience against the artificial stasis of language leads him to accentuate the paradoxes involved in giving verbal form to experience and all that such creation leaves out. Despite these differences, field poetics, with its modeling of multiple roles for language in different experiential contexts and the varied, open forms that this fluidity can generate, remains a common element in the work of Creeley, Duncan, and Levertov and differentiates them from the more restricted, often more unified or monolithic contexts of community and form articulated by the next generation.

2

Dorn's enraged satire intensifies the power imbalance between public and private voice in the force field that strained late Black Mountain poetry and spurred younger poets to develop other responses to the power of public institutions, including language. The criticism, from cool reception to outraged attack, that his work has received from poets writing both from a Romantic or Modernist Olsonian legacy and from the experimental focus of Language poetry indicates his location at a fault line in poetic culture after the early 1970s. His insistence on working at the intersection of the individual and the collective conceived as radically disjoint while asserting a raw sense of personal responsibility in a system whose agency seems to deny the individual power has become intolerable to most writers. Speaking of the community of writers drawn to the experimental techniques that came to be classified as Language poetry in the late 1970s, Lyn Hejinian writes, "We discovered each other in the intense aftermath of the Vietnam war era, having had intense experience of institutions and disguised irrationality. And by some coincidence, we all individually had begun to consider language itself as an institution of sorts, determining reasons, and we had individually begun to explore the implications of that."[42] While the Language poets are not the only group to engage the Black Mountain legacy, they are typical in their heightened awareness of institutional power and language as institutions. Younger poets tend to develop new strategies to insulate individual or local usage from institutional and to articulate their poetics in terms that depart from the fluid interaction of these public and private agents characteristic of Black Mountain field poetics.

The reception and influence of Duncan and Creeley exemplify this generational shift. De Villo Sloan maps the changing poetic landscape in his analysis of the 1984 San Francisco Bay Area "poetry war" over a Black Mountain legacy. Sloan recounts the origin of the argument in a public debate between Duncan and Barrett Watten over how to interpret Zukofsky. Because Duncan saw language as one tool among many that human beings fashion to express their evolving comprehension of a transcendent reality, he read Zukofsky's formal orderings as contributions to a cosmos beyond the limits of language. Such an ideal dimension of reference involves poetic manipulation of language in an imaginative restructuring of human reality and ultimately of cosmic community. Watten in contrast perceived language as an isolated system that absorbs the individual. He thus interpreted Zukofsky's poetry as disintegrating into separate discursive structures that reflect dominant institutional realities and their power.[43] This view disrupts the connection between poetic creation and reception, for the opacity and power of language as collective institution waylays any attempt at direct communication.

For Sloan, both factions trace their poetics in part to Black Mountain predecessors, but with different emphasis. One group, represented by David Levi Strauss, sees its poetic forms as belonging to a tradition of Whitman, Williams, the Beats, and the Black Mountain poets and emphasizes the authenticity of spoken language and the body and nature as the source of prophetic vision—both social and natural—articulated in language. For these poets, language remains a powerful tool of self-consciousness capable of registering and transforming a multitude of forces in an evolving cosmos. The other, represented by Watten, traces its origin to Black Mountain techniques, particularly the verbal and formal experimentation of Duncan and Creeley, and to European avant-garde art and poststructuralist theory. For these writers, poetry works within language as a self-contained institution that determines social reality without external reference.

Creeley's work has inspired similar double readings. Focusing on *Pieces*, Bob Perelman argues that Creeley's "insistence on self-presence does not preclude awareness of grammar and lineation" and can be read as an intersection of "personal narrative" and "elemental deconstruction." He thus places Creeley's use of language on the threshold of language as medium of personal expression and language as impersonal, self-enclosed system. For Charles Bernstein, Creeley's fragmented structures stem not from ideological convictions about language but from nostalgia for a lost self whose melancholy and instability he does not "celebrate." Bernstein sees Creeley's use of language as grounded in a biographically based "lack of self-possession." Bernstein argues that the desire for unified, stable self informs Creeley's explorations of his poetic subject matter. Although Creeley records the movement of thought from one linguistic structure to another as disrupting the self powerfully enough to prevent its unified articulation, he also registers the distortion of language by the external presences of self, nature, and history.[44] Bernstein's reading accentuates the difference in generational perceptions of language, illustrating the emergence of a stronger sense of the institutional character of language that erodes the Black Mountain understanding of the poem as tracking multiple forces in the force field.

A younger generation of Language poets reads Creeley through a conception of language as a self-enclosed institution like that outlined by Watten in his revision of Zukofsky and Duncan. Watten and Leslie Scalapino interpret Creeley's construction of self as the maneuvering of a fundamentally indeterminate personal energy behind conventional constructions or discourses. Watten reduces reference to any quantum self as an "autobiographical frame," a generic or cultural construction of self separate from any sense of personal history. For Watten, " 'The person' I speak of thus is—it has historically become—a system of feedback," autobiography merely "the work's framing." Watten emphasizes the dissolution of the person into prior social discourses in "Robert Creeley and 'The Person.'"[45] While Scalapino traces a tension in *For Love* between actual marriage and the idealized roles of the courtly love tradition, she posits "serial" writing in which thought chains from generic structure to structure without orientation to a coherent self. What she calls "[t]he mind's patterns" in "serial thinking" are "not static personality creation *because* it is only that movement." For her, the emptying of conventional reference is not loss but liberation of the mind's own space, "a very free area of deciding what to create."[46]

Both of these revisions of Black Mountain poetics depart from field poetics' location of the poem at the interface of individual imagination and collective institution and from the ambitious public role of poetry as shaper of cultural institutions that such a poetics implies. Some poets who transform field poetics resemble Levertov in denying the power of mass culture, conceiving global as well as local culture on the model of face-to-face community. Burton Hatlen demonstrates how Theodore Enslin, for example, allies himself with "the local ground," transforming his relation with his environment and his reader into an I-thou relation that makes everything familiar.[47] Enslin follows Olson's use of the force field to map the interconnection of person, polis, and geographical place but restricts this mapping to his local Maine community. He strips away conceptions of identity imported by mass institutions that do not emerge directly from individuals' daily relations in order to recover the immediate, mutually responsive identities that emerge in local relationships. Although Enslin's poems serve as models of polis, they do not attempt to engage or transform national or mass culture. Enslin remains deliberately local, publishing with local presses and not seeking a widespread audience.

Many of the nature poets with whom Levertov expressed affinity in the 1990s (Hayden Carruth, Sam Hamill, Sam Green) translate field poetics into a similar ecopoetics that nurtures local community and resists the intervention of culture beyond the local. In Levertov's words, they "intend to fit themselves into the place they have come to, modestly, rather than planning to impose their wills upon it. The covenant is with the spirit of the place as well as with one another."[48] The force field continues to provide a useful model for portrayal of nature, culture, and self as forces in the intimate interdependence of local interaction. Levertov's poetry and poetics of empathetic community both influence and parallel the emergence of poetries of ethnic and gender minority and their identity politics. Like the work of the nature writers she mentions above, these poetries tend to restore the idea of culture and the generation of linguistic meaning as local in order to resist the dominant culture. Levertov students like Jimmy Santiago Baca describe their ethnic cultures on the model of the local village resisting mass culture. Conceiving of their poetry as testimony of minority or politically embattled cultures often motivates different formal concerns than those of field poetics, such as how to incorporate collective forms or individual expressions as representative of solidarity to give form and voice to an emerging culture. Their work thus forms a bridge between the political concerns of field poetics and emerging minority literatures, signaling the new constellations of community that replace those of the New American Poetry and shape the legacy of its counterculture.

Against such debunking of mass culture to express a more authentic local and interpersonal generation of cultural and linguistic meaning, the Language poets preserve the freedom to transform the imagination by focusing on its independent materiality as impersonal medium or institution. The conception of language as impersonal institution grounds the Language poets' revision of Olson's field poetics. Four essays from the symposium "The Politics of the Referent," published in 1977 in a theoretical supplement to the L=A=N=G=U=A=G=E journal, illustrate this transformation of field poetics to define an emerging L=A=N=G=U=A=G=E poetics. In these essays, Steve McCaffery, Bruce Andrews, Ron Silliman, Ray DiPalma, and Charles Bernstein discuss language as a highly structured institution isolated from other aspects of experience. Whereas Duncan writes of poetic language as charged with cosmic energy—"language that becomes so excited that it is endlessly creative of message"[49]—McCaffery writes of language not as a force among others in the dynamic force field of reality but as a Saussurian system of signs whose materiality and inner order alone generate poetic meaning.

Refracting "Projective Verse" through a poststructuralist understanding of language as a self-contained sign system, McCaffery revises Olson's concept of the poem as energy transferred and Duncan's fluid "circuit" of language and experience to emphasize the "kinetics of mask"[50] that separates language as institution from direct personal expression or dynamic interaction with environment. McCaffery proposes a significant extension of Olsonian field theory in projective verse from the sense of the poem as occupying a mediate position as energy field, supplied by the writer and drawn from by the reader, to the concept of the poem as a rotating energy source, a translative construct in which the written text is subject to re-writing in reading, thereby refracting the energy present.[51]

Whereas Olson envisions language as a medium transferring energy from one external source to another, McCaffery's language in itself is the source of the poem's energy. The "rotating" energy field implies a self-generated energy circulating within the poem to transform authorial intent into something very different for the reader. Whereas McCaffery sees energy in "projective verse" as transferred in a close relation between writer and reader—a context for the poem that Olson reflects in the *Maximus Poems* and that Creeley, Duncan, and Levertov continue in the familiar implied audience of their poetry through the early 1960s—McCaffery attributes the primary creative energy to the written text, deemphasizing the situation of writer and reader as part of the context in which the poem's meaning emerges. As collective institution independent of its individual users, language becomes an opaque substance that interferes in individual communication, generating meanings radically different from individual intention. Like a mask, the medium alters its user's identity, concealing personal authenticity behind its surface.

A first wave of Language poets transformed Olson's cosmic field into a linguistic field or system—a word they come to prefer to field—in which meaning is removed from the flexibility of familiar, spoken usage in local community. Such a view of language as independent material reflected its status as a mass medium imposing its reality rather than a local medium whose meaning is negotiated in individual usage and spoken communication. The other images these four poets invoke to describe language reinforce this perception of poetic language as a self-contained linguistic field rather than one force in a larger force field of reality. Both Andrews and McCaffery see language as an isolated (though inexhaustible, indeterminate, infinitely complex) entity, on the analogy of the Möbius strip or Klein form. Ron Silliman's conceptualization of the social context of language analogous to that of the commodity in capitalist culture reinforces such solipsistic isolation. For Silliman, language is a product of the modern condition initiated by writing. Like the fetishized commodity, whose alienation from the means of production establishes new values severed from those of labor or use value, language in a culture of writing acquires a new life as independent medium. It loses the immediacy of speech and gesture in local communication, where face-to-face contact determines verbal meaning.[52] While some Language poets explored different conceptions of the poet-audience relation through ethnopoetics,[53] the fetishization of language as divorced from its origins in experience dominated their analysis of poetry and language in their own, capitalist culture.

It would be reductive to divide the Black Mountain legacy into exclusive focus on either individual or collective agency. Many poets of the next generation have diverged from the legacies suggested by Levertov and Dorn. Ronald Johnson draws on Zukofsky to elaborate formal artifices that insulate language from conventional usage and enable visionary transformation of his world. His mystical strain resembles Duncan's exploration of multiple kinds of form—biological, mathematical, architectural, literary, linguistic—as clues to harmony that the poet can discover in cultural inheritance and by extension in the world. Artifice becomes the source of form in a force field that includes as many branches of knowledge as Olson's. Johnson's epic *ARK* announces greater separation of art from the world than Duncan's *Passages*, his insulation of artistic structure against flood-like chaos representative of the formal concerns of many of his contemporaries. Kathleen Fraser traces ways that various women writers have transformed Olson's force field into an experimental space of the blank page to articulate a new feminist consciousness.[54] Finally, the fairly coherent movement of Language writing has branched into different forms since the 1980s, transforming a wide range of "Black Mountain" techniques, as in Susan Howe's career-long engagement of Olson's conception of the forces shaping the polis and its cultural tradition, Watten's and Silliman's critiques of the ideological implications of grammar, and Steve McCaffery's black humor and experiments with phonetic generation of meaning in performance poetry.

Christopher Beach's analysis of "poetic culture" since the 1980s (c. 1985–95) helps to explain this dispersal of field poetics and of the Black Mountain legacy into new formal and social configurations of poetry in the next generation. Beach describes U.S. poetry of the 1980s and 1990s as poised "between community and institution,"[55] between local performance and academic genre or style. While slam poetry generates specific community meaning ephemerally bound to the performance context, poetry that claims to transcend such immediacy is nurtured in university workshop poetry, which claims the universality of a confessional "scenic" I only by removing specific political context.[56] Beach calls attention to a fragmentation of poetic culture noted by other critics, among them Burton Hatlen, Geoff Ward, and Susan Vanderborg.[57] While savvier in its awareness of the institutions producing its constructions of identity, Language poetry is also produced and consumed largely in the academic institution. In contrast to little magazines of the New American Poetry like *Evergreen* and *Yugen*, which sought large-scale distribution and emulated the format of such national magazines as *Time* and *Life*,[58] Language poetry as well as slam poetries are local, consciously written for a small, often like-minded community of readers.[59] Both the innovations of the next generation of poets and the public spheres they address express the perception of a reduced public reach of poetry.

The development of field poetics in the careers of the five Black Mountain poets discussed here helps us to understand this changing institutional status of post–World War II American poetry. The belief in the fluid interaction between poetic and public voice and the corresponding claim for the public authority of poetry form the common ground that united the Black Mountain poets during their strong friendships and made the force field such a varied, productive model of poetic structure for their work. Where such claims for the ease of transaction between language and experience and for social role of poetic language can make Black Mountain poetry seem dated, they reveal an awareness and innocence of the potential of art in mass culture nearly inconceivable for the previous or the next generation. Although each perceives the interfaces between experience and language and between individual and social differently, the fluidity of interaction leads to richly varied work that emerges from the refusal to reduce language to a single scene, ideological context, or structure. In addressing his native Gloucester as prophet critiquing culture and guiding the way to a new culture, Olson makes claims for the authority of poetic vision that seem excessive today. Duncan's search for the key to history in etymology and aural correspondences in language and his attempt to construct new cultural-cosmic orders through language manipulation now seem exaggerated claims for the power of poetic language to change our understanding of reality and to influence public thought.

These poets' transformations of field poetics reflect their perception of a changing relation between poetic and public language. The heady power of a growing counterculture, its expansion due to some extent to new mass media (from the mimeograph that enabled self-publishing to news reporting of activist events)[60] inspires them to bid for poetry as a powerful force for social change and thus to create poetic forms that they believe will speak to a large public arena. While the development of field poetics in each poet's work helps us to understand how he or she perceives authoritative voice in the counterculture's increasingly massified public sphere, the group's work as a whole reveals the increasing tension between poetic and public language. The openness and vulnerability of poetry to this public culture has made the pretension to communication with a large audience seem impossible for many poets since, marginalizing the public presence of poetry and leading poets to develop new forms to preserve originality. The Black Mountain struggle to construct public voice remains an important element of the New American Poetry, for it reveals the images of public voice and authority to which other subcultures also respond, whether directly or indirectly.[61] In developing the force field as a record of social forces influencing the poet, these Black Mountain poets reveal the public life of language as a crucial element shaping post–World War II poetic form in all its idiosyncrasies and power.

Reference Matter

Notes

NOTES TO INTRODUCTION

1. Allen, "Preface," *The New American Poetry*, xii.

2. Olson, *Selected Writings*, 24–25.

3. While the Board of Fellows decided to dissolve the corporation in September 1956, Olson remained on site organizing activities until 1957. Harris, *Arts at Black Mountain*, 240.

4. See also Martin Duberman's *Black Mountain: An Exploration in Community*, which studies the institution as an example of the politics of self-government in a utopian community.

5. Other critics have defined different groupings. Maxine Combs's "A Study of the Black Mountain Poets" includes Olson, Creeley, and Duncan as major and Jonathan Williams, Ed Dorn, John Wieners, and Joel Oppenheimer as minor figures. In the last chapter of his book on Olson, Paul Christensen considers Olson's legacy in "Black Mountain poetry" as an extension and transformation of Imagism and includes Olson, Creeley, Duncan, Levertov, Blackburn, a group of "poets on the fringe," and the "Black Mountaineers," or poets who were students at the college. Christensen, *Charles Olson*. Later studies tend to group the poets differently. See, for example, Willard Fox's *Robert Creeley, Ed Dorn, and Robert Duncan* and Ekbert Faas's *Towards a New American Poetics*, which includes Olson, Creeley, Duncan, Allen Ginsberg, Gary Snyder, and Robert Bly. Allen's anthology does not include the Deep Image poets, who formed a significant voice in the poetic debate through which the Black Mountain poets and others defined their poetic views. Edward Foster's *Understanding the Black Mountain Poets* includes Olson, Creeley, and Duncan.

6. Golding, "New American Poetry," 180–211.

7. Blackburn, "The Grinding Down," 16.

8. Olson, *Mathologos*, 2: 71.

9. Creeley, in discussion with author, December 1989. Creeley's 1969 retrospective "The Black Mountain Review" reinforces this point, describing the *Origin* community that led to the founding of the *Black Mountain Review* as united

by its feeling of "distance" from the conventional poetry magazines of the time. Creeley also identifies several different "kinds of contributor." Creeley, *Collected Essays*, 507, 509–10.

10. While Allen's preface to the anthology acknowledges that his groupings are "[o]ccasionally arbitrary and for the most part more historical than actual," "justified finally only as a means to give the reader some sense of milieu and to make the anthology a more readable book," it also proposes a shared poetics for these poets: "Olson's 'Projective Verse' essays and his letter to Elaine Feinstein present the dominant new double concept: 'composition by field' and the poet's 'stance toward reality.' " Allen, "Preface," *The New American Poetry*, xiii–xiv.

11. Byrd, "Possibility of Measure," 50.

12. For analysis of this characteristic of the New American poets, see Rifkin, *Career Moves*, 7; Davidson, *Guys Like Us*, 30–48.

13. Fredman, *Grounding of American Poetry*, 22–23.

14. Paul, *olson's push*; Faas, "Charles Olson and D. H. Lawrence," 121; Faas, *New American Poetics*, 11. Enikó Bollobás focuses on a similar recording of experiential process. Bollobás, *Charles Olson*, 18. While Stephen Fredman emphasizes the construction of nature as the ground for culture more strongly than Paul and Faas, he still places the Black Mountain poets in the American Romantic tradition of nature poetry, a context I find complementary to, not exclusive of, mine. Fredman, *Grounding of American Poetry*. Fredman and Lynn Keller recognize that meditation on nature leads not only to natural rhythms but also to the distinction of mental and natural rhythm. Keller perceives nature as the model of open-ended flux but also observes that Creeley's early verse follows Olson's lineation and tendency to abstract proclamation. Keller, *Re-Making It New*, 138, 257–58. For Von Hallberg, the theory of the force field erodes the world of discrete sense objects, leading poets to reject the closed order of conventions of referential syntax. Von Hallberg, *Charles Olson*, 188–89.

15. Golding's *From Outlaw to Classic* and Rifkin's *Career Moves* are other relevant examples. The resonance of such Black Mountain formal concerns with the work of poets outside the Black Mountain circle and with the emergence of Postmodern genres or forms makes them an important focus for study. Analyzing other poets (e.g., Elizabeth Bishop, John Ashbery), Keller and Charles Altieri argue that open form records the process of experience, the only basis for form in the field's flux. Joseph Conte attributes the open-ended "serial" and "procedural" forms of the Postmodern long poem to this sense of flux. Bollobás, *Charles Olson*, 18; Altieri, *Self and Sensibility*, 139; Keller, *Re-Making It New*, 139, 257–58; Conte, *Unending Design*, 3ff. See also Peter O'Leary's reading of Duncan in a visionary tradition from H. D. to Nathaniel Mackey (*Gnostic Contagion*).

16. The body of primary resources and historical studies (memoirs, correspondence, biographies) is growing. See, for example, Fielding Dawson's *The Black*

Mountain Book, Michael Rumaker's *Robert Duncan in San Francisco*, Olson's correspondence with *Origin* editor Cid Corman, Golding's work on the negotiation behind the scenes of Don Allen's *The New American Poetry*, the William Carlos Williams–Levertov correspondence, and the Duncan-Levertov correspondence. Critical biographies include Tom Clark's *Charles Olson*, *Robert Creeley and the Genius of the American Commonplace* and *Ed Dorn*; Faas and Maria Trombacco's of Robert Creeley; and Ellingham and Killian's of Jack Spicer and his Berkeley–San Francisco circle.

Monographs on individual Black Mountain poets de-emphasize the importance of the group and place the poets in different traditions based on thematic issues. More recent studies of 1950s poetry, such as Edward Brunner's *Cold War Poetry* and Davidson's *Guys Like Us*, analyze identity formation and the role of poetic institutions across a broad spectrum of poets to dissolve boundaries not only among the "New American" subcultures but also between these and other contemporary poetry subcultures such as the "Confessional" and "Black Nationalist" poets. While Alan Golding's *From Outlaw to Classic* and Libbie Rifkin's *Career Moves* have begun to analyze ideologies shaping canonization of the period, they focus respectively on the wider counterculture of the New American Poetry and on individual poets.

17. DuPlessis and Quartermain, "Foreword," *The Objectivist Nexus*.

18. Anderson, *Imagined Communities*, 6.

19. See Golding, *From Outlaw to Classic*; Golding, "New American Poetry."

20. Rifkin, *Career Moves*, 58.

21. Spicer's biographers describe the party, citing Helen Adam's memory: "All present felt implicated in Spicer's message." Ellingham and Killian, *Poet Be Like God*, 123–37. Davidson, *Guys Like Us*, 44–45.

22. Rifkin, *Career Moves*, 20–25.

23. In studying this social emphasis in "composition by field," I follow other social interpretations of field poetics like those of Cary Nelson and Paul Breslin. Whereas these critics focus on the message of the poets' shared resistance to cultural oppression, I analyze the ways in which changing perceptions of the public sphere open to poetry generated new conceptions of creative agency and new poetic forms. This social interpretation of Black Mountain poetry complements other arguments for the sociopolitical origins of open form. Nelson argues that open form involves "a desire for freedom from both poetic tradition and social constraint" and emphasizes openness as a Whitmanic openness of poetic voice to the democratic community. Nelson, *Our Last First Poets*, 10, 99. For Nelson, this effort to identify with social rather than natural totality strained open form poetry as the poet assumed the violence and evil in the body politic during the Vietnam War. Michael André Bernstein's analysis of the Modernist and emergent Postmodern epic argues a novelistic inclusiveness that led to fragmentation and

lack of closure in Pound and Williams and stretched the poet's creation of a national poem to near formlessness in Olson's *Maximus Poems*. Bernstein, *Tale of the Tribe*, 10, 16, 273–76. Breslin's *The Psycho-Political Muse* attributes the view of poetry as a means for liberating consciousness from social repression to the allegiance of the New Left's political analysis with depth psychology (for example, in Marcuse) to dissolve the boundary between public and private and reveal the vulnerability of the self to social regulation. Breslin, *The Psycho-Political Muse*, xiii, 5, 43.

24. Beach, *Poetic Culture*.

25. Herring, "Frank O'Hara's Open Closet," 414–27.

26. By public sphere, I refer to what Seyla Benhabib, building on Jürgen Habermas, calls "discursive public space" in which ideas can be discussed. Benhabib, "Models of Public Space," 73.

27. Davidson, *Guys Like Us*, 52.

28. Breslin, *From Modern to Contemporary*, 16ff.

29. Olson, *Selected Writings*, 24.

30. See, for example, Creeley's much-quoted statement: "Coming of age in the forties, in the chaos of the Second World War, one felt the kinds of coherence that might have been fact if other time and place were no longer possible. There seemed no logic, so to speak, that could bring together all the violent disparities of that experience." Creeley, *Was That a Real Poem*, 74.

31. See the disintegration into savagery and rape of the relation between an unmarried rich couple unable to confront their unwanted pregnancy in Douglas Woolf's "The Kind of Life We've Planned"; Irene Dayton's "A Woman Leaves Her Marriage"; and treatments of madness in Kenneth Rexroth's "Artaud" and Robert Hellman's "The Quay."

32. See, for example, poems by Eberhart and Bronk in *Origin* 2.

33. *Origin* 11 (1953) is devoted to the New French writing and *Origin* 12 (1954) to the New German.

34. Enslin, "Sea Lavender," 127. See also Bronk, "Aspects of the World Like Coral Reefs," 115–16; Levertov, "The Shifting," 114; Creeley, "The Innocent," *Origin* 6, 117. One must be careful in viewing Corman's editorial selections as reflecting Black Mountain concerns, but Olson and Creeley were strenuously involved in the selection and format of the magazine, as their correspondence shows.

35. See, for example, Olson, "Purgatory Blind," *Collected Poems*, 3; Levertov, "Poem," *Collected Earlier Poems*, 7; Duncan, "Toward the Shaman," *The Years As Catches*, 6ff.; Creeley, "Poem for Beginners," *Collected Poems*, 9.

36. Seymour-Smith, "Where is Mr. Roethke?" 40–41, 45; Corman, review of Karl Shapiro's *Collected Poems*, 55. Corman, "Editorial comment," 69; Corman, "Editorial comment," 233ff.

37. Engelhardt, *End of Victory Culture*, 117, 184, 242–43.

38. Ball, "Politics of Social Science," 79–92; McCann, "The Imperiled Republic," 293–336.

39. Nelson, *Pursuing Privacy*, xi, 26. Other critics emphasize different kinds of continuities. Morris Dickstein and Dominick Cavallo emphasize the ways in which the social affluence and mobility of the 1950s led to unrealistic idealism and eventual disillusionment concerning the "American Dream." Dickstein, *Leopards in the Temple*; Cavallo, *A Fiction of the Past*.

40. Melley, *Empire of Conspiracy*, 14.

41. See, for example, Davidson, *Guys Like Us*, 197.

42. Habermas, *Structural Transformation,* 140, 214–18; Brown, *Politics Out of History*, 3–5.

43. Brunner, *Cold War Poetry,* 159, 254.

44. Ibid., 1–13.

45. DeKoven, *Utopia Limited,* 36–51.

46. Dewey, "Open Form and Collective Voice," 47–66.

NOTES TO CHAPTER 1

1. According to Ian Bell, "[t]he physics of the nineteenth century [the field theories of Faraday and Clerk Maxwell] achieved literally the dissolution of 'the solid seeming block of matter.'" Bell, *Critic as Scientist*, 127. Stephen Kern describes a similar phenomenon: "If there is no clear distinction between the plenum of matter and the void of space and if matter may be conceived as a configuration of energy alignments, then the traditional understanding of matter as made up of discrete bits with sharply defined surfaces must also be rejected." Kern, *Culture of Time and Space*, 183. Bell also describes Pound's use of science to conceive the work of art as material and thereby to give it substance in a world where worth is measured by material commodities. Bell, *Critic as Scientist*, 225–28.

A variety of writers attempted to imagine this new reality and use theories of the force field to analyze social force and process. Ronald E. Martin emphasizes the "nonempirical" and therefore "arbitrary" and "essentially figurative" character of force. Martin, *Universe of Force*, xiv. Martin traces a tradition of the social significance of the force field in the United States, from the scientific historians influenced by Herbert Spencer through naturalist writers like Frank Norris and Theodore Dreiser. Michele Pridmore-Brown shows how images derived from the new physics and electromagnetic waves and their technological applications, particularly the gramophone and radio, were used to imagine the dissolution of the independently thinking individual into a controlled, deliberately responding crowd under fascism. Her study of how this theory of fascist propaganda affects Virginia Woolf's conception of the artist as political agent analyzes another social application of the field image. Pridmore-Brown, "1939–40," 413–14. Pound advocates a similar social application, recognizing Gaudier-Brzeska's assertion that the vortex represents the energy of a particular people or culture, as culture morphology. Pound, *Gaudier-Brzeska*, 22–23, 142.

Zukofsky, in a poem in the "Anew" section (1935–44) of *ALL*, struggles to imagine the field by bending natural images perceived by the senses into appropriate metaphors for these invisible forces: "It's hard to see but think of a sea / Condensed to a speck. / And there are waves— / Frequencies of light / Others that may be heard. / The one is one sea, the other a second." Louis Zukofsky, *ALL: collected short poems*, 90. Both the pun on "see" and "sea" and the different kinds of "waves" dissolve the apparent referentiality of language. The perceived discontinuity of the scientific and phenomenal worlds no longer resolvable into a single system of language led Zukofsky to describe himself as a child in need of education, a stance that echoes Henry Adams's confession of his continual need for reeducation in the face of rapid social and scientific change in *The Education of Henry Adams*. Zukofsky's notes to the poem further identify the analogous processes of capitalist exchange and hidden rotation of magnetic force as the sources of a similarly abstract poem from the same period. The movement toward abstract or nonreferential uses of language is thus associated with the representation of social forces inaccessible to the senses. (For a fuller tracing of Zukofsky's borrowings from Henry Adams, see Quartermain, "Not at All Surprised," 203–25.)

Like Kern and Bell for the Modernists, Robert von Hallberg argues that the field's erosion of the world of sense objects leads open form poets to reject the seemingly referential order of conventional syntax. Von Hallberg, *Charles Olson*, 188–89. Don Byrd traces references to field theory in phenomenology in *Charles Olson's* Maximus, 94–95. Paul Christensen discusses the influence of field theory through Whitehead's view of "the material universe as an infinite field of particles" in *Charles Olson*, 138ff.

2. In applying the scientific model of the force field to society, Brooks and Henry Adams embrace a theory of "scientific history" prevalent in the United States in the late nineteenth and early twentieth centuries. Martin outlines the development of "scientific history" as a movement in American historiography and Henry Adams's response to it. Martin, *Universe of Force*, 97–106.

3. The following instances of other contemporary poets' uses of the field are less central in the development of each poet's thought. In *Spring and All* (1923), William Carlos Williams echoes Pound's interpretation of the force field in *Gaudier-Brzeska* to defend abstract or nonreferential use of language that liberates words and thought from their conventional patterns of meaning: "Sometimes I speak of imagination as a force, an electricity, or a medium, a place . . . its effect is . . . to liberate the man to act in whatever direction his disposition leads." Williams, *Imaginations*, 150. Like Pound, Williams changes his view of the field in the later 1930s. Williams wrote of charge and energy as social rather than individual powers, describing society as "the cyclotron of the times" during World War

II: "the poet's subject is not man so much as man as he is the product of the time . . . , and this "thing" which makes new sallies into time." Williams, *Selected Essays*, 242. Although Williams's use of the image of the field in "The Poem as a Field of Action" (1948), with its call for a new poetics based on Einstein's theory of relativity and the volatility of radioactive matter, may have inspired Olson and Creeley to develop "composition by field," Williams's explanation of the image and its significance is fairly superficial. His interpretation may be derived from Zukofsky's interpretation of the force field as an image for relative, context-bound rather than absolute measure in his writings of the 1930s.

Although most Objectivists did not use the image of the field explicitly in their poetics, they were aware of it. Mary Oppen wrote that she and George Oppen took Henry Adams's *Mont St. Michel and Chartres* (1904) with them to France in 1929 and describes the strong impression Adams's theory of history made on them. Mary Oppen, *Meaning A Life*, 134. Further, George Oppen's writings show a transformation of the Imagist dictum "direct representation of the thing" to reveal the social context and genesis of the thing as processual and positional rather than as a discrete identity in the force field. His *Discrete Series* (1934) represents the social machinery of "big Business" behind the description of the "Frigidaire" in terms of Imagist concrete and geometrical qualities. George Oppen, *Collected Poems*, 4.

Tom Sharp and Michael Davidson also analyze the Objectivists' adaptation of Imagist techniques to social themes. Sharp notes the ironic application of these techniques to artificial and decorative rather than natural objects. For Sharp, the economic hardships of the Depression forced poets to justify the value of art and influenced the Objectivists' unique combination of relevance and self-referentiality, the poetics of art as independent thing and socially relevant commentary. Sharp, "Objectivists 1927–1934," 155, 519. For Davidson, Objectivism "also attempts to address the social and economic costs of "modernization as it was experienced in the 1930s" in the tension between formal accomplishments and modernization's implied social "discourse of mastery." Davidson, "Dismantling 'Mantis,'" 521–22, 528.

4. In tracing this reception, I am concerned not with direct influence (the extent and direction of influence between Zukofsky and Olson being matter for debate among both poets and critics) but with these poets' responses to persistent issues for which the field becomes a focus. Olson mentioned Zukofsky in his record of conversations with Pound in 1945–46, but the references are brief, primarily concerning Pound's mention of Zukofsky as a friend and Zukofsky's Jewishness in relation to Pound's general perception of Jews. Although Olson mentioned Pound's performance of the "Yiddish Charleston" written for Zukofsky, Olson gives no evidence of having read the poem and does not express interest in *The Objectivist Anthology* (1932) in which it appeared. Olson, qtd. in Catherine

Seelye, *Charles Olson & Ezra Pound*, 37, 66, 79. This history does not exclude the possibility that Olson was familiar with Zukofsky's work, but it does indicate that Objectivism was not a topic of discussion with Pound and thus was probably not a part of the tradition that drew Olson to Pound at this time. As rector of Black Mountain College, Olson did try to hire Zukofsky in the early 1950s, apparently at the recommendation of Creeley and Duncan. The correspondence between Olson and Zukofsky is brief and treats mostly issues of publication, not poetics.

Zukofsky wrote in 1955 to Creeley that he did not know Olson but would probably like him because of Olson's association with Duncan, Creeley, and Jonathan Williams. Zukofsky to Creeley, November 17, 1955, Robert Creeley Papers, Department of Special Collections, University Libraries, Stanford University. Duncan wrote to Olson to inform him of the similarity between his and Zukofsky's concepts of body language. Duncan to Olson, August 19, 1954, Charles Olson Research Collection, Archives and Special Collections at the Thomas J. Dodd Research Center, University of Connecticut Libraries.

The first mention of Zukofsky in the Olson-Creeley correspondence is in Olson's letter of August 8, 1951 to Creeley and assumes Creeley's acquaintance with Zukofsky's work. Olson to Creeley, *Charles Olson and Robert Creeley*, 7: 75. The second, Olson's reference to Zukofsky's essay "Poetry (1952)," is brief. Zukofsky's essay developing Pound's concepts of melopoeia, phanopoeia, and logopoeia as the primary materials of poetry makes no mention of the field.

Olson's contact with Zukofsky seems to have been initiated by Creeley and Duncan in the mid-1950s. Duncan had been in correspondence with Zukofsky since 1947. (See, for example, Duncan's letter on the nature of Pound's ideogram. Duncan to Zukofsky, August 7, 1947, Robert Duncan Papers, Poetry Collection of the University Libraries, State University of New York at Buffalo. Creeley's letters from Zukofsky show that Creeley was interested in publishing Zukofsky's work at Black Mountain College's Divers Press. (See Creeley's early correspondence with Zukofsky, 1954–55, Robert Creeley Papers, Department of Special Collections, University Libraries, Stanford University.) For Olson's possible familiarity with some of Zukofsky's works circulated at Black Mountain College during Creeley's time there, in the summer of 1955, see Harris, *Arts at Black Mountain College*, 212.

Similarities between Olson's and Zukofsky's poetic interests are, nevertheless, striking. Celia Zukofsky noted that "Louie always felt that Olson's essay on Projective Verse was really a take-off on his own writings." Celia Zukofsky, qtd. in Terrell, "An Eccentric Profile," 73. In addition, both poets discuss poetic language as originating in the body. They share an interest in what happens between rather than in things in themselves and explore the organization of language into different spheres of discourse. I would argue that these similarities come not from direct knowledge of each other's work but from a common legacy of Pound and Williams.

5. Tom Clark documents Olson's increasing disillusionment with politics and growing belief that "[t]he modern artist could never be more than just another cog in the bureaucratic machine." Clark, *Charles Olson*, 83–94. Zukofsky experienced similar pessimism as World War II worsened. When he returned to *"A"* after the ten-year hiatus of 1938–48, he represented the overwhelming power of fascist mass culture as destructive of artistic epiphany and the artist's attempt to realize or represent it in history in *"A"*-10. Subsequent poems in *"A"* dematerialize language in order to create a space for private creation of meaning free of the destructive course of history.

6. Brooks Adams, *Theory of Social Revolutions*, 3. Although my discussion emphasizes the difference between Henry and Brooks Adams, both were ambivalent about the application of theories of force to history. Neither completely resolved the tension between individual agency and an impersonal theory of force. Brooks Adams recognizes that conceptions of truth and justice change according to social system and views these ideas as legitimating the power of the ruling class, but he argues that education should resist such self-serving conceptions of truth. For him, education in modern industrialized society should counter the specialized division of labor by teaching "a multitude of complex relations" and consequently responsibility for one's actions beyond class interest to the whole society. Brooks Adams, *Theory of Social Revolutions*, 213–17. Henry Adams wishes to return to the power of spiritual form he finds in thirteenth-century Christianity but perceives both the dynamo and capital as real forces influencing the course of modern history and his own career in the *Education*. Katherine Hayles's analysis of Henry Adams's dilemma as a historian applies to both brothers. For Hayles, Henry Adams was unsure whether the chaos he perceived in history resulted from his intellectual shortcomings or from the chaos of the external world to which he would as historian be "passive accomplice." Hayles, *Chaos Bound*, 82.

The Degradation of the Democratic Dogma (1919) records the brothers' discussion in Henry Adams's letters to his brother and Brooks's assessment of Henry's thought in his long introduction to the work, especially pp. 93ff. and 125–33. An edition by Brooks Adams of several of Henry's essays unpublished during his lifetime, the work includes a long introduction by Brooks Adams entitled "The Heritage of Henry Adams" and these essays by his brother.

7. Brooks Adams, *Theory of Social Revolutions*, 132 and *Civilization and Decay*, ix–x. Brooks Adams describes this purpose of the latter in "The Heritage of Henry Adams," *Democratic Dogma*, 109. His assertion that the ruling class presents the most powerful expression of natural force combines social theories of force with social Darwinism, another powerful nineteenth-century evolutionary model of history that sees individual survival as depending on the ability to adapt

to the current configuration of natural and social forces. Most of the writers I discuss do not distinguish between social and natural forces.

8. Brooks Adams, *Democratic Dogma*, 105–6.

9. Henry Adams to Brooks Adams, quoted in *Democratic Dogma*, 101.

10. Henry Adams, "A Letter to American Teachers of History," *Democratic Dogma*, 166.

11. Henry Adams, *Education of Henry Adams*, 428–29.

12. Henry Adams refers to "the whole mechanical consolidation of force, which ruthlessly stamped out the life of the class into which Adams [Henry] was born, but created monopolies capable of controlling the new energies that America adored." Henry Adams, *Education of Henry Adams*, 345.

13. In *Gaudier-Brzeska*, the fluidity and dynamism of Pound's vortex frees the image from representation of sensible objects and language from reference to the sensible world. Pound rejects imagistic concreteness, "copying or imitation of light on a haystack," for "a radiant node or cluster . . . a VORTEX, from which, and through which, and into which ideas are constantly rushing." *Gaudier-Brzeska* ends by citing Lawrence Binyon in support of abstraction: "FOR INDEED, IT IS NOT ESSENTIAL THAT THE SUBJECT-MATTER SHOULD REPRESENT OR BE LIKE ANYTHING IN NATURE; ONLY IT MUST BE ALIVE WITH A RHYTHMIC VITALITY OF ITS OWN." Pound, *Gaudier-Brzeska*, 88, 134.

14. Like many writers who apply theories of force to the human sciences, Pound (like Olson) uses force and energy interchangeably to indicate a natural vitality that animates consciousness as well as matter. For a discussion of the transition in the natural sciences from the concept of force as an identifiable, metaphysical absolute to that of energy as a mathematically quantifiable but qualitatively undefined measure based on such properties as heat and ability to perform work, see Berkson, *Fields of Force*, 131–36. Ronald Martin traces a similar history but demonstrates that writers in the humanities continued to use "force" to indicate what natural scientists define as energy. Martin, *Universe of Force*, 27.

15. Pound, *Make It New*, 351–52.

16. Pound seems to agree with Henry Adams's ideas but is angered by Adams's passivity and "effeminacy," which betray for Pound Adams's poor judgment of how to engage in the politics of his time. Pound, *Selected Prose,* 149; Pound, *"Ezra Pound Speaking,"* 75, 93.

17. Pound, *"Ezra Pound Speaking,"* 75, 93, 233.

18. Ibid., 265. See also 234.

19. Ibid., 307.

20. Pound, *Selected Prose,* 307.

21. Peter Nicholls argues that Pound rejects Marx due to a misreading of Marx's economics. Pound believes that Marx advocates rather than merely ana-

lyzes the phenomenon by which capital generates more capital through the accumulation of surplus value. Nicholls, *Ezra Pound*, 138–39.

22. Pound, *The Cantos*, 61.

23. Ibid., 250.

24. Ibid., 449, 519.

25. Ibid., 176.

26. Ibid., 76–79. Although the final image in "Canto XVII," that of the "[s]unset like the grasshopper flying," suggests that such ideal vision cannot be sustained in nature—only in an art that suspends disbelief—the image of nature reflected in the more enduring materials of art (stone and precious metal) suggests the possibility of full realization of paradise in the poem.

27. Ibid., 685–88.

28. For an explication of the concrete elements of some of Pound's key images, see Hong Sun's "Pound's Quest," 110–17.

29. Pound, *Cantos*, 425.

30. Ibid., 722.

31. For the role of the Adams family in *"A,"* see Ahearn, *Zukofsky's "A,"* 77ff.

32. Zukofsky, *"A,"* 106.

33. Ibid.

34. Ibid.

35. Ibid., 108.

36. Burton Hatlen argues that Marx's idea of the individual as *homo faber*, creator and not creature of history, resolves the tension present in *"A"* up to the second half of *"A"*-9 between "the shaping voice of art and the disintegrating voice of the sea of history." Hatlen, "Art and/as Labor," 234, 225. Quartermain and Davidson affirm Zukofsky's description of his unique rearrangement of historical materials as "fluorescence" (Quartermain) that makes the past new. Quartermain, "Not at All," 216–17, 225. Davidson, "Dismantling 'Mantis,'" 530–32. Byrd discusses the similar creation or "production" of meaning from the "whole visible body of language and its overt use by the tribe." In contrast to the others, Byrd emphasizes that Zukofsky resists grounding private vision in a metaphysical order and interprets it rather as creation "along the rift . . . in both private and public space." Byrd sees this quality as characteristic of Pound, Williams, Stein, Olson, and Duncan. He asserts the authenticity of speech, as opposed to writing, as these poets' solution to the influence of what he defines as the public language of writing. Byrd, "Poetry of Production," 33, 42. While I agree with Byrd that awareness of a difference between public and private language is central to these poets' creativity, I focus here on the active presence of the public in their voices. Mark Scroggins argues that "A"-9 reflects Zukofsky's shift from Marxist materialism and "gropings toward a thoroughly materialist modernism" to Spinoza's idealist influence. Scroggins, *Louis Zukofsky*, 30, 161.

37. Bruce Comens makes a similar argument that Zukofsky relinquishes authorial control of meaning to include chance correspondences as part of *"A"*'s design in "Soundings," 95. Comens's argument remains, however, on the formal level without relating chance to social forces.

38. Zukofsky, *Prepositions*, 57. Zukofsky's formulation alludes to Henry Adams's observation that modern man and woman have "married machinery" in *Education of Henry Adams*, 445–47.

39. Zukofsky, *Prepositions*, 55. Edward Schelb proposes a similarly violent production of self from a preexisting system of language. Building on Ahearn's observation that Zukofsky's form achieves a monstrous inversion of human and mechanical, Schelb argues that for Zukofsky the self too becomes a machine of words. Schelb, "The Exaction of Song," 341–42.

40. Pound calls in *The Spirit of Romance* for a "literary scholarship which will weigh Theocritus and Mr. Yeats with one balance, a scholarship based on the principle of 'standardization' which would thereby illustrate the contemporaneity of all ages." Pound, qtd. in Bell, *Critic as Scientist*, 28.

41. Zukofsky, *"A,"* 1. Even Zukofsky's presentation of the epiphany is not immediate. Although he presents the words of Christ's Passion directly, they are interspersed with the material reality of performers, concert hall, and audience, which produce and structure this particular experience of epiphany in music.

42. Zukofsky, *An "Objectivists" Anthology*, 205.

43. Zukofsky, *"A,"* 22.

44. Ibid., 23.

45. Ibid., 39.

46. See Pound, *ABC of Reading*, 37; Zukofsky, "Poetry (1952)," 49–54; and Zukofsky's observation that "Imagism and music direct the composition of the *Cantos*" but that Pound's craft is so great that this workmanship of "imagism-in-music" tends to pass unnoticed. Zukofsky, *Prepositions*, 75.

47. Zukofsky, *"A,"* 41.

48. Ibid., 60.

49. Olson, "Mystery of What Happens," TS, 1948–49, Charles Olson Research Collection, Archives and Special Collections at the Thomas J. Dodd Research Center, University of Connecticut, 20.

50. Ibid., 5.

51. Ibid., 18, 20.

52. Michael André Bernstein's *The Tale of the Tribe* interprets Olson's epic within a modernist tradition in which Williams and Pound open the epic to include history, a range of material typical of the novel, in order to encompass the collective world of modern society. Bernstein thus reads Olson's *Maximus Poems* as a looser version of *The Cantos* in their effort to include "the entire domain of public ideological utterances" (Bernstein, *Tale of the Tribe*, 230). Bernstein criti-

cizes Olson for being unable to maintain the critical distance from his sources necessary to synthesize his material and assume a didactic voice. It is precisely this
"looseness" that my analysis attempts to explain.

Von Hallberg similarly traces Olson's poetics as a response to Pound and
Williams, specifically as an effort to reconcile Pound's historical and ideal or psychological structure and Williams's structure grounded in place. Von Hallberg's
explanation of the result of this effort remains, however, on the level of philosophy, analyzing the interaction between subject and object structuring Olson's poetry. Von Hallberg, *Charles Olson*, 52–58. I will focus instead on the social origins
of the subject and object and on the larger cultural patterns informing them that
emerge from their interaction in Olson's poems.

Don Byrd, Sherman Paul, Ekbert Faas, and Paul Christensen emphasize Olson's break with this Modernist tradition, reading Olson in the context of the
"New American" poets whose works were anthologized in Donald Allen's anthology
The New American Poetry. In this context, they emphasize the effort to reintegrate
self, language, and culture into nature as what distinguishes Olson's poetics from that
of the other "New American" poets. Byrd understands Olson's polis as the "focus" of
the earth's natural energy. Byrd, "*Charles Olson's* Maximus," 24. Paul focuses on Olson's "ecological vision" of an ideal culture at one with nature. Paul, *olson's push*,
xviii. Faas links Olson's effort to those of Robert Bly, Allen Ginsberg, and Gary Snyder to recover a monism that avoids Cartesian dualism by seeing mind and nature as
one substance on the model of Chinese Buddhism. Faas, "Preamble," *Towards a New
American Poetics*, 25–27. For Christensen's view, see the last paragraph of footnote 1
of this chapter.

53. Charles Olson, *Selected Writings*, 24–25.

54. Ralph Maud records that Olson read Weil's "Beyond Personism" in *Cross
Currents* in Spring 1952 and "used [it] right away in some unpublished essays."
Maud also records that Olson was given John Pike Grady's 1956 edition of Weil's
"The Iliad; or The Poem of Force." Maud, *Charles Olson's Reading*, 282, 332. Olson probably first read Weil's essay in *Politics* in 1945 or in the pamphlet form advertised in subsequent issues of the journal (1947). The ideas from Weil
mentioned in the draft essay that became "Projective Verse" and his unpublished
1952 essay "Culture and Revolution" (Charles Olson Research Collection, Archives
and Special Collections at the Thomas J. Dodd Research Center, University of
Connecticut) also correspond to those in her essays published in *Politics*, particularly
"Factory Work."

55. Weil, *Simone Weil*, 163. Miles reprints Mary McCarthy's translation, published in *Politics*.

56. Weil, *Simone Weil*, 175.

57. Many aspects of Olson's "The Mystery of What Happens When It Happens" reflect conceptions of the physical dimensions of human life presented in

Weil's articles in *Politics*: his desire to eliminate "metaphysical" and "spiritual" "veils" of dogma that obscure the origins in physical experience of human imagination of divinity, his focus on the crucifixion as an extension of Greek sensibility, and his awareness of time as a dimension of experience formed by such cultural forces as labor and religion.

58. Although Weil, like Brooks Adams, does not distinguish force as specifically natural or social but rather describes it as an impersonal fate, she does discuss society as an interplay of forces on the model of the physical force fields. Classes within a nation and nations in the international context exert pressure on each other and seek equilibrium. Weil, "Words and War," 71, 73.

59. Olson, "Mystery of What Happens," 4–5.

60. Ibid., 3–5.

61. Ibid., 8.

62. Ibid., 15. Bérard, *Did Homer Live?*

63. In attributing this nonanthropomorphic energy to the vitality of the social organism, Olson draws on thinkers who interpret divinity as a society's expression of its collective life (e.g., Jane Harrison and Carl Jung).

64. Olson, *Selected Writings*, 24–25.

65. Olson, "Mystery of What Happens," 16.

66. Olson, *The Maximus Poems*, I:1. References to the *Maximus Poems* are to the standard pagination, which replicates that of the three volumes published separately.

67. In the early *Maximus* poems, Olson follows aspects of both Pound's *Cantos* and Williams's *Paterson*. Like Pound, Olson criticizes commercial capitalism for corrupting production and perception. Like Williams, Olson uses direct quotation from Gloucester locals to represent the life of the city. Olson condemns the culture of advertising as well as the usurious power of money as elements destructive of local culture.

68. Olson's view, placed at the end of the poem, adopts the voice of someone watching and describing what any viewer would see: "you can watch them [memorial wreaths] go out into / the Atlantic." Olson, *Maximus Poems*, I.2. In a later poem on the same ritual, Olson comments on the ritual in a single voice but again emphasizes the experience as one common to others in the community. Although no one died at sea that year, the ritual evokes the same feeling: "no difference / when men come back," because the emotion that the ritual evokes developed through centuries of the community's experience of the sea. Ibid., I.154.

69. Much of Olson's thought on usury develops from his correspondence with Creeley. As each poet developed the implications of objectism for consciousness, he reconceived thought not only in the physical, natural terms specified in "Projective Verse," but also in terms of economic activity. Creeley focuses on "Usura / as an attitude, as a color of the look, . . . as individual." Creeley to Olson, 9: 102–3, 108.

For Creeley, Pound's usury, the unnatural practice of earning money from money (rather than from labor), characterizes an essential element of thought.

70. Olson, *Maximus Poems*, I.2.

71. Ibid., I.21.

72. Olson to Creeley, 9: 54.

73. Olson, *Maximus Poems*, I.118–19, I.145.

74. Alfred North Whitehead defines eternal objects in *Process and Reality*, 40. Robert von Hallberg has traced the interaction of subject and object structuring Olson's poems to the processual understanding of object (and subject) in Whitehead's philosophy. While I agree that interaction structures Olson's poems, I will emphasize the use of the subject-object interaction to trace underlying social categories in the poems. Olson maps, for example, the evolution of concepts of usury from the deity Agyasta to Ezra Pound in the *Maximus Poems*, II.23.

75. Olson alludes to Robert Graves's image of the Celtic poet as recorder of the battle capable of stopping the fighting and thus of intervening in the immediate flow of experience to record the events. Graves, *The White Goddess*, 22. This idea of the poet-historian as intervening to record shapes Olson's concept of history in the *Maximus Poems*.

76. Olson, *Maximus Poems*, II.14.

77. Ibid., II.15.

78. Ibid., I.82. Olson's writings about the poem and readings at the time indicate that the poem is composed primarily from dream material. Olson's record of a flow of relatively unbroken, perhaps unconscious thought seems to be an effort to trace personality using D. H. Lawrence's model of a "tram-car" driven by the "circuits" of force established by its accumulation of affective connections with external objects. Lawrence, *Fantasia of the Unconscious*, 131. Olson to Creeley, November 28, 1951, shows that he was reading this work at the time of composition of "The Twist." 8: 187.

79. Olson, *Maximus Poems*, I.85.

NOTES TO CHAPTER 2

1. Creeley, *Collected Poems*, 21.

2. Levertov, *Collected Earlier Poems*, 10.

3. Duncan, *The Years As Catches*, 28.

4. Duncan, *Derivations*, 73.

5. Levertov, *Collected Earlier Poems*, 5, 24.

6. Ibid., 7.

7. Creeley's letter to Jacob Leed c. 1949 discusses Melville's "noble act of violence" in an existentialist framework and the reality of the imagination as an act in the world. A following letter, also dated 1949, admires Lawrence's " 'living' contact with other people and with one's surroundings which . . . is to me primary in

a realization of one's self." Creeley to Leed, [194?], Folder 23; Creeley to Leed from Hotel Brunswick, [194?], Folder 23; Robert Creeley Papers, Archives and Special Collections at the Thomas J. Dodd Research Center, University of Connecticut Libraries.

8. Creeley, *Collected Poems*, 17.

9. Ibid., 6, 13.

10. Duncan, *Years As Catches*, 40.

11. Duncan, *Derivations*, 44, 53.

12. For poems on dissolution into nature, see Olson, "You, Hart Crane" (Olson, *Collected Poems*, 4) and Creeley, "Hart Crane" and "Hart Crane 2" (Ibid., 23, 109). For poems on the coldness of physical decomposition, see Olson's "Pacific Lament" and "Burial Ground" (Ibid., 15, 27).

13. This hiatus was productive for Levertov. Although she did not publish a book, she continued to write and seek publication in literary reviews. The period also corresponds to her adaptation to life in the United States and to motherhood.

14. Creeley, *Collected Poems*, 20.

15. Olson, *Collected Poems*, 300.

16. Moraru, " 'Topos/typos/tropos,' " 255–57.

17. Levertov, *Collected Earlier Poems*, 35.

18. Duncan, *Selected Poems*, 35–36.

19. Olson, "Mayan Heads," 27. For a fuller reading of Olson's interpretation of Mayan petroglyphs that reinforces his idealization of language as referring to and transmitting the energy of nature, see Bertonneau, "Life in a Human Universe," 119, 129.

20. Olson, *Maximus Poems*, 16.

21. Creeley to Olson, 4: 24–25.

22. Olson, *Additional Prose*, 48.

23. Creeley, "Introduction" [to Olson's *Selected Writings*], original typed manuscript in letter to Olson, February 12, 1965, p. 2, Charles Olson Research Collection, Archives and Special Collections at the Thomas J. Dodd Research Center, University of Connecticut Libraries. Later revision printed as "Introduction to Charles Olson: *Selected Writings* I," in Creeley, *Quick Graph*, 174–78. The introduction finally published provides more biographical and historical background that places Olson in a Modernist tradition stemming from Pound as well as Williams. James Laughlin may have been instrumental in Creeley's revisions, for Creeley wrote to Olson that Laughlin was "boggled" by the first version. Creeley to Olson, February 24, 1965, Olson and Creeley, *Charles Olson and Robert Creeley*.

24. Olson, qtd. in Creeley, "Introduction" [to Olson's *Selected Writings*], original typed manuscript in letter to Olson, February 12, 1965, p. 2, Charles Olson Research Collection, Archives and Special Collections at the Thomas J. Dodd Research Center, University of Connecticut Libraries.

25. Olson to Creeley, 5: 76.

26. Olson, *Maximus Poems*, 155-56.

27. Creeley, Draft response to Olson, May 7, 1952, Charles Olson Research Collection, Archives and Special Collections at the Thomas J. Dodd Research Center, University of Connecticut Libraries.

28. Creeley to Olson, June 29, 1952, Olson and Creeley, *Charles Olson and Robert Creeley*. Lynn Keller traces Williams's definition of self through sexual desire as a strong influence in Creeley's early work. Keller, *Re-making It New*, 139–42.

29. Creeley to Olson, May 4, 1950, Olson and Creeley, *Charles Olson and Robert Creeley*.

30. See, for example, Olson's letter to Louis Martz, included in Olson to Creeley, 7: 64–71 and Creeley's ensuing discussion of the letter.

31. Gelpi, *A Coherent Splendor,* 310.

32. Von Hallberg discusses this divided legacy of the Modernist long poem in *Charles Olson*, 50ff.

33. Margaret Dickie analyzes the failure of the metaphors of man and city to provide structural unity in *Paterson*. Dickie, *Modernist Long Poem*, 86–88. Pound orders the world into his ideal forms of beauty only by abandoning the rubble of history for selective natural beauty.

34. For critics who read Olson's *Maximus Poems* as a revolutionary integration, see Don Byrd's description of their logic of "space-time" and interpenetration of individual with natural place. Byrd, *Charles Olson's* Maximus, 100, 130–31; Sherman Paul, *olson's push,* 33, 129; and Brian Conniff's analysis of Olson's effort to place subject and object on equal terms. Conniff, *Lyric and Modern Poetry*, 64.

35. Randy Prus and Gary Grieve-Carlson discuss Olson's parataxis and contiguity as strategies through which to undo the metaphysical hierarchy implicit in hypertaxis. Olson's choice of parataxis derives at least in part from Havelock's *Preface to Plato*, which contrasts Plato's language as logos of an ideal order underlying the structure of reality with Homer's geography and history as experientially based cultural memory. For Prus, the *Maximus Poems*, particularly the third volume, use "logorhythmic parataxis" to render geography rather than rhetoric the poem's primary ordering structure. Prus, *Olson's Dance,* 8. Grieve-Carlson argues that "Olson's view of history is marked by a strong sense of contiguity, leveling the hierarchy of ideal over real. Men and gods are bound together intimately." Grieve-Carlson, *Cracked Tune*, 278. While I agree with these analyses of Olson's style, I emphasize the disjunction as well as the integration that this leveling of hierarchies introduces.

36. Whitehead, *Science and the Modern World*, 75.

37. Holsapple, "Williams, Whitehead," 79, 86. Holsapple traces Williams's reading of Whitehead and integration of Whitehead's philosophy into his works.

38. Whitehead, *Process and Reality*, 34, 214–15.

39. Pound, *The Cantos*, 429.

40. George Butterick traces Olson's use of *intaglio* to Pound and Dante. Butterick, *Guide to* Maximus Poems, 429.

41. Olson, *Maximus Poems*, 308.

42. Whitehead, *Process and Reality*, 288. Whitehead's idea of evolution parallels that of Hermann Weyl, a mathematician who also influenced Olson. Weyl argues that the time structure of mental operations is more important to their outcome than spatial structure. Weyl, *Philosophy of Mathematics*, 32.

43. Olson's conception of a temporally developing and changing universe led to a poem whose structure changes through time, the text as a whole lacking spatial unity. As such, the *Maximus Poems* depart from what Joseph Frank calls the "space-logic" of Modernism, which defines an "atemporal form of Time" through spatial relations to grasp "moments in their permanent essence." Frank, "Spatial Form," Part I, 229, 235–36. Although such a Modernist space-logic describes well the use of place in *Paterson* and order of heaven and earth in Pound's later *Cantos*, it does not distinguish Modernist from postmodern structure. Marjorie Perloff discusses a different kind of primary space ordering textual images visually in the work of postmodern poets like Steve McCaffery. Perloff, *Radical Artifice*, 78.

44. Olson, *Maximus Poems*, 306.

45. Ibid., 429.

46. Ibid., 492.

47. Butterick, *Guide to* Maximus Poems, 616–17.

48. Olson, *Maximus Poems*, 492–93.

49. Ibid., 385.

50. Ibid., 383.

51. Ibid., 320.

52. Ibid., 386.

53. Unable to build bridges between the cosmic and the individual, Olson focused more on process in the individual, who became increasingly private and isolated. Albert Glover describes a parallel between the nostalgia and isolation in Pound's later *Cantos* and Olson's later *Maximus Poems* through Olson's striking references to Pound's imagery in "Evolution in Ezra Pound's Poetics," 64–65.

54. Olson, *Maximus Poems*, 5.

55. Hesiod, "Theogony," in *Hesiod and Theognis*, 33.

56. Olson, *Maximus Poems*, 257.

57. Ibid., 489.

58. Ibid., 414.

59. Charles Olson, "Maximus at the Reach," in "Poems," 29. The poems in this selection, not included in the three-volume *Maximus Poems*, express despair

darker than the published volumes. Olson's "Antimaximus II" poem criticizes the perversion of American speech (22). "So Has Suffering Offended" describes his disenchanted vision, "looking out of eyes / I never wanted seeking to speak from a heart / fallen" (25). Whereas in the earlier poems the sea represented a natural power to be tapped by human culture, Olson here portrays the threat of a sea deity, which requires violent suppression: "he pierces her heart / through her mouth open / to devour him" (31).

60. Olson, *Maximus Poems*, 448.

61. Penny Tselentis-Apostolidis describes the poem's tension between faithful representation of place and prophetic resistance to a contemporary Gloucester that is losing its local integrity to a national mass culture. Tselentis-Apostolidis, "Olson's Geographic Methodology," 135.

62. Olson, *Maximus Poems*, 400.

63. Ibid., 401.

64. Ibid., 405, 407.

65. As his perception of the distance between individual and collective processes creating human nature grew, Olson focused increasingly on the interface between individual and world process. He sought patterns in the flux of experience as the basis for understanding the relation between individual, evolving cosmic whole, and the forces of creation. Whereas the first and second volumes of the *Maximus Poems* open with maps of the city of Gloucester and of Gondwanaland (the original single landmass from which the continents formed), respectively, the third volume shows a map of New England formed by a single line indicating the coastline. Rather than positing distinct elements, Olson reveals only the interface between the two, leaving their specific topography and other boundaries open. Just as land and sea, when mapped, are indistinguishable except at their boundary, so Olson distinguishes the form of self not as a discrete entity but as the boundary between other forces.

66. Olson, *Maximus Poems*, 528.

67. Olson to Creeley, 2: 165. For Catherine Stimpson, "Olson's trust in language distinguishes him from many post-Modernists." Catherine Stimpson, "Charles Olson," 154.

68. Olson, *Selected Writings*, 27–30.

69. Charles Olson, "RIME, or notes on Verse pre-Chaucer and post-Pound" original typed mss., [c. 1953], Robert Creeley's Olson Materials, Charles Olson Research Collection, Archives and Special Collections at the Thomas J. Dodd Research Center, University of Connecticut Libraries. For further discussion of the significance of pun for Olson and a summary of scholarship on it, see Bollobás, *Charles Olson*, 47–49.

70. Creeley, *Collected Poems*, 205.

71. Creeley, *Quick Graph*, 34.

72. Creeley to Jacob Leed, from Hotel Brunswick, [194?], Folder 23, Robert Creeley Papers, Archives and Special Collections at the Thomas J. Dodd Research Center, University of Connecticut Libraries. It is interesting that Creeley in a later interview repudiated existentialism as "incredibly self-destructive." Creeley, *Contexts of Poetry*, 46.

73. Creeley to Olson, June 22, 1951, Olson and Creeley, *Charles Olson and Robert Creeley*.

74. Creeley to Olson, August 19, 1953, Olson and Creeley, *Charles Olson and Robert Creeley*.

75. Creeley, "Alfred North Whitehead," Robert Creeley Papers, Lilly Library, Indiana University, Bloomington.

76. Creeley, *Collected Poems*, 105.

77. Ibid., 109.

78. Ibid., 110.

79. Alice Entwhistle, "Creeley and Crane," 93–95.

80. Creeley, *Collected Poems*, 196.

81. Creeley, *Contexts*, 31.

82. Creeley, *Collected Poems*, 162.

83. Ibid., 159.

84. Lynn Keller, *Re-making It New*, 139. Other critics have discussed the distinction between public and private voice in Creeley's poetry. Brian Conniff interprets both Creeley's and Olson's poems as speaking from "the wall between the private and the public, the 'single' and the 'many,' Olson moving awkwardly outward and Creeley forsaking the public world for the personal but finding the wall between them "distressingly slight." Whereas I focus on both public and private forces in the self, Conniff sees a real boundary between public and private language. For him, Creeley's poems try to break through to a common public world rather than to resist the influence of the public world on the individual. Conniff, *Lyric and Modern Poetry*, 106–8. Stephen Fredman emphasizes the rigidity of social language in Creeley's poetry but sees his poetic creativity as "playful differentiation among systems." Stephen Fredman, *Poet's Prose*, 78. While this phrase characterizes later works by Creeley well, it does not convey the anxiety and entrapment that pervade *For Love*.

85. Creeley, *Collected Poems*, 257.

86. Ibid., 165.

87. Ibid., 194.

88. Ibid., 235.

89. Ibid., 218.

90. Ibid., 119.

91. Ibid.

92. Ibid., 180.

93. Ibid., 182.

94. Creeley, *Contexts*, 173.

95. Creeley to Olson, June 13, 1952, Olson and Creeley, *Charles Olson and Robert Creeley*.

NOTES TO CHAPTER 3

1. Although Olson, Creeley, and Corman discuss and disagree on poetics from their earliest correspondence, poetics are only part of the motivation. Olson and perhaps Creeley are driven by economics as well, Olson in particular hoping that the magazine will serve as advertising for Black Mountain College.

2. Duncan, "Interview with Mary Emma Harris," 1. Robert Duncan Papers, Poetry Collection of the University Libraries, State University of New York at Buffalo.

3. Corman, *Origin* 2, 69; *Origin* 4, 233. The decision to include statements of poetics in *Origin*, particularly those of the editor, comes from Creeley and Pound, whom Creeley consults about how to start a little magazine. Pound is adamant about a magazine needing a coherent poetics and explicit standards. Creeley thus pushes Corman to define his poetics as editor throughout their early correspondence and, despite their frequent arguments, reiterates his respect for Corman's autonomy as editor even if it disagrees with that of major contributors.

4. Creeley to Cid Corman, March 9, 1951, Cid Corman Manuscripts, Lilly Library, Indiana University, Bloomington.

5. Brunner, *Cold War Poetry*, 1–14.

6. Their letters from the time leading up to the reading express this common purpose, as does the number of poems the poets write for each other. Olson dedicates the first volume of his *Maximus Poems* (1956) to Creeley. Creeley includes poems to Olson and Duncan in *The New American Poetry*. Levertov's statement of poetics in the same anthology mentions Creeley and Duncan as "the chief poets among my contemporaries." Levertov in Allen, *New American Poetry*, 412.

7. Creeley, *Quick Graph*, 211.

8. Williams, *Collected Poems of Williams*, 2: 53. For the many references in Creeley's poetics to Williams's "Preface" to *The Wedge*, see Creeley, *Quick Graph*, 24, 26, 32, 44, 120. Williams's preface to *The Wedge* (1944), so influential for Creeley and Duncan, asserts that the relation between poetry and society is "complex," that a poem may relate to society in many ways. Against utilitarian Marxist and scientific views of poetry as necessary only until an ideal society has been realized, Williams's "Writer's Prologue to a Play in Verse" articulates the importance of literature to the self's formation in any society. The "Prologue" constructs the audience's relation to the work of art as a participatory "composition with code" that teaches individual improvisation on given forms of language. Williams, *Collected Poems*, 2: 53, 59–62.

Williams's articulation of poetry's social or political purpose as conscious individual use of language follows the turn away from advocacy for a political program in the Pound-Williams tradition of Modernism. If Pound and H. D. advocate their theories of political reform as authoritative poet-prophets, the next generation, Objectivists like Zukofsky and Oppen, feel poetry cannot be a force in group activism and tend not to write poetry during their periods of political activism.

9. Duncan, as transcribed by Creeley, "ROBERT DUNCAN: talking late," Robert Creeley Papers, Department of Special Collections, University Libraries, Stanford University.

10. Duncan to Creeley, January–February 1956, Robert Creeley Papers, Department of Special Collections, University Libraries, Stanford University.

11. Levertov, *Collected Earlier Poems*, 10.

12. Levertov, "The Poem as Counterforce," typescript, n.d., William Carlos Williams Papers, Beinecke Rare Book and Manuscript Library, Yale University.

13. Donna Krolik Hollenberg cites painters' influence on Levertov's work of this period as well. Hollenberg states that Levertov (as I will argue for Creeley and Duncan) "turned in her poetry to the materiality of the visual arts to express spiritual energy and force." Hollenberg, "History as I desired it," 519.

14. Olson, *Selected Writings*, 21, 24.

15. Thomas Bertonneau argues that Olson's view of language as referring to nature links him to a referential rather than Postmodern constructivist conception of language. Bertonneau, "Life in Human Universe," 119. Although Creeley and Duncan do not fully reject a view of language as transmission of natural energy, their emphasis on the artificial character of language marks a significant difference from Olson's.

16. Duncan, "Preface," "Homage to Coleridge," p. 1. Robert Duncan Papers, Poetry Collection of the University Libraries, State University of New York at Buffalo.

17. Creeley, *Quick Graph*, 196.

18. Coleridge, *Biographia Literaria*, 1: 202.

19. In a retrospective on Black Mountain College, Creeley writes of the crucial influence of Abstract Expressionism during his time at the college. See John Yau, "Active Participant," 50ff.

20. Creeley, *Was That a Real Poem*, 78. Duncan, *Fictive Certainties*, 69. Although she does not visit Black Mountain College, Levertov becomes familiar with these artists while living in New York at this time. She too incorporates "Projective Verse" into her poetics by modeling her representation on that of painters. The early poems that seek to incorporate Olson's idea of isolating different forces at work in the poem use the painter's gaze to objectify the subject. See, for example, her letters to Duncan circa 1955 in *Letters of Duncan and Levertov* and "Kresch's Studio," *Collected Earlier Poems*, 12.

21. Duncan also discussed this influence in his interview with Mary Emma Harris. Robert Duncan Papers, Poetry Collection of the University Libraries, State University of New York at Buffalo.

22. Duncan, "Interview with Mary Emma Harris," Robert Duncan Papers, Poetry Collection of the University Libraries, State University of New York at Buffalo, 10–11.

23. Ibid., 21.

24. Greenberg, "The Avant-Garde and Kitsch," in John O'Brian, ed., *The Collected Essays and Criticism.*

25. Creeley, *Quick Graph*, 341.

26. Ibid., 196, 339, 357. For Creeley's early interest in abstraction, see his letters to Olson on the importance of art as "the destruction of its own reference," Creeley to Olson, February 16, [1952], 9: 127; Creeley, "René Laubiès," essay enclosed in letter to Olson, February 23, 1952, 1: 165–66. Creeley is interested in the "color" of words and their use like color in abstract rather than representative painting. Creeley to Olson, November 7, 1950, 3: 158.

27. Creeley, "The Painters," n.d., Robert Creeley Papers, Archives and Special Collections at the Thomas J. Dodd Research Center, University of Connecticut Libraries. Creeley's typescript gives "Fontrousse par Aix en Provence" as the address, dating the typescript c. 1951–52.

28. Rosenberg, qtd. in Doss, *Benton, Pollock, and Politics*, 383.

29. Harold Rosenberg as quoted in Doss, 382–83. Doss concludes that "the action of individuality was asserted as the goal of revolution, rather than revolution (political or social) being the goal of the individual" (Doss, 383). Her analysis of this internalization of political activity in private acts to transform individual consciousness resonates with Paul Breslin's critique of post-1950s poetic activism. Breslin observes that poets since the 1950s practice a "radical psycho-politics" that "tend[s] to take refuge in symbolic but politically ineffectual protest." Breslin, *The Psycho-Political Muse*, xii, 17, 83.

30. Duncan to Creeley, April 9, 1955, Robert Creeley Papers, Department of Special Collections, University Libraries, Stanford University.

31. Duncan, *Fictive Certainties*, 65–66. Also published in "From a Notebook." Michael André Bernstein interprets the "chasm" Mallarmé establishes between literature and other "deployments of language" as a sign of fear that art will be contaminated by public declamation and ideology. Bernstein, *Tale of the Tribe*, 227.

32. Duncan to Creeley, March 28, 1959, Robert Creeley Papers, Department of Special Collections, University Libraries, Stanford University.

33. Clyfford Still, qtd. in Rose, *Readings in American Art*, 140–42.

34. Jess, *Jess: A Grand Collage*, ed. Michael Auping, 22.

35. This rearrangement remains part of Duncan's mature poetics. By 1971, Duncan has developed a poetics that echoes this artistic transformation of given

cultural material. His writing and Olson's "us[e] something like the same enormous amount of material that's accumulated in what we know of as literature . . . , the culture that litters our whole scene." Duncan, "Interview with Mary Emma Harris," Robert Duncan Papers, Poetry Collection of the University Libraries, State University of New York at Buffalo, 25. Collage replaces ideogram as Duncan's principle of composition, distinguishing his work from that of Pound and Olson. While interviewing Duncan in 1985, Michael André Bernstein observes that "there is a huge difference between a collage principle and an ideogram principle." For Bernstein, the ideogram principle "doesn't allow for interferences. It can take different elements but it always has to blend them into a unity." Duncan agrees and responds that Pound and Olson are not collagists for social reasons. "And here Pound really is a non-collagist. When he is faced with the problem of society he sees it *contaminated* with other elements. . . . One feels a challenge and wants it to be eliminated. Those things are there to be eliminated." Whereas Pound seeks to purge or transcend the social elements that would disrupt his art, Duncan advocates a continuum and interaction between the independence or "interference" of cultural media and the artist's transformative power. Bernstein and Robert Duncan, in Michael André Bernstein and Burton Hatlen, "Interview with Robert Duncan," 117–18.

36. Auping, *Jess: A Grand Collage*, 20. Although Duncan frequently adopts Jess's language, Jess comments that in this case the influence goes the other way. Jess traces his paste-ups to Duncan's disruption of the poetic image in order to give it new meaning. Other critics have commented on Duncan's view of language as an autonomous agent. Joseph G. Cronick distinguishes Olson's *muthos* as a people's expression of its collective emotion from Duncan's view of language as a nonanthropomorphic agent in poetry. Cronick, "Duncan and the Truth," 193–98. R. S. Hamilton analyzes Duncan's use of language as a means to cultivate awareness of language as socio-ideological construction. Hamilton, "After Strange Gods," 227.

Creeley's work has also been interpreted in these divergent ways. Jerry McGuire summarizes these tendencies in "No Boundaries: Robert Creeley," 92–118.

Charles Altieri and Rosalind Krauss represent idealist and deconstructionist poles defining this opposition. For Altieri, Modernist abstraction is a "self-reflexive heroism" whose apparent impersonality presents a "formal" model of how individuals can express the creative potential of psychic energies. Altieri also gives a historical argument for the reasons that abstraction emerges in the Modernist period (Altieri, *Painterly Abstraction*, 33–34, 371, 376, 385). Whereas Altieri views the subject of the painting as ideal psychic energy, Krauss views this subject as the socially constructed process of representation. She emphasizes the prevalence of the grid in abstract painting as a depiction of the cultural structure of Cartesian space that shapes our image of thought. For Altieri, the collage represents a selection and reordering of material fragments that fuse them into the artist's imaginative forms. For Krauss, in contrast, Picasso applies newspaper to canvas "to construct the sign of space as penetrable or transparent." She defines collage as "a systematic exploration of the conditions of representability entailed by the sign." The juxtaposition of elements thus exposes the specific character of each as sign, not a figure of the artist's imagination. Krauss, *Originality of the Avant-Garde*, 8–23, 34. In collage, color and line do not vanish into the objects they represent but retain a separate identity as the particular materials and kind of space from which art is constructed.

37. For the distinction between Pound's natural or cosmic image and Zukofsky's fugue, see Scroggins, *Louis Zukofsky*, 182, 217. Sandra Kumamoto Stanley emphasizes the attention to historical change and thus relativism as an important difference between Pound and Zukofsky. Stanley, *Louis Zukofsky*, 33.

38. Zukofsky, "Preface," *An "Objectivists" Anthology*, 14.

39. Duncan had corresponded with Zukofsky since the 1940s. Creeley published parts I and II of *Bottom* in *Black Mountain Review* 7, initiating a lively correspondence with Zukofsky in 1955–56. In his letters to Duncan, Creeley reports enthusiastically of reading *"A"* and *Bottom*. Creeley to Duncan, August 20, 1959, and February 24, 1964, Robert Duncan Papers, Poetry Collection of the University Libraries, State University of New York at Buffalo. Bob Perelman argues Zukofsky's importance as a model of the poet as activist for Creeley, Duncan, and Dorn and as a model of masculinity for Olson in *The Trouble with Genius*, 224.

40. See also Edward Schelb's remarks on the formal disunity of Zukofsky's early political lyrics in "The Exaction of Song," 337–38.

41. Zukofsky, *"A,"* 119.

42. Ibid., 112, 117.

43. Ibid., 112, 117, 119.

44. Ibid., 234.

45. Ibid., 124.

46. Zukofsky, *Bottom*, 130.

47. Zukofsky, *"A,"* 150.

48. Ibid., 157–58.

49. Zukofsky, *Bottom*, 33. Zukofsky cites Plato's forms and Freud's division between primitive sense knowledge and "higher" forms of spiritual development in *Moses and Monotheism* as examples of the Western tradition's distinction between sensory perception and abstract knowledge (Zukofsky, *Bottom*, 54, 68).

50. Zukofsky, *Bottom*, 86.

51. Ibid., 88–89.

52. Burton Hatlen relates Zukofsky's meditation on love, sight, and language in *Bottom* to the division between history and private being in *"A."* Zukofsky begins with the assumption that language is allied with history, but sight with an

immediate individual yet ineffable mode of perception that can only be communicated in approximate social language. Although love seeks to mediate between sight and language to adjust thought to sense perception, such mediation is only partly successful. Hatlen describes Zukofsky's poetry as an effort to work at the boundary between language and sight. The result is a "poetics of absence" in which both thing and subject are mere "traces," "present only in their absence." Language as a surface of words becomes the only true presence. Hatlen concludes with a suggestion that this use of language initiates an exploration of language in itself as the only presence in the poem. The end of Hatlen's essay points to the Language poets as the heirs of this exploration of language in itself. Creeley and Duncan form part of an intermediary generation in this tradition. Burton Hatlen, "Zukofsky, Wittgenstein, Poetics," 73–79, 91–92.

53. Creeley, *Quick Graph*, 53.

54. Creeley to Duncan, October 6, 1955, Robert Duncan Papers, Poetry Collection of the University Libraries, State University of New York at Buffalo. In the late 1950s and 1960s, partly through its publication in Cid Corman's second series of *Origin*, Zukofsky's poetry enjoys a revival among many poets of the New American Poetry. In addition to Duncan and Creeley, poets as varied as Gary Snyder and Amiri Baraka (then LeRoi Jones) profess admiration for Zukofsky's work.

55. As early as his reviews of Kline and Laubiès, Creeley emphasized the role of the flat canvas and texture of paint in determining painting's unique visual form. While alienation from the ordinary is liberating, it also imposes constraints on the artist. For Kline, the medium seems to have a life of its own. "There seems to be something that you can do so much with paint and after that you start murdering it." Kline, quoted in Rose, *Readings in American Art*, 132.

56. Creeley, *Collected Poems*, 286.

57. Ibid., 285.

58. Ibid., 270.

59. Heather McHugh, "Love and Frangibility," 16. Alan Golding describes *"A"* as a struggle with language as presence versus absence. For Golding, this awareness of language as both presence and absence distinguishes Creeley's long poem from Objectivist poetics and poems like Oppen's *Discrete Series*. Golding, *The Objectivist Nexus*, 102.

60. Creeley, *Collected Poems*, 294.

61. Ibid., 271.

62. Ibid.

63. Ibid., 283.

64. Creeley to Olson, February 3, 1960, Olson and Creeley, *Charles Olson and Robert Creeley*.

65. Creeley, *Collected Poems*, 338–39.

66. Ibid., 432.

67. Ibid., 383.

68. Ibid.

69. Ibid., 422–23.

70. Ibid., 444–45.

71. Damon, *Dark End of the Street*, 178.

72. Duncan, "The Homosexual in Society," 40.

73. Duncan, *Years As Catches*, 86–87.

74. Ibid., 28.

75. Duncan, Black Mountain College Notebook, n.p., Robert Duncan Papers, Poetry Collection of the State University Libraries, State University of New York at Buffalo.

76. Duncan, in Bernstein and Hatlen, "Interview with Robert Duncan," 101.

77. Peter Quartermain discusses Stein's use of linguistic "shifters" (Roman Jakobson's term) at the sentence level in Quartermain, *Disjunctive Poetics*, 40–41.

78. Stein, *Three Lives*, 13, 62.

79. Duncan, *Derivations*, 33, 36, 44.

80. Ibid., 45. Jayne Walker traces Duncan's apprenticeship to Stein and the objectification he learns from it in "Exercises in Disorder: Duncan's Imitations of Gertrude Stein," *Scales of the Marvelous*, 24–28.

81. Despite his plans, Duncan did not republish "The Homosexual in Society" at this time. It was republished in 1973 in *Fag Rag* 5, 3–20.

82. Duncan, "The Homosexual in Society," 39.

83. Duncan, *Opening of the Field*, 96.

84. See, for example, the roles of Duncan's mother in "My Mother Would be a Falconress" and of Denise Levertov during the Vietnam War period poetry.

85. Johnston, *Precipitations*, 63–72, 98.

86. Duncan, "The H. D. Book, Part I: Chapter 2," *Coyote's Journal* 8 (1967): 30. Among poems defining this cosmology are "Often I Am Permitted to Return to a Meadow" and "Poem Beginning from a Line by Pindar," *Opening of the Field*, 7, 69.

87. Duncan read *Zarathustra* at Black Mountain College and credits it as the inspiration for the *Structure of Rime*. Duncan, "Interview with Mary Emma Harris," Robert Duncan Papers, Poetry Collection of the University Libraries, State University of New York at Buffalo, 2–3. Duncan to Levertov, 48.

88. Nietzsche, *Thus Spake Zarathustra*, 8, 19, 23, 25.

89. Duncan, *Opening of the Field*, 11.

90. Ibid., 18, 30, 33.

91. Mossin, *Scenes of Intent*, 47–48.

92. Duncan, *Opening of the Field*, 17.

93. Rumaker, *Robert Duncan*, 78. Rumaker's essay, an earlier version of which was published in *Credences* in 1978, contrasts Duncan's strategy with that of other writers who focus on documenting the horrors of street life for homosexuals in the 1950s and the failure of public spaces to encourage gay liberation. Keenaghan, "Vulnerable Households."

94. Duncan, *Opening of the Field*, 36–37.

95. Ibid., 44, 45.

96. Damon traces such whimsical and often burlesque punning as character-istic of homosexual poetry of the San Francisco Renaissance. Damon, *Dark End of the Street*, 142ff.

Sight functions differently for Duncan than for Creeley. Whereas Creeley sees the world of discrete material objects as fundamentally different from the rela-tional system of notes composing music, Duncan sees the two modes of being as similar, both structured like an open sign system. For Duncan, both provide a lib-erating dissolution of the everyday order of things. By rendering Goya's painting of Cupid and Psyche in his own words, for example, Duncan dissolves and recon-figures this Christian heterosexual figure into an image of knowledge generated from sexual desire. He thus reinterprets Goya's aura of fallen materiality to make a place for his own erotic attraction to Cupid, whose body now represents a power to generate knowledge, "hot luminescence at the loins of the visible." Duncan, *Opening of the Field*, 62. This translation of figures from artistic tradition into lan-guage becomes a "passionate dispersion" (Ibid., 63) reminiscent of Coleridge's dissolving and re-creating secondary imagination.

97. Duncan, *Opening of the Field*, 41–42.

98. Ibid., 95.

99. Ibid., 96.

100. Duncan to Rago, July 15, 1964, *Poetry* Manuscripts, Lilly Library, Indiana University, Bloomington.

101. Duncan, *Bending the Bow*, 49.

102. Ibid., 48

103. Ibid., 49.

104. Ibid., 50.

105. Ibid., v.

106. Duncan to Creeley, February 19, 1964, Robert Creeley Papers, Depart-ment of Special Collections, University Libraries, Stanford University.

107. Creeley to Duncan, February 24, 1964, Robert Duncan Papers, Poetry Collection of the University Libraries, State University of New York at Buffalo.

NOTES TO CHAPTER 4

1. Duncan to Creeley, June 4, 1979. Robert Creeley Papers, Department of Special Collections, University Libraries, Stanford University. Duncan's contrast is with Louis Zukofsky's and Charles Olson's need to establish or propose order.

2. Brunner, *Cold War Poetry*, 123–24.

3. Creeley participated in antiwar protest but chose not to write overtly politi-cal poetry. He expressed respect for protest poems like Duncan's "The Multiver-sity" and Ginsberg's war poems but felt that poets' primary responsibility was not

politics, seeing "the government of words as our responsibility." "I feel that writing is primarily the experience of language, and the diversity of contexts, and the diversity of changes and significations." Creeley fears political contribution may be confused with a "typicality" he wishes to avoid, "the insistent didacticism of attitude, the locked mind that enters almost immediately." Creeley, *Tales Out of School*, 33–35, 103–5.

Susan Vanderborg argues that Olson's effort to construct "a communal text that redefined its own borders to incorporate marginal voices and narratives" influences "the development of a more overtly political poetics by writers in the projectivist tradition," including Duncan, Levertov, and Baraka. Vanderborg, *Paratextual Communities*, 25–30.

My emphasis on the audience implied in these poems develops from Evelyn Fox Keller's analysis of scientific objectivity as a form of knowledge that creates a world of objects by denying "the very real indeterminacy between subject and object." Keller, *Gender and Science*, 70. Dorothy Nielsen traces a similar emphasis on intersubjectivity from Levertov's "allegiance to Hasidim," which leads her to establish a mystical I-thou relation to the concrete image rather than to emphasize objectification in the style of Williams, Zukofsky, and Olson. Nielsen, "Mystical/Political Poetry," 90–93.

4. Levertov to Duncan, 234.
5. Ibid., 158.
6. Ibid., 504.
7. Duncan to Levertov, 239.
8. Levertov to Duncan, 179.
9. Duncan to Levertov, 244.
10. Ibid., 245.
11. For the composition history of "The H. D. Book," see Bertholf, "Editor's Introduction," *A Great Admiration*, viii.
12. Duncan, "The H. D. Book, Part I: Chapter 2," 142.
13. Duncan, "From the H. D. Book," II.5, 343; and "The H. D. Book: Part II Nights and Days. Chapter 4," 44–47.
14. Duncan, "Two Chapters from H. D.," 98.
15. To trace H. D.'s concept of this occult tradition through her many works informed by it requires more space than I can give it here. Other critics have studied the concept of spiritual tradition in H. D.'s work. Adalaide Morris establishes the primacy of a " 'we' rather than 'I' in H. D.'s poetic voice, a hermetic band, clan, or tribe that submerges the ego in community with others." Morris, "A Relay of Power," 65. Susan Stanford Friedman describes a similarly conservative role of tradition. For Friedman, H. D.'s *The Walls Do Not Fall* "builds an image of a community ('we') dedicated to preserving the ancient traditions that the cultural mainstream ('you') continually mocks." Friedman, *Psyche Reborn*, 213.

16. H. D., *Collected Poems 1912–1944*, 514. In a letter to Levertov, Duncan writes that the occult tradition possesses knowledge superior to that of the contemporary age, a knowledge which enables the poet to act in the higher interests of collective humanity. Quoting from *La Kabbala Pratique*, Duncan draws a parallel between poet and Kabbalist as voices of the collective imagination: "Le but de l'Art est donc, *pratiquement,* de mettre l'Adepte en liaison psychique avec les Plans Supérieurs et les Intelligentes qui y résident. En outre, d'agir altruistement et occultement sur les semblables, au mieux des intérêts supérieurs de la Collectivité humaine." Duncan to Levertov, 349. The higher reality of language developed by poets thus gains an authority to guide current history and usage with its meanings.

17. Duncan, "from the H. D. Book, Part II Chapter 5 (section one)," 344.

18. Duncan, "The H. D. Book," I.2, 127–28. In contrast to conventional forms, "paradigms of thought and feeling agreed upon by reasonable and sensible men," Duncan posits "the matter of idealistic form, where, in contrast to the models of conventional verse which are social in their origin, the poet strives to conform to eternal paradigms, and each individual poem may be conceived of as having an eternal perfect form of its own" in an interview with L. S. Dembo. In keeping with Duncan's resistance to universal truths, these eternal forms are not general paradigms but the perfection of the individual's imagination. Duncan included his partially revised typescript of this interview in a letter to Levertov, July 14, 1967, Denise Levertov Papers, Department of Special Collections, University Libraries, Stanford University.

Duncan's conception of ideal forms closely resembles Pound's ideograms as eternal paradigms. Michael André Bernstein has written of Duncan's turn to tradition in "The H. D. Book" as an effort to create his own canon "in the absence of a relatively homogeneous and stable hierarchy of values." Bernstein, "Bringing it all back home," 178, 185, 189. Bernstein's analysis describes well Duncan's relation to Pound's Modernism and Duncan's effort to preserve the influence of occult thought in Modernism. It does not, however, adequately explain the role of tradition in relation to Duncan's immediate social context, a role significant to his departure from a Poundian conception of tradition and crucial to his subsequent writing. First, Duncan is concerned not with stability of value but with plurality of meaning. He seeks to resist what he sees as the State's desire to create a democracy of consensus through control of individual opinion rather than a pluralistic democracy in which individuals are free to form and express their own opinions. Second, although Duncan cites Pound's city Dioce and temple in *Thrones* as forerunners, he resists Pound's view of tradition as the fragmentary incarnation in history of stable ideal and eternal forms. Duncan's tradition more closely resembles H. D.'s occult tradition as a living spirit world evolving concurrently with contemporary history and expressing the truth of that history. This conception of concurrent evolution informs Duncan's understanding of the relation between literary and contemporary society as it develops during the war. Duncan, "The H. D. Book," I.2, 127–28.

19. Duncan, "Nights and Days," Part II.1 of "The H. D. Book," 101–2, 115.

20. Duncan, "The H. D. Book," I.2, 27.

21. Duncan, *Roots and Branches*, 12, 76. This theme pervades "A Sequence of Poems for H. D.'s Birthday, September 10, 1959" and "Two Presentations." Duncan represents his adoptive father as a carpenter who would have him follow a trade and his adoptive mother as an obstacle to his knowledge of a spirit mother.

22. Duncan to Levertov, 472.

23. Duncan, "Beginnings: Chapter 1 of the H. D. Book, Part I," 29.

24. Duncan, *Roots and Branches*, 48.

25. Ibid., 47.

26. Levertov to Duncan, 301.

27. Levertov, "H. D.: An Appreciation," 182. In addition to this presence of tradition, Levertov praises H. D.'s technical ability, the "icily passionate precision" brought to the dark mystery of the cosmos, a precision of "the music, the play of sound, that arises miraculously out of fidelity to the truth of experience" in the crucial issue of "the interplay of psychic and material life." Ibid., 182–86.

28. Levertov goes on to write that she calls herself an American poet but feels that European (rather than only English) poets belong to her heritage. Poetic "'voice' does not speak only in the often slipshod imprecise vocabulary with which one buys the groceries but with all the resources of one's life." Levertov's change of view is palpable. She had written to Williams in 1954, "I get bored by my own English-style formalities—they feel stuffy sometimes)." Levertov to Williams, MacGowan, ed., 12, 99–101.

In 1961, Levertov wrote Duncan of her need to articulate her poetics. "This has been a year for me of preoccupation to some extent with the formulation of (or organization of) theory." Levertov to Duncan, 304. Her "September 1961" meditates on the aging of Pound, Williams, and H. D. and the uncertainty of their legacy and her own direction. Levertov, *Poems 1960–1967*, 81.

29. Levertov to Duncan, 445.

30. Levertov, *Poems 1960–1967*, 3–5.

31. Levertov to Duncan, 499.

32. See, for example, "Six Variations," Levertov, *Poems 1960–1967*, 18–20. Sections v and vi alternate sharp, short "i" and fluid long "o" sounds to accentuate the contrast between the surface brilliance of concrete things and the depth of human sorrow apart from this visible world.

33. Levertov, *Poems 1960–1967*, 13.

34. Levertov, *Poems 1968–1972*, 121–22, 123.

35. Levertov to Duncan, 532.

36. Duncan to Levertov, 540.

37. Marjorie Perloff's "Poetry in a Time of War" (208–11) traces the early stages of this debate, in which Duncan criticizes Levertov's short early war lyrics for relinquishing poetic craft to propagandistic moral message. I would like to focus on the later debate over Levertov's long poem "Staying Alive" and thus to contextualize the debate in the discussion of the poet's public role that grounds Duncan's and Levertov's esthetic decisions.

38. Robert Duncan, *Bending the Bow*, v. Peter O'Leary traces Duncan's conception of violence and creativity to his personal mythology. I will focus here on the way in which Duncan forms this strongly personal theory of violence in relation to media figures. O'Leary, *Gnostic Contagion*, 114–70.

39. Duncan, *Bending the Bow*, i.

40. Ibid., 10.

41. Ibid., 11.

42. Ibid., iv.

43. Ibid., 12.

44. Ibid., 12–13.

45. Ibid., 12.

46. Ibid., 115.

47. Ibid., 42–43.

48. Ibid., 115.

49. Ibid., 81, 183.

50. Ibid., 83.

51. Ibid., 115.

52. Ibid., v.

53. Duncan's letters of the mid-1960s show his active reading of the Romantics in addition to H. D., Olson, and Williams as he begins *Passages*. Letters to Levertov quote Whitman's "As I Ponder'd in Silence" as a source for Duncan's thinking about war (Duncan to Levertov, 466–67). He also considers Wordsworth and "the Romantics" in general, who for him protest the undemocratic or disenfranchising law as destructive of "self-esteem" (Ibid., 541–42).

54. Shelley, *Prometheus Unbound*, 125.

55. I would argue that both *Prometheus Unbound* and *Bending the Bow* exhibit degrees of escape and entrapment.

56. Duncan, *Bending the Bow*, 36.

57. Ibid., 41.

58. Ibid., 42.

59. Ibid., 44.

60. Damon, 189.

61. Johnson, *Robert Duncan*, 109.

62. Duncan, *Bending the Bow*, 77.

63. Ibid., 128–29.

64. Zukofsky, *"A,"* 234.

65. Duncan, *Bending the Bow*, 132.

66. Ibid., 131.

67. Duncan's theory of history as developed in the late 1960s in "The H. D. Book" presents a similar understanding of the individual as a persona created by history rather than as an autonomous person. Following H. D.'s Freudian theory of history as the evolution of a collective consciousness which it is the poet's gift to remember, Duncan interprets social upheaval as the eruption of repressed material from the past. H. D. collapsed psychological and political experiences of the war, interpreting her inner crises during World War II as those of European civilization. Drawing on Freud, she explained her psychological crises through collective myths of the race, extending the belief that nothing of the past was lost, but only repressed. Although forgotten, the past remains present and exerts its pressure in the present. Because the individual psyche is formed by its historical circumstances, it inherits and relives the unresolved tensions of the collective psyche. In works like *The Walls do not Fall* and *Palimpsest*, H. D. searches for the origins of personal crisis in unresolved past crises, seeing her life in London as a replay of earlier Roman and Christian dramas. Likewise, for Duncan, "[t]he poet's task is thus to arouse in contemporary consciousness reverberations of old myth, to prepare the ground so that when we return to read we will see our modern texts charged with a plot that had already begun before the first signs and signatures."

"Soul and Eros are primordial members of the cast. To imagine ourselves as souls is to become engaged in all the mystery play, the troubled ground of a poetry that extends beyond the reaches of any contemporary sense. Eros and Psyche are personae of a drama or dream that determines, beyond individual consciousness, the configurative image of the species." Duncan, "The H. D. Book," I.3, 67–68.

68. Duncan, *Bending the Bow*, 126.

69. Mackey, "from *Gassire's Lute*," part II, 163.

70. Perloff, *Poetry On and Off the Page*, 219–21. Burton Hatlen traces George Oppen's similar challenge to Levertov's use of poetry to advocate a particular opinion in "Feminine Technologies," 9–14.

71. Duncan, *Fictive Certainties*, 142–47.

72. Ibid., 136, 139, 142; *Bending the Bow*, v.

73. Duncan, *Ground Work; Before the War*, 36.

74. Ibid., 43–44.

75. Ibid., 41.

76. Ibid., 42.

77. Ibid., 41

78. Ibid., 40.

79. Levertov, *Poems 1968–1972*, 124.

80. The "burning babe" of "Advent 1966" is one of the many instances of common imagery in the poems of Duncan and Levertov. Their use of similar images and even words—scale and melody, interim, chalice, birthing, dramatic structure, spider and cloth—reveal the extent to which they inhabit a shared world and to which their poetry emerges from their dialogue with each other.

81. Levertov, *Poems 1968–1972*, 129.

82. Ibid., 130.

83. Ibid.

84. Ibid., 16.

85. Ibid., 139.

86. Ibid., 183.

87. Levertov, *Letters of Duncan and Levertov*, 682.

88. Levertov, *Poems 1968–1972*, 137.

89. Ibid., 107.

90. Ibid., 160.

91. Ibid., 184.

92. Ibid., 176.

93. Ibid., 174–76.

94. Ibid., 149.

95. Ibid., 159.

96. Ibid., 151–53.

97. Donna Krolik Hollenberg argues that the search for solutions to this problem also informs Levertov's late political poetry. For Hollenberg, Levertov seeks "to mirror and transcend the confusion and angst of a person caught in a world of catastrophe" and does so through ekphrasis informed by nuanced selection of concrete details. Hollenberg, "History as I desired it," 519-37.

98. Cary Nelson, *Our Last First Poets*, 16.

99. Altieri, *Self and Sensibility*, 126–28. For a more thorough review of the critical reception of Levertov's political poetry, see Rodgers, *Denise Levertov*, 47–56.

100. Levertov, *Poems 1968–1972*, 149.

101. Lorrie Smith, "Songs of Experience," in Gelpi, ed., *Denise Levertov*, 186–88. Dorothy Nielsen alters the terms of this debate by emphasizing the I-thou relation between subjects as more typical of Levertov's treatment of images than it is of imagist objectification. For Nielsen, Levertov's political poetry of empathy grows from her earlier treatment of the natural, concrete image. Nielsen, "Mystical/Political Poetry," 89–90.

102. Levertov, *Poems 1968–1972*, 173–74.

103. Ibid., 150.

104. Ibid., 170.

105. Ibid., 150.

106. Ibid., 155.

107. Marx and Engels, *Manifesto of the Communist Party*, 17. Levertov commented that she took this line from a contemporary popular song by *The Doors*. Levertov, pers. comm., August 3, 1994.

108. Levertov, *Poems 1968–1972*, 153.

109. Ibid., 155.

110. Ibid., 147.

111. Ibid., 159.

112. Ibid., 187.

113. Ibid., 181–82.

114. Ibid., 188.

115. Ibid., 130.

116. Ibid., 155.

117. Ibid., 147.

118. Ibid., 188.

119. Ibid., 184.

120. Ibid., 186.

121. Duncan to Levertov, 607.

122. Ibid., 612.

123. Marjorie Perloff has traced the history of this correspondence more fully in *Poetry On and Off the Page*, 208–21.

This divergence is partially a product of earlier differences. Levertov, with her emphasis on the personal and concrete, consistently resisted Duncan's emphasis on accident in composition. For a discussion of how their war poetry extends their earlier poetics, see the chapters on Duncan and Levertov in Mersmann, *Out of the Vietnam Vortex*, esp. 89–90, 103–110, 173–81. Although Mersmann discusses how each poet's perception of the war as destructive of poetic form reveals a close association of poetic form with other forms of life, he also demonstrates how Duncan's and Levertov's war poetry grows out of their earlier poetic temperaments.

Some of the correspondence concerning the argument I present is documented by Levertov in "Some Duncan Letters—A Memoir and a Critical Tribute," *Light Up the Cave*, 196–232. Here Levertov also recalls her earlier disagreement with Duncan over the graphic presentations of violence in her war poetry, which Duncan took to be repressed anger at men in a sexualized revenge fantasy. Duncan's conflation of the international war with the war between the sexes follows H. D.'s thematization of World War II as a war of masculine and feminine on the home front in both *Asphodel* and *Helen in Egypt*. On war as a contest between men and women, see Susan Stanford Friedman's "Creating a Women's Mythology," *Signets*, 373–405. Levertov resented Duncan's Freudian playing out of meanings and insistence on the inner sources of her anger in this war of the sexes rather than in the protest and outrage at the political situation.

Mackey also summarizes the Duncan-Levertov quarrel in "from *Gassire's*

Lute," part IV, 218–19. While Duncan's psychoanalytic interpretations of Levertov's political poetry reflect his wartime understanding of history, I will focus on the conflicting ways each claims authority to speak publicly as a poet, particularly on the different relation each establishes between poetic tradition and the contemporary historical community.

124. Duncan to Levertov, 609–10.

125. Ibid., 611.

126. Ibid., 661, 669.

127. Ibid., 661.

128. Ibid., 666.

129. Ibid., 673–74.

130. Ibid., 619.

131. Ibid., 670.

132. Ibid., 660.

133. Ibid., 669.

134. By the mid-1960s, Duncan and Levertov differed on the nature of poetic agency. Levertov initially resisted the looser structure of *Passages* as an abdication of poetic control of meaning. Duncan claimed that he wished "to disconnect, to unweave" meaning in an attempt "to open my work up to material that lies just beyond my recognition of use as I work" and thereby work toward a new meaning not initially known (Duncan to Levertov, 466).

Interestingly, Levertov articulates a loose formal structure similar to Duncan's in *Passages* as the goal of her *Olga Poems,* "to approach the focal point from different distances & in different moods," resulting in a formal "wheel of sorts" (Levertov to Duncan, 471).

Whereas Duncan seeks to submerge personal agency in a wider process of world creation, Levertov would retain conscious individual control of meaning. In the same way, Duncan's malaise at contemporary events emerges in poetry as "contagion" (Duncan, *Bending the Bow,* 32), an identification of poetry with history. Levertov objects and would maintain personal voice apart from history, insisting that poetry maintains an ideal realm separate from history and capable of articulating a perfection beyond. Her reply to Duncan ("Poetry is a possibility without which humans are incomplete. This is health, not sickness" [Levertov to Duncan, 465]) indicates the possibility that poetry may help to resist infection from public events and thus to fulfill a higher ideal of human nature.

135. Levertov to Duncan, 677.

136. Ibid., 683.

137. Ibid., 682.

138. Ibid., 684.

139. Duncan, *Ground Work: Before the War,* 46.

140. Ibid., 53.

141. Habermas, *Structural Transformation*, 181ff.
142. Brown, *Politics Out of History*, 3–5.
143. Levertov, *Poems 1968–1972*, 165; Duncan, *Ground Work: Before the War*, 46.
144. Brown, *Politics Out of History*, 52–53.
145. Ibid., 56.
146. Sisko, "To Stay Alive," 52–54. Although I agree with this aspect of Sisko's argument, I disagree with her analysis of Levertov's conception of poetry as that of the recording "camera eye" as the source of this incompatibility of poetry with political activism.
147. Duncan, *Fictive Certainties*, 27.
148. Duncan, *Bending the Bow*, v.

NOTES TO CHAPTER 5

1. Dorn to Levertov, June 3, 1959, Denise Levertov Papers, Department of Special Collections, University Libraries, Stanford University. Creeley was a member of Dorn's examination committee for graduation at Black Mountain College.
2. Dorn, "Interview with John Wright," 121–22.
3. Ibid., 138.
4. Levertov, *Life in the Forest*, 62. Cary Nelson interprets this change in Levertov's *The Freeing of the Dust* as a recognition of the power of ideology to influence individuals that she had denied in her earlier writing. Nelson, *Our Last First Poets*, 25. While I agree with Nelson's explanation, I focus on this awareness as the motive for Levertov's return to the personal as the basis of political reform in her subsequent work.
5. Levertov, *Light Up the Cave*, 118. One must interpret Levertov's theory of political poetry as a response to the negative critical reception of *To Stay Alive* (see discussion of this reception in Chapter 4) and of others' political poems during the war. Critics felt her poetic treatment of political topics crude and inferior to her previous work. Her defense focuses on the lyric power of political statement. "The question, can a political poem be poetry? seems to me a wholly modern one" (Levertov, *Light Up the Cave*, 117). In an essay on Neruda, Levertov argues that "there is no inherent contradiction between the spheres of poetry and (revolutionary) politics, . . . that it is indeed their basic relatedness that is inherent" (Ibid., 135).
6. Levertov, *Light Up the Cave*, 120–21.
7. Ibid., 128.
8. Ibid.
9. Ibid., 123.
10. Levertov, *Life in the Forest*, vii.
11. Pavese, *Hard Labor*, 191.
12. Ibid., 195, 202. In a 1972 interview with Ian Reid, Levertov comments on

other attempts to move away from a single speaker in her experimentation with "a Russian conversation poem" in which more than one voice is heard. Brooker, *Conversations with Denise Levertov*, 74.

13. The "Homage to Pavese" section of *Life in the Forest* imitates Pavese more directly by recovering childhood innocence and memories based in beliefs of cultural tradition, as in the definition of hope gleaned from a naive reading of Chekhov with a friend in "Chekhov on the West Heath." I focus on the later sections of the volume, in which Levertov incorporates Pavese's poetics into her idea of political poetry.

14. Levertov, *Life in the Forest*, 126–27.

15. Ibid., 134.

16. Levertov, *Candles in Babylon*, 35.

17. Ibid.

18. Diane LeBlanc argues that Levertov's compound words reflect a patriarchal dualism that divides the self and that Sylvia transcends in the course of the poem. LeBlanc notes that there are more compounds in the first half of the poem than the second and argues that this expresses Sylvia's maturation toward an undivided self. However, the divisions and compound words are not always gendered and do not seem to reflect the gender divisions of a patriarchal culture. Sylvia uses "cowfriend" (the female Kaya), "dogbrothers," "She-human," and "He-human," terms that express relations to both masculine and feminine characters. I emphasize that the decrease in compounds is not nearly as significant as their continued presence and significance in articulating Sylvia's understanding of self through relation to others in her environment. (The number of "standard compounds" decreases from fourteen to eight, but the number of compound neologisms and hyphenated words varies only by two and four, respectively). Further, hybridity need not represent division, and the interplay between recognition of similarity and difference is integral to a communal self-understanding enriched by diversity. LeBlanc, "Pilgrimage, Duality, and Quest," 106–21.

19. Levertov, *Candles in Babylon*, 25–26.

20. Ibid., 29.

21. Ibid., 39.

22. Ibid., 30.

23. Ibid., 31.

24. Hedda Marcus writes of the importance of empathy in *Pig Dreams* but emphasizes its value in revealing a universally natural or animal "unity of all creatures" rather than the comprehension of difference. Marcus, "Into the Wild," 79–80.

25. Levertov, *Candles in Babylon*, 38.

26. Ibid., n.p.

27. Ibid.

28. Ibid., 4.

29. Ibid., 5.
30. Ibid., 15.
31. Ibid., 19.
32. Audrey Rodgers discusses the increasing emphasis on the relation between outer world and sensitive perceiver and the importance of place in *Candles in Babylon* but focuses on Levertov's representation of the radical difference between crisis and calm rather than on the dynamic between them. Rodgers, *Denise Levertov*, 146, 160.
33. Levertov, *Candles in Babylon*, 57.
34. Ibid., 58.
35. Ibid., 100.
36. Ibid., 77–78.
37. Ibid., 92–93.
38. Ibid., 93.
39. Ibid.
40. Ibid.
41. Ibid., 95.
42. Ibid., 101.
43. Ibid., 91.
44. Ibid., 112.
45. Ibid., 113.
46. Ibid., 108.
47. Ibid., 108–9.
48. Ibid., 111.
49. Ibid.
50. Ibid., 113.
51. Ibid., 114.
52. Ibid., 115.
53. Albert Gelpi, "Introduction," *Denise Levertov*, 5.
54. Dorn to Levertov, January 21, 1960, and January 31, 1961, Levertov, Denise Levertov Papers, Department of Special Collections, University Libraries, Stanford University.
55. Dorn, *Views*, 69.
56. Fox and Frobenius, qtd. in Edward Dorn, *Views*, 83.
57. Dorn, *Collected Poems*, 46–47.
58. Dorn to Levertov, November 24, 1958, Levertov, Denise Levertov Papers, Department of Special Collections, University Libraries, Stanford University.
59. Von Hallberg, *American Poetry and Culture*, 206–8. What draws Dorn initially to Jones's work is its engagement with the mechanisms of culture that create local place, the measure Dorn also respects in Olson (Dorn, *Views*, 71). Unlike Olson, however, Jones emphasizes ideology rather than geography as the primary force shaping place. Dorn's review of Jones's *The Dutchman and the Slave* focuses

on the absorption of characters into the ideologies with which they are associated. Dorn quotes a long debate from the play concerning whether political rhetoric refers to specific individuals or an abstract group. He concludes that "social anthropology is a false endeavor in the sense that when you look at a certain feature you're supposed to associate it with the catalogue of which it is a part, before I ever knew even on casual terms a negro I was misled to think of them as a problem that wanted a 'sensible' solution" (Dorn, *Views*, 76–77). Dorn is interested in Jones's exploration of the relation between individual and category. Von Hallberg goes on to interpret *Gunslinger*'s narrative and logical discontinuities as continuing this decontextualization. Von Hallberg, *American Poetry and Culture*, 212–17.

James Elmborg covers similar ground in tracing Dorn's rejection of the "I" as a political subject. Elmborg, *Pageant of Its Time*, 56–61.

60. Dorn, *Views*, 118–19.

61. Ibid., 36.

62. Dorn, *Interviews*, 54.

63. Dorn, "Interview with Roy K. Okada," 140.

64. Brian McHale relates Dorn's reversal of the relation between literal and figurative to Menippean satire as a pervasive element in 1960s literature. McHale, *Obligation Toward the Difficult Whole*.

65. Dorn, *Gunslinger*, 3.

66. Slinger distinguishes between death and the loss of a unique life that mere "mortals" associate with death. "I die, he said / which is not the same as Mortality" (Ibid., 32). Slinger also attributes his slowing down to the angle of the sun, returning to a linguistic and thus human source of natural phenomena. However, he reveals the apparent motion of the sun to be the motion of the earth that he causes when he speaks. "You say the Sun moves!? / Not exactly. Yet when I say what I say, / The Earth Turns" (Ibid., 80).

67. Ibid., 37.

68. Ibid., 70.

69. Davidson, "To eliminate the draw" in Wesling, *Internal Resistances*, 115–16.

70. Dorn, *Interviews*, 50. Davidson discusses the significance of the views of the specific philosophers Dorn chooses, all of whom oppose the Cartesian model of ego. Davidson, in Wesling, *Internal Resistances*, 119–20.

71. Dorn, *Gunslinger*, 46.

72. Ibid., 49.

73. Ibid., 48.

74. Ibid., 55.

75. Ibid., 57–58.

76. Ibid., 48.

77. Ibid., 39.

78. Ibid., 89.
79. Ibid., 90–91.
80. Ibid., 109.
81. Ibid., 136.
82. Ibid., 137.
83. Ibid., 5.
84. Ibid., 163.
85. Ibid., 132.
86. Ibid., 164.
87. Ibid., 153.
88. Ibid., 154.
89. Ibid., 156.
90. Ibid., 180–81.
91. Ibid., 167.
92. Ibid., 200.
93. Ibid., 135.
94. Ibid., 150.
95. Ibid., 155.
96. Foster, "Kick[ing] the Perpendiculars," 79, 84, 102.
97. Dorn, *Gunslinger*, 50.
98. Ibid., 57.

NOTES TO THE CONCLUSION

1. Creeley to Duncan, December 6, 1978, Robert Duncan Papers, Poetry Collection of the University Libraries, University Libraries, State University of New York at Buffalo. In the same letter, Creeley asserts that he now finds *Gunslinger* brilliant. He states his sense of a common purpose with Dorn as a follower of Olson in the interest of preserving the unity of a poetic tradition stemming from Olson and now under attack in the poetic and academic communities.

2. Duncan, "Interview with Mary Emma Harris," Robert Duncan Papers, Poetry Collection of the University Libraries, University Libraries, State University of New York at Buffalo, 16. Ellipses in brackets refer to my omission; all others are Harris's notation of pauses in Duncan's speech.

3. Duncan, "Interview with Mary Emma Harris," Robert Duncan Papers, Poetry Collection of the University Libraries, University Libraries, State University of New York at Buffalo, 17. Dorn notices a similar departure from what he calls the subjective or objective "locality" he sees in Pound's *Cantos*, Williams's *Paterson*, and Olson's *Maximus Poems* and characterizes *Gunslinger* as a poem of the West, which "keeps shifting under your feet and that was intolerable to [Olson]." Dorn thus articulates his difference from Olson as unconcern for totality. Dorn, "Interview by Kevin Bezner," 43.

4. Duncan, "Interview with Mary Emma Harris," Robert Duncan Papers, Poetry Collection of the University Libraries, University Libraries, State University of New York at Buffalo, 18.

5. Duncan to Creeley, December 12, 1978, Robert Creeley Papers, Department of Special Collections, University Libraries, Stanford University.

6. Jenkins, "*Gunslinger*'s Ethics of Excess," 210; Dorn, "Interview with John Wright," 127. James Elmborg argues, less persuasively, that Dorn's writing "from 'outside'" employs "scientific detachment to avoid an overly emotional portrayal that might seem self-righteous or hysterical." While Dorn does resist sentimental emotion in protest, I believe this comes less from his fear of excess emotion than from his sense that individual emotion has nothing to do with agency in the public arena. Elmborg, *"Pageant of Its Time"*, 32–34.

7. Dorn, "Interview with Kevin Bezner," 43.

8. Dorn, *Abhorrences*, 66.

9. Ibid., 16.

10. Duncan, *Ground Work: Before the War*, 137ff.; Levertov, *Breathing the Water*, 89; Creeley, "Preface," in Levertov, *Selected Poems*, xiii–xvi.

11. Levertov, *Door in the Hive*, 44.

12. Levertov, *Evening Train*, 81–83.

13. Levertov, *Door in the Hive*, 53.

14. Levertov, *Breathing the Water*, 81–82.

15. Levertov, *Door in the Hive*, 53.

16. Ibid., 29.

17. Levertov, *Sands of the Well*, 53.

18. Ibid., 54–55.

19. This is not a criticism, for I am discussing poetry, not a methodology for political activism.

20. Levertov, *Sands of the Well*, 114.

21. Duncan, *Ground Work: Before the War*, 22.

22. Collis, "Frayed Trope of Rome," 145.

23. Duncan, *Ground Work: Before the War*, 56.

24. Ibid., 59.

25. Ibid., 96–97.

26. Ibid., 104.

27. Ibid., 107–08.

28. Duncan, *Ground Work II*, 6.

29. Finkelstein, "Late Duncan," 362.

30. Duncan, *Ground Work II*, 8.

31. Davidson, *Ghostlier Demarcations*, 191–93.

32. Duncan, *Ground Work II*, 45.

33. Ibid., 39, 51, 54, 90.

34. Creeley, *Presences*, n.p.

35. Coleridge, qtd. in Creeley, *Echoes*, n.p.

36. Creeley, *Later*, 6–7.

37. Ibid., 17.

38. Ibid., 18.

39. Ibid., 20.

40. Ibid., 25–26.

41. Ibid., 68.

42. Hejinian, "Interview with Tyrus Miller," 34.

43. Sloan, "Crude Mechanical Access," 241–42, 247.

44. Charles Bernstein, "Creeley's Eye," 138.

45. Watten, "Robert Creeley," 138–39.

46. Scalapino, "Thinking Serially," 46–48.

47. See Levertov and the nature poets and Christian poets she mentions in "Some Affinities of Content," Levertov, *New & Selected Essays*, 1–21; Hatlen, "Toward a Common Ground," 255.

48. Levertov, *New & Selected Essays*, 8. Levertov criticizes Language poetry as failing to respect communal meanings, as "ignor[ing] the consensus of understanding of what words denote; I find that arrogant, a kind of elitism that denies the human communion." "Interview with Jean W. Ross," in Brooker, *Conversations*, 169.

49. Johnson, *Robert Duncan*, 26.

50. McCaffery, "Death of the Subject," n.p. Andrews also uses the image of a Möbius strip in "Text and Context," n.p.

51. McCaffery, "Death of the Subject," n.p.

52. Silliman, "For Open Letter," n.p. Although many Language poets explore other models of poetic communication, particularly from non-Western cultures, they rarely apply these models to their own writing. Silliman's capitalist model of linguistic fetishism seems to dominate the construction of the reader-writer relation in their conception of Western writing. See, for example, Jerome Rothenberg's contribution in Bernstein, *Politics of Poetic Form*.

53. See, for example, work published in *Sulfur* and early essays in *The Politics of Poetic Form*.

54. Fraser, *Translating the Unspeakable*, 149ff.

55. Beach, *Poetic Culture*.

56. Ibid., 91–92.

57. Hatlen, "Toward a Common Ground"; Geoff Ward, "Before and After Language," in Kelly, *Poetry and the Sense of Panic*, 170–71; Vanderborg, *Paratextual Communities*, 98.

58. I have traced the popular format of such little magazines as *Evergreen* and *Yugen* elsewhere. Dewey, "Open Form and Collective Voice," 47–66.

59. On the elite audience of Language writing, see Silliman, "For Open Let-

ter," n.p. Altieri echoes Silliman's self-consciousness in stating the gap between the revolutionary ideals and the actual effect of Language poetry. The "disrup[tion] of the syntactic forms by which hegemony is maintained . . . do[es] not directly affect any of the agendas we pursue in public life or the specific commitments we make to actual political communities." Altieri, "Afterword," in DuPlessis and Quartermain, *The Objectivist Nexus*, 313.

60. Davidson emphasizes the role of such machines in *Ghostlier Demarcations*. Todd Gitlin traces changes in the political counterculture's strategies, from debate-style argumentation and manifestoes to sound-bite-oriented media events in *The Whole World Is Watching*.

61. See, for example, Lehman's *The Last Avant-Garde*, Ellingham and Killian's *Poet Be Like God*, and Terrell Scott Herring's "Frank O'Hara's Open Closet," 414–27.

Bibliography

Adams, Brooks. *The Law of Civilization and Decay: An Essay on History.* New York: The Macmillan Company, 1896.

————. *The Theory of Social Revolutions.* New York: The Macmillan Company, 1913.

Adams, Brooks, and Henry Adams. *The Degradation of the Democratic Dogma.* New York: The Macmillan Company, 1919.

Adams, Henry. *The Education of Henry Adams.* Edited by Ernest Samuels. Boston: Houghton Mifflin Company, 1973.

Ahearn, Barry. *Zukofsky's "A": An Introduction.* Berkeley: University of California Press, 1983.

Alighieri, Dante. Inferno. Vol. 1 of *The Divine Comedy.* Translated by Allen Mandelbaum. New York: Bantam Books, 1980.

Allen, Donald, ed. *The New American Poetry 1945–1960.* New York: Grove Press, 1960.

Altieri, Charles. *Painterly Abstraction in Modernist American Poetry: The Contemporaneity of Modernism.* Cambridge: Cambridge University Press, 1989.

————. *Self and Sensibility in Contemporary American Poetry.* Cambridge: Cambridge University Press, 1984.

Anderson, Benedict. *Imagined Communities: Reflections on the Origin and Spread of Nationalism.* Rev. ed. London: Verso, 1991.

Andrews, Bruce. "Text and Context." *L=A=N=G=U=A=G=E.* Supplement Number One (June 1980): n.p.

Auping, Michael, ed. *Jess: A Grand Collage.* Buffalo, NY: Albright Knox Art Gallery, 1993.

Ball, Terence. "The Politics of Social Science in Postwar America." In *Recasting America: Culture and Politics in the Age of Cold War,* edited by Lary May, 79–92. Chicago: University of Chicago Press, 1989.

Beach, Christopher. *Poetic Culture: Contemporary American Poetry between Community and Institution.* Evanston: Northwestern University Press, 1999.

Bell, Ian F. A. *The Critic as Scientist: The Modernist Poetics of Ezra Pound.* London: Methuen, 1981.

Benhabib, Seyla. "Models of Public Space: Hannah Arendt, the Liberal Tradition, and Jürgen Habermas." In *Habermas and the Public Sphere*, edited by Craig Calhoun, 73–98. Cambridge: The MIT Press, 1992.

Bérard, Henri. *Did Homer Live?* Translated by Brian Rhys. New York: E. P. Dutton & Co., 1931.

Berkson, William. *Fields of Force: The Development of a World View from Faraday to Einstein.* New York: John Wiley and Sons, 1974.

Bernstein, Charles. "Creeley's Eye and the Fiction of the Self." *Review of Contemporary Fiction* 15, no. 3 (1995): 137–40.

———, ed. *The Politics of Poetic Form: Poetry and Public Policy.* New York: Roof, 1990.

Bernstein, Michael André. " 'Bringing it all back home': Derivations and Quotations in Robert Duncan and the Poundian Tradition." *Sagetrieb* 1, no. 2 (1982): 176–89.

———. *The Tale of the Tribe: Ezra Pound and the Modern Verse Epic.* Princeton: Princeton University Press, 1980.

Bernstein, Michael André, and Burton Hatlen. "Interview with Robert Duncan." *Sagetrieb* 4, nos. 2–3 (1985): 87–135.

Bertholf, Robert J., and Ian W. Reid, eds. *Robert Duncan, Scales of the Marvelous.* New York: New Directions, 1979.

Bertonneau, Thomas F. "Life in a Human Universe: Charles Olson's (Post) Modernism in Context (An Anthropoetics)." *Sagetrieb* 13, no. 3 (1994): 117–52.

Blackburn, Paul. "The Grinding Down." *Kulchur* 3, no. 10 (1963): 9–19.

Bollobás, Enikő. *Charles Olson.* New York: Twayne Publishers, 1992.

Breslin, James. *From Modern to Contemporary: American Poetry, 1945–1965.* Chicago: Chicago University Press, 1984.

Breslin, Paul. *The Psycho-Political Muse: American Poetry since the Fifties.* Chicago: University of Chicago Press, 1987.

Bronk, William. "Aspects of the World Like Coral Reefs." *Origin* 7 (1952): 115–16.

Brooker, Jewel Spears, ed. *Conversations with Denise Levertov.* Jackson: University of Mississippi Press, 1998.

Brown, Wendy. *Politics Out of History.* Princeton: Princeton University Press, 2001.

Brunner, Edward. *Cold War Poetry: The Social Text in the Fifties Poem.* Urbana: University of Illinois Press, 2001.

Butterick, George. *A Guide to* The Maximus Poems *of Charles Olson.* Berkeley: University of California Press, 1978.

Byrd, Don. "*Charles Olson's* Maximus: *An Introduction.*" PhD diss., University of Kansas, 1971.

———. "The Poetry of Production." *Sagetrieb* 2, no. 2 (1983): 7–43.

———. "Possibility of Measure." *Boundary 2* 2, nos. 1–2 (1973–74): 39–53.

Carter, Steven. "Fields of Spacetime and the "I" in Charles Olson's *The Maximus Poems*." In *American Literature and Science*, edited by Robert J. Scholnick, 194–208. Lexington: University of Kentucky Press, 1992.

Cavallo, Dominick J. *A Fiction of the Past: The Sixties in American History*. New York: Palgrave, 1999.

Christensen, Paul. *Charles Olson: Call Him Ishmael*. Austin: University of Texas Press, 1979.

Clark, Tom. *Charles Olson: The Allegory of a Poet's Life*. New York: W. W. Norton & Co., 1991.

———. *Ed Dorn: A World of Difference*. Berkeley: North Atlantic Books, 2002.

———. *Robert Creeley and the Genius of the American Commonplace*. New York: New Directions, 1993.

Coleridge, Samuel Taylor. *Biographia Literaria*. 2 vols., edited by John Shawcross. Oxford: Oxford University Press, 1968.

Collis, Stephen Scott. "'The Frayed Trope of Rome': Poetic Architecture in Robert Duncan, Ronald Johnson, and Lisa Robertson." *Mosaic: A Journal for the Interdisciplinary Study of Literature* 35, no. 4 (2002): 143–62.

Combs, Maxine. "A Study of Black Mountain Poets." PhD diss., University of Oregon, 1967.

Comens, Bruce. "Soundings: The 'An' Song Beginning "*A*"-22." *Sagetrieb* 5, no. 1 (1986): 95–106.

Conniff, Brian. *The Lyric and Modern Poetry: Olson, Creeley, Bunting*. New York: Peter Lang, 1988.

Conte, Joseph M. *Unending Design: The Forms of Postmodern Poetry*. Ithaca: Cornell University Press, 1991.

Corman, Cid. Editorial Comment. *Origin* 2 (1951): 69.

———. Editorial Comment. *Origin* 4 (1951–52): 233ff.

———. Manuscripts. Lilly Library. University of Indiana at Bloomington.

———. Review of Karl Shapiro's *Collected Poems 1940–1953*. *Black Mountain Review* 3 (1957): 55.

Creeley, Robert. *The Collected Essays of Robert Creeley*. Berkeley: University of California Press, 1989.

———. *The Collected Poems of Robert Creeley 1945–1975*. Berkeley: University of California Press, 1982.

———. *Contexts of Poetry: Interviews 1961–1971*. Edited by Donald Allen. Bolinas: Four Seasons Foundation, 1973.

———. *A Day Book*. Exp. ed. New York: Charles Scribner's Sons, 1972.

———. *Echoes*. New York: New Directions, 1993.

———. "The Innocent." *Origin* 6 (1952): 117.

———. *Later*. New York: New Directions, 1979.

———. *Memory Gardens*. New York: New Directions, 1986.

———. *Mirrors*. New York: New Directions, 1983.

———. Papers. Special Collections. Lilly Library, University of Indiana Library.

———. Papers. Special Collections. Stanford University Libraries.

———. Papers. Special Collections. Washington University Libraries.

———. Papers. Thomas J. Dodd Research Center. University of Connecticut Libraries. University of Connecticut at Storrs.

———. *Presences: A Text for Marisol*. New York: Charles Scribner's Sons, 1976.

———. *A Quick Graph: Collected Notes and Essays*. Edited by Donald Allen. Bolinas: Four Seasons Foundation, 1970.

———. *Tales Out of School: Selected Interviews*. Ann Arbor: University of Michigan Press, 1993.

———. *Was That a Real Poem & Other Essays*. Edited by Donald Allen. Bolinas: Four Seasons Foundation, 1979.

———. *Windows*. New York: New Directions, 1990.

Cronick, Joseph. "Robert Duncan and the Truth That Lies in Myth." *Sagetrieb* 4, nos. 2–3 (1982): 191–207.

Damon, Maria. *The Dark End of the Street: Margins in American Vanguard Poetry*. Minneapolis: University of Minnesota Press, 1993.

Davidson, Michael. "Dismantling 'Mantis': Reification and Objectivist Poetics." *American Literary History* 3, no. 3 (1991): 521–41.

———. *Ghostlier Demarcations: Modern Poetry and the Material World*. Berkeley: University of California Press, 1997.

———. *Guys Like Us: Citing Masculinity in Cold War Poetics*. Chicago: University of Chicago Press, 2004.

———. *The San Francisco Renaissance: Poetics and Community at Mid-century*. Cambridge: Cambridge University Press, 1989.

Dawson, Fielding. *The Black Mountain Book*. Exp. and rev. ed. Rocky Mount, North Carolina: Wesleyan College Press, 1991.

Dayton, Irene. "A Woman Leaves Her Marriage." *Black Mountain Review* 3 (1952).

DeKoven, Marianne. *Utopia Limited: The Sixties and the Emergence of the Postmodern*. Durham: Duke University Press, 2004.

Dewey, Anne. "The Relation between Open Form and Collective Voice: The Social Origins of Processual Form in John Ashbery's *Three Poems* and Ed Dorn's *Gunslinger*." *Sagetrieb* 11, nos. 1 and 2 (1992): 47–66.

Dickie, Margaret. *On the Modernist Long Poem*. Iowa City: University of Iowa Press, 1986.

Dickstein, Morris. *Leopards in the Temple: The Transformation of American Fiction*. Cambridge: Harvard University Press, 2001.

Dorn, Edward. *Abhorrences*. Santa Rosa: Black Sparrow Press, 1990.

———. *The Collected Poems, 1956–1974*. Exp. edition. San Francisco: Four Seasons Foundation, 1983.

————. *Gunslinger*. Edited by Marjorie Perloff. Durham: Duke University Press, 1989.

————. "Interview with John Wright." *Chicago Review* 39, no. 1 (1992): 102–47.

————. "Interview with Kevin Bezner." *American Poetry Review* 21, no. 5 (1992): 43.

————. "Interview with Roy K. Okada." In *Interviews with Contemporary Writers, Second Series, 1972–1982*, edited by L. S. Dembo, 130–47. Madison: University of Wisconsin Press, 1983.

————. *Interviews*. Edited by Donald Allen. Bolinas: Four Seasons Foundation, 1980.

————. Papers. Thomas J. Dodd Research Center. University of Connecticut Libraries. University of Connecticut at Storrs.

————. *Views*. Edited by Donald Allen. San Francisco: Four Seasons Foundation, 1980.

Doss, Erika. *Benton, Pollock, and the Politics of Modernism: From Regionalism to Abstract Expressionism*. Chicago: University of Chicago Press, 1991.

Duberman, Martin. *Black Mountain: An Exploration in Community*. New York: Dutton, 1972.

Duncan, Robert. "Beginnings: Chapter 1 of the H. D. Book, Part I." *Coyote's Journal* 5/6 (1966): 8–31.

————. *Bending the Bow*. New York: New Directions, 1968.

————. *Derivations: Selected Poems 1950–1956*. London: Fulcrum Press, 1968.

————. *Fictive Certainties*. New York: New Directions, 1985.

————. "From the H. D. Book, Part II Chapter 5 (section one)." *Stony Brook* 3/4 (1969): 336–47.

————. *Ground Work: Before the War*. New York: New Directions, 1984.

————. *Ground Work II: In the Dark*. New York: New Directions, 1987.

————. "The H. D. Book, Part I: Chapter 2." *Coyote's Journal* 8 (1967): 27–35.

————. "The H. D. Book: Part II Nights and Days. Chapter 4." *Caterpillar* 7 (1969): 27–60.

————. "The Homosexual in Society." In *Robert Duncan: A Selected Prose*, edited by Robert J. Bertholf, 38–50. New York: New Directions, 1995.

————. Letter to Henry Rago. July 15, 1954. "Poetry" Mss., Correspondence. Lilly Library. University of Indiana.

————. "Nights and Days." *Sumac* 1, no. 1 (1968): 101–46.

————. *The Opening of the Field*. New York: New Directions, 1960.

————. Papers. The Poetry Collection of the University Libraries. State University of New York at Buffalo.

————. *Roots and Branches*. New York: New Directions, 1964.

————. *Selected Poems*. Edited by Robert J. Bertholf. New York: New Directions, 1993.

———. *A Selected Prose*. Edited by Robert J. Bertholf. New York: New Directions, 1995.

———. "Two Chapters from H. D." *TriQuarterly* 12 (1968): 67–98.

———. *The Years As Catches: First poems (1939–1946)*. Berkeley: Oyez Press, 1966.

Duncan, Robert, and H. D. *A Great Admiration: H. D. and Robert Duncan Correspondence 1950–1961*. Edited by Robert J. Bertholf. Venice, CA: The Lapis Press, 1992.

Duncan, Robert, and Denise Levertov. *The Letters of Robert Duncan and Denise Levertov*, edited by Robert J. Bertholf and Albert Gelpi. Stanford: Stanford University Press, 2004.

DuPlessis, Rachel Blau, and Peter Quartermain, eds. *The Objectivist Nexus: Essays in Cultural Poetics*. Tuscaloosa: University of Alabama Press, 1999.

Ellingham, Lewis, and Kevin Killian. *Poet Be Like God: Jack Spicer and the San Francisco Renaissance*. Middletown: Wesleyan University Press, 1998.

Elmborg, James K. *"A Pageant of Its Time": Edward Dorn's* Slinger *and the Sixties*. New York: Peter Lang, 1998.

Engelhardt, Tom. *The End of Victory Culture: Cold War America and the Disillusioning of a Generation*. Amherst: University of Massachusetts Press, 1995.

Enslin, Theodore. "Sea Lavender." *Origin* 7 (1952): 127.

Entwhistle, Alice. "Creeley and Crane: 'The kick/ of the foot against.'" *The Cambridge Quarterly* 27, no. 2 (1998): 87–106.

Faas, Ekbert. "Charles Olson and D. H. Lawrence: Aesthetics of the Primitive Abstract." *Boundary 2* 2, nos. 1–2 (1973–74): 113–26.

———, ed. *Towards a New American Poetics: Essays and Interviews*. Santa Barbara: Black Sparrow Press, 1978.

Faas, Ekbert, and Maria Trombacco. *Robert Creeley: A Biography*. Hanover: University Press of New England, 2001.

Finkelstein, Norman. "Late Duncan: From Poetry to Scripture." *Twentieth Century Literature: A Scholarly and Critical Journal* 51, no. 3 (2005): 341–72.

Foster, Edward. *Understanding the Black Mountain Poets*. Columbia: University of South Carolina Press, 1994.

Foster, Thomas. "'Kick[ing] the Perpendiculars Outa Right Anglos': Ed Dorn's Multiculturalism." *Contemporary Literature* 38, no. 1 (1997): 78–105.

Fox, Willard. *Robert Creeley, Ed Dorn, and Robert Duncan: A Reference Guide*. Boston: G. K. Hall, 1989.

Frank, Joseph. "Spatial Form in Modern Literature." Part I. *Sewanee Review* 53, no. 2 (1945): 201–39.

Fraser, Kathleen. *translating the unspeakable: Poetry and the Innovative Necessity*. Tuscaloosa: University of Alabama Press, 2000.

Fredman, Stephen. *The Grounding of American Poetry: Charles Olson and the Emersonian Tradition*. Cambridge: Cambridge University Press, 1993.

————. *Poet's Prose: The Crisis in American Verse*. Cambridge: Cambridge University Press, 1983.

Friedman, Susan Stanford. *Psyche Reborn: The Emergence of H. D.* Bloomington: Indiana University Press, 1981.

Friedman, Susan Stanford, and Rachel Blau DuPlessis, eds. *Signets: Reading H. D.* Madison: University of Wisconsin Press, 1990.

Gelpi, Albert. *A Coherent Splendor: The American Literary Renaissance 1910–1950*. Cambridge: Cambridge University Press, 1989.

————, ed. *Denise Levertov: Selected Criticism*. Ann Arbor: University of Michigan Press, 1993.

Gitlin, Todd. *The Whole World Is Watching: Mass Media in the Making and Unmaking of the New Left*. Berkeley: University of California Press, 2003.

Glover, Albert. "Evolution in Ezra Pound's Poetics of History and Charles Olson's Special View." *Paideuma* 24, nos. 2–3 (1995): 57–67.

Golding, Alan. *From Outlaw to Classic: Canons in American Poetry*. Madison: University of Wisconsin Press, 1996.

————. "The New American Poetry Revisited, Again." *Contemporary Literature* 39, no. 2 (1998): 180–211.

Graves, Robert. *The White Goddess: A Historical Investigation*. Amended and exp. ed. New York: Farrar, Straus and Giroux, 1948.

Greenberg, Clement. *The Collected Essays and Criticism*. 2 vols., edited by John O'Brian. Chicago: University of Chicago Press, 1986.

Grieve-Carlson, Gary. "The Cracked Tune That Chronos Sings: W. B. Yeats, Charles Olson, and the Idea of History." PhD diss., Boston University, 1988.

H. D. *Collected Poems 1912–1944*. Edited by Louis L. Martz. New York: New Directions, 1983.

Habermas, Jürgen. *The Structural Transformation of the Public Sphere: An Inquiry into a Category of Bourgeois Society*. Translated by Thomas Burger and Frederick Lawrence. Cambridge: The MIT Press, 1991.

Hamilton, R. S. "After Strange Gods: Duncan Reading Pound and H. D." *Sagetrieb* 4, nos. 2–3 (1982): 225–40.

Harris, Mary Emma. *The Arts at Black Mountain College*. Cambridge: The MIT Press, 1987.

Hatlen, Burton. "Art and/as Labor: Some Dialectical Patterns in "*A*"-1 through "*A*"-10." *Wisconsin Studies in Contemporary Literature* 25, no. 2 (1984): 205–34.

————. "'Feminine Technologies': George Oppen Talks at Denise Levertov." *The American Poetry Review* 22, no. 3 (1993): 9–14.

————. "Toward a Common Ground: Versions of Place in the Poetry of Charles Olson, Edward Dorn, and Theodore Enslin." *Sagetrieb* 15, no. 3 (1996): 243–61.

————. "Zukofsky, Wittgenstein, and the Poetics of Absence." *Sagetrieb* 1, no. 1 (1982): 63–93.

Hayles, N. Katherine. *Chaos Bound: Orderly Disorder in Contemporary Literature and Science*. Ithaca: Cornell University Press, 1990.

Hejinian, Lyn. "Interview with Tyrus Miller." *Paper Air* 4, no. 2 (1989): 34–42.

Hellman, Robert. "The Quay." *Black Mountain Review* 1 (1954).

Herring, Terrell Scott. "Frank O'Hara's Open Closet." *Publications of the Modern Language Association* 117 (2002): 414–27.

Hesiod. *Theogony*. In *Hesiod and Theognis*. Translated by Dorothea Wender. Harmondsworth: Penguin Books, 1973.

Hollenberg, Donna Krolik. "'History as I desired it': Ekphrasis as Postmodern Witness in Denise Levertov's Late Poetry." *Modernism/modernity* 10 (2003): 519–37.

Holsapple, Bruce. "Williams, Whitehead and *The Embodiment of Knowledge*: 'A New Order of Knowing.'" *Sagetrieb* 9, no. 3 (1990): 57–96.

Jenkins, Grant. "*Gunslinger*'s Ethics of Excess: Subjectivity, Community, and the Politics of the Could Be." *Sagetrieb* 15, no. 3 (1996): 207–42.

Johnson, Mark Andrew. *Robert Duncan*. Boston: Twayne Publishers, 1988.

Johnston, Devin. *Precipitations: Contemporary American Poetry as Occult Practice*. Middletown: Wesleyan University Press, 2002.

Keenaghan, Eric. "Vulnerable Households: Cold War Containment and Robert Duncan's Queered Nation." *Journal of Modern Literature* 28, no. 4 (2005): 57–90.

Keller, Lynn. *Re-Making It New: Contemporary American Poetry and the Modernist Tradition*. Cambridge: Cambridge University Press, 1987.

Kelly, Lionel, ed. *Poetry and the Sense of Panic: Critical Essays on Elizabeth Bishop and John Ashbery*. Amsterdam: Rodopi, 2000.

Kern, Stephen. *The Culture of Time and Space 1880–1918*. Cambridge: Harvard University Press, 1983.

Krauss, Rosalind E. *The Originality of the Avant-Garde and Other Modernist Myths*. Cambridge: The MIT Press, 1985.

Lawrence, David Herbert. *Fantasia of the Unconscious: Psychoanalysis and the Unconscious*. London: Penguin Books, 1960.

LeBlanc, Diane C. "Pilgrimage, Duality, and Quest in Denise Levertov's 'Pig Dreams.'" *Essays in Literature* 18, no. 1 (1991): 106–21.

Lehman, David. *The Last Avant-Garde: The Making of the New York School of Poets*. New York: Doubleday, 1998.

Levertov, Denise. *Breathing the Water*. New York: New Directions, 1987.

———. *Candles in Babylon*. New York: New Directions, 1982.

———. *Collected Earlier Poems 1940–1960*. New York: New Directions, 1979.

———. *A Door in the Hive*. New York: New Directions, 1989.

———. *Evening Train*. New York: New Directions, 1992.

———. "H. D.: An Appreciation." *Poetry* 100 (1962): 182–86.

———. *Life in the Forest*. New York: New Directions, 1978.

———. *Light Up the Cave*. New York: New Directions, 1981.

———. *New & Selected Essays*. New York: New Directions, 1992.

———. *Oblique Prayers*. New York: New Directions, 1984.

———. Papers. Department of Special Collections. University Libraries. Stanford University Libraries.

———. *Poems 1960–1967*. New York: New Directions, 1983.

———. *Poems 1968–1972*. New York: New Directions, 1987.

———. *Sands of the Well*. New York: New Directions, 1996.

———. *Selected Poems*. Preface by Robert Creeley. Edited by Paul Lacey. New York: New Directions, 2002.

———. "The Shifting." *Origin* 6 (1952): 114.

———. *This Great Unknowing: Last Poems*. Edited by Paul Lacey. New York: New Directions, 1999.

Levertov, Denise, and William Carlos Williams. *The Letters of Denise Levertov and William Carlos Williams*. Edited by Christopher MacGowan. New York: New Directions, 1998.

Mackey, Nathaniel. "From *Gassire's Lute*: Robert Duncan's Vietnam War Poems." Part II. *Talisman* 6 (1991): 141–66.

———. "From *Gassire's Lute*: Robert Duncan's Vietnam War Poems." Part IV. *Talisman* 8 (1992): 189–221.

Marcus, Hedda. "Into the Wild: The Role of Animal Nature in the Work of a Poet in the American Tradition—Denise Levertov's *Pig Dreams*." *The Nassau Review* 6, no. 3 (1992): 76–82.

Martin, Ronald. *American Literature and the Universe of Force*. Durham: Duke University Press, 1981.

Marx, Karl, and Friedrich Engels. *The Manifesto of the Communist Party*. Moscow: Foreign Language Publishing House, 1872.

Maud, Ralph. *Charles Olson's Reading: A Biography*. Carbondale: Southern Illinois University Press, 1996.

McCaffery, Steve. "The Death of the Subject: The Implications of Counter-Communication in Recent Language-Centered Writing." *L=A=N=G=U=A=G=E*. Supplement Number One (June 1980): n.p.

McCann, Sean. "The Imperiled Republic: Norman Mailer and the Poetics of Anti-Liberalism." *English Literary History* 67 (2000): 293–336.

McGuire, Jerry. "No Boundaries: Robert Creeley as Post-Modern Poet." *Sagetrieb* 1, no. 3 (1982): 92–118.

McHale, Brian. *The Obligation Toward the Difficult Whole: Postmodernist Long Poems*. Tuscaloosa: University of Alabama Press, 2004.

McHugh, Heather. "Love and Frangibility: An Appreciation of Robert Creeley." *The American Poetry Review* 26 (1997): 9–16.

Melley, Timothy. *Empire of Conspiracy: The Culture of Paranoia in Postwar America*. Ithaca: Cornell University Press, 2000.

Mersmann, James F. *Out of the Vietnam Vortex: A Study of Poets and Poetry against the War*. Lawrence: University of Kansas Press, 1974.

Moraru, Christian. " 'Topos/typos/tropos': Visual Strategies and the Mapping of Space in Charles Olson's Poetry." *Word & Image* 14, no. 3 (1998): 253–66.

Mossin, Andrew. "Scenes of Intent: Community, Lyric Subjectivity and the Formation of Poetic Career: Robert Duncan, Robin Blaser, Charles Olson, Nathaniel Mackey." PhD diss., Temple University, 1998.

Nelson, Cary. *Our Last First Poets: Vision and History in Contemporary American Poetry*. Urbana: University of Illinois Press, 1981.

Nelson, Deborah. *Pursuing Privacy in Cold War America*. New York: Columbia University Press, 2002.

Nicholls, Peter. *Ezra Pound: Politics, Economics and Writing: A Study of* The Cantos. London: Macmillan, 1984.

Nielsen, Dorothy. "The Mystical/Political Poetry of Denise Levertov: Rereading 'Advent 1966.' " *Sagetrieb* 14, no. 3 (1995): 89–106.

Nietzsche, Friedrich. *Thus Spake Zarathustra*. Translated by Thomas Common. New York: The Modern Library, 1954.

O'Leary, Peter. *Gnostic Contagion: Robert Duncan and the Poetry of Illness*. Middletown: Wesleyan University Press, 2002.

Olson, Charles. *Additional Prose: A Bibliography on America: Proprioception and Other Notes and Essays*. Edited by George F. Butterick. Bolinas: Four Seasons Foundation, 1974.

———. *The Collected Poems of Charles Olson*. Edited by George Butterick. Berkeley: University of California Press, 1987.

———. *Letters for Origin 1950–1970*. Ed. Albert Glover. New York: Grossman, 1970.

———. *The Maximus Poems*. Edited by George F. Butterick. Berkeley: University of California Press, 1983.

———. "Mayan Heads." *Black Mountain Review* 2 (1954): 26–28.

———. *Muthologos: The Collected Lectures and Interviews*. 2 vols., edited by George Butterick. Bolinas: Four Seasons Foundation, 1971.

———. Papers. Thomas J. Dodd Research Center. University of Connecticut Libraries. University of Connecticut at Storrs.

———. "Poems." *The Worcester Review* 11.2 (1989): 1–48.

———. *Selected Writings of Charles Olson*. Edited by Robert Creeley. New York: New Directions, 1966.

Olson, Charles, and Cid Corman. *Charles Olson and Cid Corman: Complete Correspondence, 1950–1964*. 2 vols., edited by George Evans. Orono: National Poetry Foundation, 1999.

Olson, Charles, and Robert Creeley. *Charles Olson and Robert Creeley: The Complete Correspondence*. 9 vols., edited by George F. Butterick. Santa Rosa: Black Sparrow Press, 1980–90.

Oppen, George. *The Collected Poems of George Oppen*. New York: New Directions, 1975.

Oppen, Mary. *Meaning A Life*. Santa Barbara: Black Sparrow Press, 1978.

Paul, Sherman. *olson's push: origin, black mountain, and recent american poetry*. Baton Rouge: Louisiana State University Press, 1978.

Pavese, Cesare. *Hard Labor*. Translated by William Arrowsmith. Baltimore: The Johns Hopkins University Press, 1979.

Perelman, Bob. *The Marginalization of Poetry: Language Writing and Literary History*. Princeton: Princeton University Press, 1996.

———. *The Trouble with Genius: Reading Pound, Joyce, Stein, and Zukofsky*. Berkeley: University of California Press, 1994.

Perloff, Marjorie. *Poetry On and Off the Page: Essays for Emergent Occasions*. Evanston: Northwestern University Press, 1998.

———. *Radical Artifice: Writing Poetry in the Age of Media*. Chicago: University of Chicago Press, 1991.

Pound, Ezra. *ABC of Reading*. New York: New Directions, 1960.

———. *The Cantos*. New York: New Directions, 1969.

———. *"Ezra Pound Speaking": Radio Speeches of World War II*. Edited by Leonard W. Doob. Westport: Greenwood Press, 1978.

———. *Gaudier-Brzeska: A Memoir*. New York: New Directions, 1960.

———. *Make It New: Essays by Ezra Pound*. London: Faber and Faber, 1934.

———. *Selected Prose 1909–1965*. Edited by William Cookson. New York: New Directions, 1973.

Pridmore-Brown, Michele. "1939–40: Of Virginia Woolf, Gramophones, and Fascism." *Publications of the Modern Language Association* 113, no. 3 (1998): 408–21.

Prus, Randy. "Olson's Dance: The Poetics of Place in American Poetry." PhD diss., State University of New York at Buffalo, 1989.

Quartermain, Peter. *Disjunctive Poetics: From Gertrude Stein and Louis Zukofsky to Susan Howe*. Cambridge: Cambridge University Press, 1992.

———. "Not at All Surprised by Science: 'Louis Zukofsky's First Half of *A-9*.'" In *Louis Zukofsky: Man and Poet*, edited by Carroll Terrell, 203–25. Orono: The National Poetry Foundation, 1979.

Rexroth, Kenneth. "Artaud." *Black Mountain Review* 1 (1954).

Rifkin, Libbie. *Career Moves: Olson, Creeley, Zukofsky, Berrigan, and the American Avant-Garde*. Madison: University of Wisconsin Press, 2000.

Rodgers, Audrey T. *Denise Levertov: The Poetry of Engagement*. Rutherford: Fairleigh Dickinson Press, 1993.

Rose, Barbara, ed. *Readings in American Art 1900–1975*. New York: Praeger Publishers, 1975.

Rumaker, Michael. *Robert Duncan in San Francisco*. San Francisco: Grey Fox Press, 1996.

Scalapino, Leslie. " 'Thinking Serially' in *For Love*, *Words* and *Pieces*." *Talisman* 8 (1992): 42–48.

Schelb, Edward. "The Exaction of Song: Louis Zukofsky and the Ideology of Form." *Contemporary Literature* 31, no. 3 (1990): 335–53.

Scroggins, Mark. *Louis Zukofsky and the Poetry of Knowledge*. Tuscaloosa: University of Alabama Press, 1998.

Seelye, Catherine, ed. *Charles Olson & Ezra Pound: An Encounter at St. Elizabeth's*. New York: Grossman Publishers, 1975.

Seymour-Smith, Martin. "Where Is Mr. Roethke?" *Black Mountain Review* 1 (1951): 40.

Sharp, Tom. "Objectivists 1927–1934: A Critical History of the Work and Association of Louis Zukofsky, William Carlos Williams, Charles Reznikoff, Ezra Pound, George Oppen." 2 vols. PhD diss., Stanford University, 1982.

Shelley, Percy Bysshe. *Prometheus Unbound: A Variorum Edition*. Edited by Lawrence John Zillmer. Seattle: University of Washington Press, 1959.

Silliman, Ron. "For Open Letter." *L=A=N=G=U=A=G=E*. Supplement Number One (June 1980): n.p.

Sisko, Nancy. "To Stay Alive: Levertov's Search for a Revolutionary Poetry." *Sagetrieb* 5, no. 2 (1986): 47–60.

Sloan, De Villo. " 'Crude Mechanical Access' or 'Crude Personism': A Chronicle of One San Francisco Bay Area Poetry War." *Sagetrieb* 4, nos. 2–3 (1985): 241–54.

Smith, Lorrie. "Songs of Experience: Denise Levertov's Political Poetry." In *Denise Levertov: Selected Criticism*, edited by Albert Gelpi. Ann Arbor: University of Michigan Press, 1993.

Stanley, Sandra Kumamoto. *Louis Zukofsky and the Transformation of a Modern American Poetics*. Berkeley: University of California Press, 1994.

Stein, Gertrude. *Three Lives*. Norfolk: New Directions, 1933.

Stimpson, Catherine. "Charles Olson: Preliminary Images." *Boundary 2* 2, nos. 1–2 (1973–74): 151–72.

Sun, Hong. "Pound's Quest for Confucian Ideals: The Chinese History Cantos." In *Ezra Pound and China*, edited by Zhaoming Qian, 96–117. Ann Arbor: University of Michigan Press, 2003.

Terrell, Carroll. "An Eccentric Profile." In *Louis Zukofsky: Man and Poet*, edited by Carroll Terrell, 203–25. Orono: The National Poetry Foundation, 1979.

Tselentis-Apostolidis, Penny. "On Olson's Geographic Methodology: Quoting, Naming, Pacing and Mapping." *Sagetrieb* 12, no. 2 (1993): 119–36.

Vanderborg, Susan. *Paratextual Communities: American Avant-Garde Poetry since 1950*. Carbondale: Southern Illinois University Press, 2001.

Von Hallberg, Robert. *American Poetry and Culture 1945–1980*. Cambridge: Harvard University Press, 1985.

———. *Charles Olson: The Scholar's Art*. Cambridge: Harvard University Press, 1978.

Ward, Geoff. "Before and After Language: The New American Poetry." In *Poetry and the Sense of Panic: Critical Essays on Elizabeth Bishop and John Ashbery*, edited by Lionel Kelly, 169–81. Amsterdam: Rodopi, 2000.

Watten, Barrett. "Robert Creeley and the Politics of the Person." *Poetics Journal* 9 (1991): 138–43.

Weil, Simone. "Factory Work." *Politics* 34 (1946): 369–75.

———. *Simone Weil: An Anthology*. Edited by Sian Miles. New York: Weidenfeld and Nicholson, 1986.

———. "Words and War." *Politics* 26 (1946): 69–73.

Wesling, Donald. *Internal Resistances: The Poetry of Ed Dorn*. Berkeley: University of California Press, 1985.

Weyl, Hermann. *Philosophy of Mathematics and Natural Science*. Rev. and augmented ed. Translated by Olaf Helmer. Princeton: Princeton University Press, 1949.

Whitehead, Alfred North. *Process and Reality: An Essay in Cosmology*. Corrected ed. Edited by David Ray Griffin and W. Sherburne. London: The Free Press, 1978.

———. *Science and the Modern World*. New York: The Free Press, 1967.

Williams, William Carlos. *The Collected Poems of William Carlos Williams. Volume II 1939–1962*. Edited by Christopher MacGowan. New York: New Directions, 1988.

———. *Imaginations*. Edited by Webster Schott. New York: New Directions, 1970.

———. Papers. Beinecke Library. Yale University Library.

———. *Selected Essays of William Carlos Williams*. New York: New Directions, 1954.

Woolf, Douglas. "The Kind of Life We've Planned." *Black Mountain Review* 2 (1954).

Wordsworth, William. *The Thirteen-Book Prelude*. Vol. 1. Edited by Mark L. Reed. Ithaca: Cornell University Press, 1991.

Yau, John. "Active Participant: Robert Creeley and The Visual Arts." In *In Company: Robert Creeley's Collaborations*. Edited by Amy Cappellazzo and Elizabeth Licata. Greensboro: The Castellani Art Museum of Niagara University and Weatherspoon Art Gallery, University of North Carolina at Greensboro, 1999.

Zukofsky, Louis. "*A.*" Berkeley: University of California Press, 1978.

———. *ALL: collected short poems*. New York: W. W. Norton & Co., 1966.

———. *Bottom: On Shakespeare*. Berkeley: University of California Press, 1963.

———. "Poetry (1952)." *Montevallo Review* 1, no. 3 (1952): 49–54.

———. *Prepositions: The collected critical essays of Louis Zukofsky*. New York: Horizon Press, 1967.

———, ed. *An "Objectivists" Anthology*. New York: Folcroft Library Editions, 1975.

Index